The Fourth Industrial Revolution

Alan Nankervis • Julia Connell
Alan Montague • John Burgess
Editors

The Fourth Industrial Revolution

What Does it Mean for Australian Industry?

Springer

Editors
Alan Nankervis
Centre for Organisational Change
and Agility (COCA)
Torrens University
Adelaide, SA, Australia

School of Management and Law
Curtin University
Perth, NSW, Australia

Alan Montague
School of Management
RMIT University
Melbourne, VIC, Australia

Julia Connell
Newcastle Business School, College
of Human and Social Futures
University of Newcastle,
Newcastle, NSW, Australia

John Burgess
Torrens University
Adelaide, SA, Australia

ISBN 978-981-16-1613-6 ISBN 978-981-16-1614-3 (eBook)
https://doi.org/10.1007/978-981-16-1614-3

This Springer imprint is published by the registered company Springer Nature Singapore Pte Ltd.
The registered company address is: 152 Beach Road, #21-01/04 Gateway East, Singapore 189721, Singapore

Preface

This book explores the core themes of the Fourth Industrial Revolution (4IR), highlighting the digital transformation that has been occurring in society and business. Although an extensive literature has recently emerged that examines the impact of technological change, this has not to date included a focus on the impact of Fourth Industrial Revolution (4IR) technologies on industry sectors in Australia. This book sets out to fill that gap by exploring a broad range of Australian industry sectors in relation to the new technologies associated with the 4IR. Representing an interface between technologies in the physical, digital and biological disciplines, the chapters investigate emerging technologies such as: artificial intelligence, robotics, the Internet of Things, autonomous vehicles, 3D printing, nanotechnology; biotechnology, materials science, energy storage and quantum computing. In particular, the book focuses on new technologies being implemented across eight industry sectors (categorised by the Australian and New Zealand Industrial Classification of Industries – ANZSIC) and multiple stakeholders' predictions concerning the associated changes to labour markets, jobs and skills. The eight industry sectors featured in the book are: agriculture and mining; manufacturing and logistics; health, medical and nursing; education; retail; financial services; government services; and tourism and hospitality.

Industry-specific chapters report on the findings of collaborative research studies where the potential impact of the 4IR on labour markets, occupations, future workforce competencies and skills is explored. The catalytic effect of the COVID-19 pandemic is also considered in relation to its impetus for transitions towards more automated functions in many of the industries discussed in the book. The authors stress the urgency of addressing the key implications identified for Australia's governments and industry so that Australia can make a positive impact in an era where technological advances are having, and will continue to have, an unprecedented impact.

Adelaide, SA, Australia Alan Nankervis

Newcastle, NSW, Australia Julia Connell

Melbourne, VIC, Australia Alan Montague

Adelaide, SA, Australia John Burgess

Quote

Automation, Artificial Intelligence (AI), and the Internet of Things (IoT) are having an impact almost everywhere, in all industries, jobs and everyday life. Given this pace of change, it is important to understand and anticipate what this means for the future: jobs, youth, government and society more broadly, so that everyone has an opportunity to participate in the digital economy.

(Cisco and Oxford Economics, 2019: 3)

Acknowledgement

The editors gratefully acknowledge the professional contribution of Christine Armstrong, whose research assistance was invaluable in bringing the volume to an efficient conclusion.

Contents

Editors and Contributors

About the Editors

John Burgess is an adjunct professor, Centre for Organisational Change and Agility, Torrens University, Adelaide. His research interests include HRM practices of multinational enterprises, graduate work readiness, human resource development in emerging economies, and the future of work. His most recent book, co-edited with Kantha Dayaram, Linda Lambey, John Burgess and Tri Wulida Afrianty, is *Developing the Workforce in an Emerging Economy: The Case of Indonesia*, Routledge, Abingdon, 2020. john.burgess@torrens.edu.au

Julia Connell is EMBA/Newcastle Business School director (Sydney Campus), University of Newcastle. She has published numerous refereed journal articles/book chapters and co-edited 16 special issue journal volumes and 8 books to date. Many publications have focused on the future of work and technology, change/people development, organisational effectiveness, vulnerable workers/precarious jobs and also issues related to higher education. julia.connell@newcastle.edu.au

Alan Montague was a senior lecturer at RMIT University Melbourne. His research and vocational experience within a rich working life links skill/vocational shortages, government policies relating to education and industry, employment/education program policy development, and management and workforce planning. His research also extends to critical commentary on corporate ethics and the impact of artificial intelligence on organisations and jobs. His research is undertaken predominantly through the lens of human resource management (HRM). alanjmontague@gmail.com

Alan Nankervis is an adjunct professor of human resource management at Torrens University (Adelaide) and Curtin University (Perth). His research interests include strategic HRM, comparative Asian HRM, graduate work-readiness and artificial intelligence across the Asia Pacific. He is the lead author of Australia's best-selling HRM text and is chair of the Australia HR Institute's National (Course) Accreditation Committee. a.nankervis@curtin.edu.au

Contributors

Timothy Bartram is a professor of management at RMIT University. His expertise is in human resource management, high performance work systems and healthcare management. Tim's research work has culminated in 119 refereed journal publications. Publications include articles in *Human Resource Management*, *Human Resource Management Journal*, *Journal of Management Studies*, *The British Journal of Industrial Relations*, *The International Journal of Human Resource Management*, *British Journal of Management*, *Applied Psychology: An International Review*, *Journal of Business Ethics*, *Journal of Advanced Nursing*, *BMC Health Services*, *Personnel Review*, *Journal of Industrial Relations*, *Relations Industrielles* and *Health Care Management Review*. timothy.bartram@rmit.edu.au

Patricia Pariona Cabrera is a PhD student, lecturer/tutor, and research assistant at RMIT University. Her thesis topic is in the area of workplace violence in aged care. Her interests include human resource management, clinical psychology and healthcare management. She has published in the *Journal of Vocational Education and Training*, *Relations Industrielles*, *Journal of Advanced Nursing* and *Asia Pacific Journal of Human Resources*. patricia.pariona-cabrera@rmit.edu.au

Roslyn Cameron is director of the Centre for Organisational Change and Agility (COCA) at Torrens University, Australia. She is a member of the AHRI Advisory Research Panel in Australia. Roslyn has been the recipient of several large-scale workforce development research grants and an array of smaller scale research grants related to skilled migration, workforce readiness/employability and future skilling/future of work for the 4th Industrial Revolution, totalling $1.9m. She has over 90 publications. Ros.cameron@torrens.edu.au

Jillian Cavanagh is a senior lecturer in HRM at RMIT University. Her research expertise includes human resource management, healthcare management, Indigenous health and well-being, and disability management. She has published in *Personnel Review*, *International Journal of Human Resource Management*, *Journal of Vocational Education and Training*, *Relations Industrielles*, *Journal of Business Ethics* and *Journal of Advanced Nursing*. jillian.cavanagh@rmit.edu.au

Chi-Tsun Cheng is a senior lecturer in manufacturing, materials and mechatronics, School of Engineering, RMIT University, Melbourne, Australia. He serves as associate editor for the *IEEE Transactions on Circuits and Systems II, IEEE Access* and *IEICE Nonlinear Theory and Its Applications*. His research interests include wireless sensor networks, Internet of Things, Industry 4.0 Technologies, cloud computing and additive manufacturing. ben.cheng@rmit.edu.au

Mark Dean is research and data officer at the Australian Apprenticeships and Traineeships Information Service, undertaking research projects and data analysis around emerging areas of importance in the vocational education and training (VET) sector. Prior to this, Mark was an academic at Flinders University where his research and teaching focused on the political economy of Industry 4.0 and the future of work, particularly in advanced manufacturing and service industries. Mark's PhD research critically examined the political economy of industrial transformation and industry policy in Australia. mark.bernard.dean@gmail.com

Lisa Dethridge has produced media for web, film, television, theatre, radio, print, telecoms and 3D virtual environments in Australia and the United States. She supervised research in virtual environments, artificial intelligence, games, robotics and online global collaboration at the RMIT University School of Media and Communication. Dethridge designs story worlds, avatars and scripts for multi-user virtual environments and has developed screen material for major and independent studios and networks including Fox, Warner, Working Title, MTV, CBS, NBC, Ted Turner CNN, Granada, SBS and Tesltra. Lisa is author of numerous research articles on innovation technology. Her PhD is in media ecology from New York University. Dr Dethridge is now semi-retired but continues her research work and supervision in an honorary capacity. lisa.dethridge@rmit.edu.au

Subas P. Dhakal is a senior lecturer at the UNE Business School, University of New England (UNE), Armidale. He is a management academic with expertise in the field of sustainability. His research interests include: future of education and employment, social responsibility, and Sustainable Development Goals in the Asia Pacific Region. Subas.dhakal@une.edu.au

Venesser Fernandes lectures and researches in the field of educational leadership studies. She is particularly focussed on research pertaining to organisational change and development within educational institutions across Australia and internationally with her focus extending to the impact of artificial intelligence on pedagogy and andragogy. venesser.fernandez@monash.edu.au

Kai-Yin Fok received his BSc (Hons.) degree in Internet and multimedia technologies and his PhD degree in electronic and information engineering from The Hong Kong Polytechnic University, Kowloon, Hong Kong, in 2014 and 2019, respectively. His research interests include optimisation techniques in additive manufacturing, evolutionary algorithms, NLP, and OCR. kyfok@ieee.org

Nuwan Ganganath received his BSc degree with first class honours from the University of Moratuwa, Sri Lanka, in 2010, MSc degree from the University of Calgary, Canada in 2013, and PhD degree from the Hong Kong Polytechnic University, Hong Kong in 2016. He is currently an adjunct research fellow at the University of Western Australia, Australia. manganganath@gmail.com

Victor Gekara is an associate professor in the College of Business and Law at RMIT University. He is also the director of the Global Transport and Logistics Research Group (GTL) and the founding leader of the Skills, Training and Industry Research Network (STIR). His research interests and expertise are broadly located at the intersection between workplace technological change and the future of work and workforce skills. In this space, he has developed and led several major research projects and published on the implications of technological and digital transformations on work and industry skills demand and the role and capacity of vocational education and training to meet these changes. victor.gekara@rmit.edu.au

Aida Ghalebeigi is an academic in the Department of Logistics and Supply Chain Management at RMIT University. Her research focus and expertise are in the behavioural and social aspects of supply chains such as diversity in the businesses, workforce studies and power relations within the supply chain. Aida.ghalebeigi@rmit.edu.au

Beni Halvorsen is a lecturer in HRM at RMIT University. His recent interests include HRM, employee turnover and healthcare management. He has published in *Personnel Review*, *International Journal of Human Resource Management* and *International Journal of Manpower*. beni.halvorsen@rmit.edu.au

Narges Kia is a sessional lecturer at RMIT University and Deakin University, Australia. She received her PhD in 2020. Her research interests include human resource management and leadership. She has recently published in *Personnel Review*. narges.kia@rmit.edu.au

Roslyn Larkin is a senior lecturer in employment relations at the Newcastle Business School, University of Newcastle, Australia. Research interests include: knowledge management, international HRM, ethical leadership, university governance. Roslyn.larkin@newcastle.edu.au

Tsz-Kwan Lee [Glory] is a lecturer in computer science at the School of Information Technology, Deakin University, Australia. Her research interests include machine learning, video quality assessment, 2D/3D video coding, multimedia technologies, signal processing and video transcoding. glory.lee@deakin.edu.au

Francesco Maisano is an experienced teacher and seminar leader at RMIT University Melbourne. His academic research streams include artificial intelligence and its implications on the workforce and sustainability reporting, as well as professional identity in small practice accountants and the effect professionalism has on small practice accountants. Francesco has further experience in directing and managing his own company for a decade, with experience in accounting, strategic management and business growth. frank.maisano@rmit.edu.au

Ashish Malik is an associate professor at the University of Newcastle, Australia. Ashish's research is at the interface of strategy, HRM and innovation management in an international context. He serves as an associate editor of the *Journal of Business Research*, *Asia Business & Management* and *IIM – Society and Management Review*, and is a member of the editorial review boards of *Human Resource Management Review* and the *Journal of Knowledge Management*. His research appears in journals, such as the *Journal of Knowledge Management*, *Journal of Business Research*, *Journal of International Management*, *Human Resource Management Review*, *Industrial Marketing Management*, *International Journal of Human Resource Management and Applied Psychology: An International Review*. Ashish.malik@newcastle.edu.au

Hannah Meacham is a lecturer in HRM at Monash University. Her recent interests include HRM and disability management. She has recently published in *Personnel Review*, *Human Resource Management* and *Journal of Business Ethics*. Hannah.meacham@monash.edu.au

Al Rainnie is an adjunct senior research fellow at the University of South Australia and is also co-editor-in-chief of the *Economic and Labour Relations Review*. Al's research has covered small firms, restructuring Central Europe, labour process analysis, spatiality, global production networks and global destruction networks. His latest book (with Andy Herod), *Work, Workers and Waste* will be published by Edward Elgar in 2021. al.f.rainnie@gmail.com

Vishal Rana is a lecturer in management at the Australian Institute of Business, Adelaide, Australia. He is a Professional Member of Australian Human Resource Institute (AHRI). Dr Rana is the founder of Mental Health Tech, a start-up that is developing a software as a service (SaaS) based platform to predict symptoms of depression by monitoring speech in real time. He is also the founder of an education tech start-up that is developing a platform to provide online markers with real-time sentimental analysis of their feedback to ensure a constructive tone and feedback to the students. Dr Rana's research interest is in the ethics of artificial intelligence and the future of work. Vishal.rana@aib.edu.au

Wajeeha Shaikh is a PhD candidate at RMIT, Melbourne. Her thesis is titled 'The Practices of Library Practitioners and the Shaping of Performance in Victorian Local Government Libraries'. wajeeha.shaik@rmit.edu.au

Jan Svanberg is an associate professor at the University of Gävle in Sweden and has been a proud research fellow at RMIT University, Melbourne, since 1st September 2019. His research is in accounting and he has obtained several grants for conducting research on the application of artificial intelligence on problems in accounting and auditing. This research is now conducted in long-term cooperation with several colleagues at RMIT University and some of the leading researchers in Sweden in artificial intelligence. jan.svanberg@hig.se

Richard Tay is a chartered professional engineer (CPEng) in Australia, a fellow of the Institute of Transportation Engineers and the Chartered Institute of Logistics and Transport, and a senior fellow of the Economic Society of Australia. His expertise is in multidisciplinary theory and evidence-based approaches to improving transportation safety, efficiency, accessibility and sustainability. He serves on the editorial board of many transportation journals, and as an expert in many government taskforces and committees. richard.tay@rmit.edu.au

Chapter 1
Introduction

John Burgess, Julia Connell, Alan Nankervis, and Alan Montague

Abstract Although an extensive literature has been developed that examines the impact of technological change, to date this has not included a focus on the impacts of the Fourth Industrial Revolution (4IR) technologies on industry sectors in Australia. This book sets out to fill that gap by exploring a broad range of Australian industry sectors categorised by the Australian and New Zealand Standard Industrial Classification of Industries (ANZSIC). It explores the types of new technologies associated with the 4IR being implemented across eight sectors; and multiple stakeholders' predictions about the potential changes to the associated labour markets, jobs, and skills.

Keywords 4IR · Covid-19 · Structural change · Technological change

Introduction

The nature and technical capabilities of industry sectors differ, as do their labour requirements in terms of jobs, tasks, and skills. Within the context of the range of technologies linked to the 4IR, the purpose of this book is to examine the actual and projected changes that are taking place across Australian industry sectors by addressing the following questions in each chapter:

J. Burgess
Torrens University, Adelaide, SA, Australia

J. Connell (✉)
Newcastle Business School, College of Human and Social Futures, University of Newcastle, Newcastle, NSW, Australia
e-mail: julia.connell@newcastle.edu.au

A. Nankervis
Centre for Organisational Change and Agility (COCA), Torrens University, Adelaide, SA, Australia

School of Management and Law, Curtin University, Perth, NSW, Australia
e-mail: a.nankervis@curtin.edu.au

A. Montague
School of Management, RMIT University, Melbourne, VIC, Australia

A. Nankervis et al. (eds.), *The Fourth Industrial Revolution*,
https://doi.org/10.1007/978-981-16-1614-3_1

(a) What are the characteristics of each industry sector, and its current strengths and weaknesses?
(b) What key technologies are currently impacting on the sector and what technologies are likely to have a future impact on the sector?
(c) What is the impact of technological change on the size and composition of the sector's workforce?
(d) What is the impact of technological change on the skill requirements of the sector?
(e) Are there active programs in place to support organisations and workers to accommodate the predicted technological changes? And
(f) What programs and policies are required to address the predicted changes within the sector?

In addition to outlining the topics and key questions explored in this book in relation to 4IR technologies in the selected industry sectors in Australia, this chapter incorporates a range of definitions and concepts. It begins with the nature and challenges of the 4IR before briefly considering changes in jobs, work, skills and potential new occupations and their associated new skills that have emerged. The chapter outlines structural changes in Australia, the global context of the 4IR, the framework used to structure each chapter, and the research methods used to guide authors' investigations, before providing a summary of each chapter.

What Is the Fourth Industrial Revolution (4IR)?

There has been considerable debate about the nature of what has been referred to as the Fourth Industrial Revolution (4IR) or Industry 4.0. The term 4IR was coined by Klaus Schwab, the founder of the World Economic Forum (WEF 2016), who suggested that the 'velocity, scope, and systems impact (of the 4IR) is evolving at an exponential rather than a linear pace' (Schwab 2016), with new and emerging technologies distinguishing it from previous industrial revolutions. Schwab's (2016) conceptualisation and rationale have been promoted by many authors (see Brynjolfsson and McAfee 2017; Cedefop 2019; EIU 2018; Finextra and Intel 2017; Fluss 2017; Scarpetta 2017), and the term 4IR has since acquired common parlance status. The four industrial revolutions referred to in Schwab's framework are:

> The First Industrial Revolution used water and steam power to mechanize production. The Second used electric power to create mass production. The Third used electronics and information technology to automate production. Now a Fourth Industrial Revolution is building on the Third, the digital revolution that has been occurring since the middle of the last century. It is characterized by a fusion of technologies that is blurring the lines between the physical, digital, and biological spheres (Schwab 2016: webpage).

These four stages of technological development cover a period of around two hundred years. However, the 4th revolution has evolved only the past two decades. The short duration between stages 3 and 4 are symptomatic of the speed and extent of technological change, with the 4th stage being built upon the technological developments of the 3rd stage, leading Schwab to comment:

> There are three reasons why today's transformations represent not merely a prolongation of the Third Industrial Revolution but rather the arrival of a Fourth and distinct one: velocity, scope, and systems impact. The speed of current breakthroughs has no historical precedent. When compared with previous industrial revolutions, the Fourth is evolving at an exponential rather than a linear pace. Moreover, it is disrupting almost every industry in every country. And the breadth and depth of these changes herald the transformation of entire systems of production, management, and governance (Schwab 2016: webpage).

The 4IR is not country or industry specific. It permeates the globe and has the potential to impact on all communities at different stages of development, and in various industry sectors. However, it is unlikely to have a significant impact on countries that have poor infrastructure to support ICT; large labour surpluses; large populations in rural areas or an extensive subsistence and informal economy (Ayentimi and Burgess 2018). The developing world is simultaneously experiencing forces other than technological change which are poised to impact labour markets (Bandura and Hammond 2018). First, it is 'rapidly urbanizing, creating challenges for cities in terms of infrastructure, job creation, and basic social services. Second, different regions are following varied demographic transition paths that will affect the number of potential workers, the composition of the workforce, and the types of jobs created' (Bandura and Hammond 2018: 3). It can also be argued that the emergence of the COVID-19 pandemic may have accelerated the implementation of these innovative technologies in some countries and sectors. This is evident as employers strive to reduce their staffing costs by replacing them with artificial intelligence or machine learning technologies, whilst in others economic factors may constrain such imperatives. As outlined in the chapters in this book there are already significant differences between the various Australian industry sectors in relation to their recovery from the pandemic and their subsequent intentions and capacity to utilise these new technologies.

On the positive side, the 4IR has been promoted as providing significant benefits to organisations and their managers through creating opportunities to deliver increased and higher quality products and services at a considerably cheaper cost, with enhanced speed and improved reliability (Acemoglu and Restrepo 2017; Arnold et al. 2018; Dilsizian and Siegel 2014). Conversely, the anticipated negative consequences of the 4IR have primarily focused on its threats to labour markets, workplaces, jobs (both quantity and quality), skills and employees more generally through the expectation that these new technologies will lead to massive job disruption, significant job losses and employee de-skilling (Bandura and Hammond 2018; Brynjolfsson and McAfee 2017; Finextra and Intel 2017; Fluss 2017, Marrengo 2019). That said, it has been pointed out that computerisation automates tasks, rather than jobs, and consequently the nature of most jobs is likely to change rather than disappear due to automation (Arntz et al. 2016; Susskind 2020).

Nations and industries can potentially encompass all four 'revolutions' through the processes of international trade and investment and the global spread of digital technology and the internet. However, the 4IR concept is not without its critics. The problems are linked to technological determinism, under which, there are no points of resistance to the changes and the underlying conditions supporting technological change are constant. For example, Rainnie and Dean (2019) state that the literature on Industry 4.0 deals with technology, and the problem-solving of digital transformation issues and embedding firms within production systems. It canvasses issues of standardisation and communication and making the business and consumer case for the digitalisation of manufacturing production. Attention to the impact of (the 4IR) on more pressing human dimensions of digitally-driven industrial change is significantly lacking (p. 17).

What Are the 4IR Transforming Technologies?

In a survey of 371 leading global companies, the World Economic Forum (WEF 2016) identified the main technologies that are driving changes to work, working, jobs, skills, and the future of work (FOW). These technological changes are listed below in order of those regarded by survey respondents as being the most significant changes for their organisation and industry:

1. Mobile internet and cloud technology
2. Advances in computing power and Big Data
3. New energy supplies and technologies.
4. The Internet of Things through remote sensors, communications, and processing power in industrial and household equipment
5. Crowdsourcing, the sharing economy, and peer-to-peer platforms
6. Advanced robotics and autonomous transport
7. Artificial intelligence and machine learning
8. Advanced manufacturing and 3D printing
9. Advanced materials, biotechnology, and genomics

These technologies have potential applications across all industries supporting new production processes, new industries, new ways of working or providing entertainment and consumption. They also support efficiency improvements and productivity increases while changing the skill mix required for many industry sectors. The technological possibilities are extensive. Many of the technologies are transformative and disruptive to existing production employment and distribution arrangements within industry sectors, raising questions linked to the impact of the technologies on jobs and living standards, and how the benefits of these technologies will be supported and distributed. Schwab (2016) discusses the potential inequities that could arise as follows:

> …inequality represents the greatest societal concern associated with the Fourth Industrial Revolution. The largest beneficiaries of innovation tend to be the providers of intellectual and physical capital—the innovators, shareholders, and investors—which explains the rising gap in wealth between those dependent on capital versus labor. Technology is therefore

one of the main reasons why incomes have stagnated, or even decreased, for a majority of the population in high-income countries.

Are All Jobs and Sectors Equally Affected by Technological Change?

The displacement effects of technology will depend on the type of technological applications; the skill composition of jobs; and the extent to which the technologies can be supported and implemented. In Australia, a report produced by Cisco and Oxford Economics (2019: p. 3) suggested that the greatest displacement effects, that is the substitution of technology for jobs over the period 2018–2028, will occur in the following sectors: transport (12.4%); construction (11.2%); mining (10.7%); agriculture (10.4%); utilities (9.5%) and manufacturing (9.4%). Specifically, based on the modelling, 12.4% of equivalent full-time jobs in the transport sector will be displaced by technology over the coming decade with the aggregate displacement effect resulting in 630,000 full-time jobs across the economy. In terms of the most vulnerable sectors due to technological job displacement the report commented that:

> …the relative vulnerability of these sectors to technology-driven displacement is a result of the nature of their work. Workers spend more time operating vehicles, handling objects and controlling machines, all of which have the potential to be completed more efficiently with the application of new and existing technologies, such as advanced robotics and machine learning' (Cisco and Oxford Economics 2019: 9).

In general terms this refers to craft, trades, and transport jobs that are mainly performed by male workers in positions such as drivers, machine operators, mechanics, carpenters, technicians, and warehouse workers.

The Intersection of Structural Changes and the 4IR

One of the challenges in assessing the impact of the 4IR is that, in addition to technological changes there are structural changes that will impact on the level and growth of demand for output and jobs, and the composition of production and employment. Returning to the WEF (2016) discussion of the 4IR, their survey asked respondents from leading global companies to identify what they regarded as the primary demographic and socio-economic factors driving change in their organisations. The most significant factors identified were as follows, with the percentage referring to the proportion of respondents who identified the factor as the most important change:

- Changing work environments and flexible working arrangements (44%): remote working, co-working; teleconferencing; increased sub-contracting.

- Rise of the middle class in emerging markets (23%); rising living standards, especially in Asia, to drive and change the composition of global demand.
- Climate change, natural resource constraints and the transition to a greener economy (23%): innovation in energy development and storage; controls over carbon emissions.
- Rising geopolitical volatility (21%): implications for global trade and investment; increased expenditure on defence and policing.
- Consumer concerns about ethical and privacy issues (16%): ethical investment funds; NGO monitoring of human rights; fair trade and supply chain assessments; on-line privacy.
- Longevity and ageing (14%): especially in advanced economies. Implications for health, labour force participation, education, savings, and international migration.
- Young demographics in emerging markets (13%): population growth in emerging economies with pressures on education, youth labour markets; and implications for international migration.
- Women's rising aspirations and economic power (12%): increased labour force participation; increased household incomes; breaking down gender barriers to participation and
- Rapid urbanisation (8%): pressures on infrastructure and the environment; congestion and commuting.

Aggregating structural changes alongside technological changes will indicate the combined impact on jobs and skill requirements in the coming years. The job displacement effects of technological change are offset by increasing demand due to population and income growth. Automated check-out machines and online shopping will reduce the demand for sales staff in supermarkets and department stores, but as the population and income expands, there will likely be requirements for additional supermarkets and department stores.

The (2019) Cisco and Oxford Economics report forecast the net changes in jobs for the period 2018–2028 by sector in Australia, adding together the technological and income effects. The income effects represent the projected growth in the economy and its impact on sector output and jobs. Combining the two effects (the positive income effects and the adverse displacement effects from technological change) the three sectors that will have contributed the most jobs over the decade were forecast to be (presented in thousands of full-time equivalent jobs): healthcare (79.5); hotels and restaurants (21.6) and wholesale and retail trade (20.5). The three sectors with the most significant net job loss were: construction (73.2); manufacturing (33.3) and transport (26.1).

However, the forecasts were undertaken prior to the COVID-19 pandemic and are therefore unlikely to accurately reflect post-2020 workforce conditions. Such steady-state growth forecasts are of course eroded by unexpected changes and crises (such as bushfires, wars, earthquakes and flooding) which impact on growth, trade, investment, and the uptake of new technologies.

Impact of the 4IR on Work, Skills and Occupations

The WEF (2016) report found that changes in both where and how work is conducted will be one of the major developments from technological change. COVID-19 has forced organisations and workers to embrace mobile technologies and working away from central workplaces as options. Prior to the COVID-19 pandemic, approximately 24% of Australian workers reported working some hours from home. However, between March and April 2020, that number almost doubled, with 48% of workers transitioning to remote work (ABS 2020). In their analysis of future jobs, Ross et al. highlighted new ways of working, including technological versus geographical proximity in work and workplace identity; web intermediated work; co-working and offshoring. They argued that technological developments not only affect job and skill profiles, but also potentially how work is carried out, where and when it is conducted and for whom the work is performed. Internet technologies reconstruct the nature of the workplace, the employer, and the employment relationship. The 4IR promises to fundamentally transform the ways in which we interact with machines, and in addition, the way that machines learn, improve, and build on their own performance. The benefits of these new digital technologies may be considerable (Lu and Burton 2017). However, their impact on future work processes, training needs and workforce structures, as well as the ethical frameworks for their implementation, demand equal consideration by all stakeholders likely to be involved in decisions about their usage in various industry sectors and organisations.

The WEF (2016, 22) analysis on the future of work concluded that:

> …in the face of rapidly rising computing power, an ability to work with data and make data-based decisions will become an increasingly vital skill across many job families as employers scramble to build a workforce with solid skills in data analysis and presentation (e.g. through visualization) and the amount of potentially useful digital information generated and stored keeps increasing exponentially.

This analysis of global firms indicates that skillsets will need to change, and as a result, the potential for skills mismatches will increase as educational and training programs lag behind the skill changes required for the new technologies. Across the industries surveyed, the three primary skills identified were complex problem-solving skills, social skills, and process skills with the largest increase in future skills being cognitive abilities.

Ongoing Structural Change in Australia

Technological change is continuous and disruptive. However, it is not only technology that is changing; the underlying conditions that influence production, investment, and employment are also changing. While technology and automation have the potential to displace labour, other factors increase production and jobs. For example, underlying wealth and income growth lead to increased trade, and demographic change. As communities become wealthier, they demand products and services that are supported by higher incomes – for example, hospitality and travel. Technology also drives down the cost of products, such as consumer electronics that become more affordable with increased demand. Demographic change alters the composition of production. Australia is ageing, and with it, the ageing community requires additional leisure and health services (Devasahayam et al. 2018; Federal Treasury 2010). The proportion of total participation in the labour market by mature-aged persons (aged 55 years and over) 'increased from 9.1%in May 1989 to 19.3% in May 2019 (Department of Employment, Skills, Small and Family Business 2019: 5). This upward trend reflects the ageing population as life expectancy steadily increases over time (Department of Employment, Skills, Small and Family Business 2019). An important demographic factor in Australia is also net immigration as it offsets ageing since the migrant cohort is, on average, younger than the general population and migrants also provide a source of skilled labour (Devasahayam et al. 2018). Moreover, the younger immigrant cohort increases the demand for such services as housing and schooling (Devasahayam et al. 2018). However, a significant decrease in migration during and following the COVID-19 pandemic will undoubtedly affect this demographic trend in Australia.

In the last thirty years, Australia's labour market has undergone a structural change with a significant shift from production industries to labour-intensive service industries and higher-skilled occupations. Technological advances over the last three decades have resulted in a changing labour market, with amplified automation supporting jobs that 'are non-routine in nature and require people to have skills that are not easily replicated by a machine (such as social skills, emotional intelligence, creativity and advanced reasoning)' (Department of Employment, Skills, Small and Family Business 2019:1). The shift to services and automation, as discussed earlier, has been prominent since 1989–2019.

In 1989, manufacturing was the largest Australian industry sector in terms of employment, accounting for 15.2% of total persons employed (Department of Employment, Skills, Small and Family Business 2019). In 2019 – three decades later, employment in manufacturing has fallen by 316,600 (or 27.2%) and is the seventh-largest employing industry, accounting for 6.6% of the total workforce. In the face of the long-term decline recorded in this industry sector, manufacturing does however remain a substantial employing industry, as 848,700 workers were employed in May 2019 (Department of Employment, Skills, Small and Family Business 2019). Occupations commensurate with the highest skill level (usually requiring a bachelor's degree or higher) accounted for 45.1% of total employment growth over the past three decades. By contrast, occupations commensurate with the lowest skill level (usually requiring Certificate I or secondary education) accounted for only 9.4% of total employment growth (Department of Employment, Skills, Small and Family Business 2019: 3).

The extent and complexity of structural change in Australia and its impact on the labour market have been captured by several studies (Adeney 2018; Connolly and Lewis 2010; Heath 2016). Adeney (2018) indicated that there are internal sectoral changes that are shifting production from goods and distribution to service production, especially in the business and professional services sectors. These have resulted in a consequential shift in skill requirements across the economy towards business and professional skills- jobs that require high-level cognitive skills.

Further, Heath (2016) demonstrated that the changing composition of jobs can be divided by skill sets into routine and cognitive. Routine jobs involve homogenous and repetitive tasks and are associated with relatively short training periods. Cognitive jobs are characterised by complex and multiple tasks, involve autonomy, and require extensive training. Some routine jobs require cognitive skills, for example, customer inquiry, complaints, and service centres. Using this classification, Heath (2016) argued that the jobs that are increasing have non- routine and cognitive attributes. While the sectoral change will generate changes in the compositions of jobs, together with other conditions such as technology, there are likely to be changes to the skill composition of both existing and new jobs. Across each industry sector the underlying structural conditions determining output and employment differ. These include income, demographic, international and policy conditions. Technology can displace not only labour but can also change the skill requirements for the industry. As a result, when considering the impact of the range of technologies associated with the 4IR, consideration also needs to be given to the other conditions that are changing the demand for labour and skills.

Positioning Australia in the Global Context of the 4IR

The WEF (2016) survey of global corporations reported that the four main barriers that organisations faced in addressing projected skills needs were insufficient understanding of disruptive changes, resource constraints, pressure from shareholders, and workforce strategies unaligned with innovation strategies. Large, sophisticated, and international organisations with embedded human resource management (HRM) programs and strategies were regarded as not being prepared for the workforce and skill changes associated with the 4IR.

The 2019 Australian Industry Group (AIG) report *The Fourth Industrial Revolution – Australian Businesses in Transition* stated that 'Australian businesses are currently transitioning to the Fourth Industrial Revolution (or Industry 4.0)' (p. 5). The report indicated that progress towards Industry 4.0 has been evident mostly from leading local and multinational firms that have been 'doing amazing things with new technology and leading the way for others' (AIG 2019: 5), while the gap between these firms and most other businesses is substantial in terms of the integration of technological advances into productive pursuits. A research report by Renjen (2020) for a *Deloitte Review* focused on exploring readiness to leverage the 4IR to benefit customers, employees, communities, and other key stakeholders. Drawing on findings from 1600 C-level executives surveyed across nineteen countries, in addition to personal interviews, it was reported that many executives lack confidence in their organisations' readiness to influence and harness the opportunities offered by the 4IR.

For Australia, the findings indicate that only 2% of Australian business leaders felt confident that they could exploit the changes associated with the 4IR, compared with 14% of executives globally (Renjen 2020). That said, the Australian CEOs surveyed were reportedly the most confident concerning the skills and abilities of their current workforce to adapt to the necessary changes. Specifically, 71% of Australian executives (compared with 40% globally) reported that they have people in place with the right skills to maximise their potential. This was the highest percentage of any country surveyed. The two statements appear to be paradoxical, however, as it begs the question as to why CEOs lack the confidence to exploit the necessary changes required for the 4IR if they believe they have employees with the right skills to do so.

An earlier study by the Economist Intelligence Unit (EIU 2018) resulted in the creation of the Automation Readiness Index (ARI) where Australia was ranked 10th out of a total of twenty-five countries. The Automation Readiness Index compares countries on their preparedness for the age of intelligent automation. In assessing the existence of policy and strategy in the areas of innovation, education and the labour market, the study found that little policy was in place that specifically addresses the challenges of AI- and robotics-based automation (EIU 2018: 5).

Countries were compared according to their relative 'readiness' status for automation. Readiness relates to the ability to develop and apply automated solutions, together with their capacity to support the innovation process (through education) and translate it into programs that support workplace adjustment and upskilling. The ARI ranked the selected countries against these criteria. The Index focuses on three policy areas: innovation policy (government and industry); education policy (secondary, vocational, and higher education systems) and labour market policy (government, industry and educational systems) – (EIU 2018). These were informed by fifty-two indicators that were combined to provide a score by each criteria. Across the three key areas that influence readiness, Australia's rankings were: innovation environment (7/25), education policies (11/25), and labour market policies (10/25).

The Economist Intelligence Unit Report (2018: 7) included two key findings, namely:

> Automation thus points toward the augmentation of work, potentially leading to greater job satisfaction, as well as to outright displacement. Humans will continue to play a role in designing or operating these systems, and it is expected that many activities will continue to require the distinct skills of humans. Work performed by people will be continuously redefined, requiring the constant updating of skills. Governments, businesses, educators, labour unions and civil society organisations all have roles to play in developing an understanding of what the impacts of automation are likely to be and to plan initiatives that will help their societies adapt.

A subsequent study conducted in Australia reported on the level of preparedness amongst Australian human resource management (HRM) professionals related to the impact of the 4IR on organisations, workplaces, jobs and skills, as well as on their professional roles and competencies (Nankervis et al. 2019). Survey findings indicated that, while most HRM professionals felt that 4IR technologies would be useful for their organisations and assist with improving job performance, increasing productivity and making jobs easier for employees, not many intended to use these technologies soon. Many survey respondents also reported that they were not impressed with the lack of current Australian government 4IR strategies and policies. This sentiment is also evident in the Australian Industry Group (AIG 2019:3) report:

> People are right to demand solutions. Real solutions need substance and rigour. There is a growing risk worldwide that anger, distrust, and the need to be seen to be doing something lead to populist or heavy-handed proposals on trade, regulation, and technology. That would undermine the foundations both of global growth and Australia's strong performance over recent decades. Australia needs to achieve inclusive growth. Making the most of the Fourth Industrial Revolution is essential to that goal.

The Framework for Evaluating the 4IR

Critical reviews of the 4IR and the future of work (FOW) highlight the absence of nuanced analyses such as how the new technologies impact the gendered division of labour, the spatial distribution of jobs across regions and countries, and the quality of jobs (Rainnie and Dean 2019). To develop a systematic link between the 4IR and the FOW, there is a need for an analytical starting point and a framework to evaluate the implications for work and skills development. The 4IR is a typology that classifies technological change as a sequential process that is linked by keystone technological developments. However, within the 4IR framework there are contextual and social conditions that intervene to disrupt, regulate, or circumvent the introduction and adoption of new technologies. Three such conditions are infrastructure access and quality; government policies; and industry/labour regulations. Accessing the platform economy becomes difficult if there is only unreliable or limited web and energy access. Industry regulations. policies and procedures governing competition, product standards, immigration, procurement, education and skill development and certification all impact on the processes and consequences of technological change. Labour regulations that proscribe set conditions for employment and redundancy, occupational health, and safety, and limit the unfettered application of technology towards labour displacement and the downgrading of employment conditions mitigate the impact of change.

The focus in this volume is not directly on the 4IR or the FOW. Instead, it is on the impact of technological change within the identified industry sectors, covering the full spectrum from new products and processes, automation, artificial intelligence, internet and platform technologies, data mining, industry, labour and skill needs. At the industry level, the technology, product and labour market conditions and institutional conditions differ. Behind the technological changes, as explained above, there are other conditions that impact differently on industry products and labour markets. These include global and national growth rates, the demographic profile of the population, the levels and skill composition of migration, patterns of income and consumer expenditure, and the skill and educational profile of the population. Hence, making predictions linked to the 4IR must consider the other conditions that impact on future product and labour markets.

The Research Method

Each chapter in this book addresses the research questions outlined in the introduction and draws on multiple data sources. The analysis is exploratory in nature, mainly drawing on secondary sources from the key stakeholder groups associated with the relevant industry sector. Documentary analysis is used extensively in business and public policy research. However, it should be noted that such documents have potential biases and may present the views of one stakeholder among many. With regard to this book, most of the documents utilised are in the public domain and can be authenticated and they represent organisational, rather than private perspectives. Bryman and Bell (2011: 545) maintain that documents can be analysed according to their authenticity by asking questions such as: authenticity (is the evidence genuine?); credibility (is the evidence free from error and distortion?); representation (is the evidence consistent with similar evidence?); and meaning (is the evidence unambiguous?).

The range of documents sourced and presented is not consistent across the chapters, as the stakeholders are different, and the volume and quality of official data also differs. The purpose of the analysis is to critically assimilate and interpret the documentary material (Bryman and Bell 2011: 561) to help answer the core research questions. To support the research questions the approach to the research reported in this book is summarised by the following points:

A. The 4IR is a set of technological possibilities whose relevance and application across industries form the basis for the research.
B. Technological change is not the only condition impacting on product and labour markets; any analysis of the impact of 4IR should be cognisant of other conditions that will impact on industry employment and skill needs.
C. Industries share common technologies, product and labour market conditions, and institutional conditions, so they represent a suitable framework in which to discuss the impact of technological change on employment and skills.
D. In some cases, standard industry classifications may be unsuitable for capturing production and employment generated through the platform economy, as the 4IR technologies not only generate new products and processes but also restructure industries and blur the boundaries between industries.
E. The identification of salient stakeholders in the selected industries provides a basis for the collection of data and for providing a range of informed perspectives towards assessing the core research questions (Nankervis et al. 2019).

F. The relevant salient stakeholders comprise those groups who have a vested interest in the industry sector and who can influence industry job and skill profiles. These groups include organisations, industry associations, professional associations, trade unions, training and education institutions, state and federal government agencies.

The Organisation of the Book

The chapters in the book are organised by industry sector, broadly following the ANZSIC industry classification. The purpose of the industry classification system is to 'to organise data about business units. It provides a standard framework under which business units carrying out similar productive activities can be grouped together, with each resultant group referred to as an industry' (ABS 2006: webpage).

The industry classifications are grouped broadly to encompass a range of industries. Under the broad groupings, there are subdivisions that are broken down into greater detail where the activities become more uniform. The ABS provides an example – manufacturing as the broad classification, which can be broken down to food product manufacturing, then to meat and meat product manufacturing, and then to meat processing. Here, the industry groupings use the broad classifications, and some of them are aggregated as in the case of agriculture, mining, and construction.

The chapters do not cover all major industry groupings, consequently, there are some notable absences. These include: professional, scientific, and technical services; and administrative and support services. Moreover, the coverage of the selected industries is incomplete, for example the public sector analysis is confined to local government; and the analysis of education is confined to universities. The boundaries between industries are fluid as new business models, products and production processes emerge that are associated with the 4IR. There is greater integration across industries through IT and supply chains, and services are increasingly becoming an important component of those sectors that were previously associated with producing physical goods, such as manufacturing and construction. The ordering of the chapters follows the ANZSIC codes from agriculture through to education and health. Each chapter is structured to provide an overview of the structural developments within the sector, especially in terms of employment and skills; this is followed by a discussion of the key technologies that are impacting production and employment within the sector. This is followed by an analysis of how jobs, work and skills are changing in the sector; and finally, the chapters consider the challenges and opportunities that the technological changes have generated in each sector, together with an evaluation of how the key stakeholders in that sector are responding to these challenges.

The chapters are presented in order of the ANZSIC broad industry divisions:

1. Agriculture, Forestry and Fishing; Mining; Construction

2. Manufacturing
3. Utilities
4. Retail Trade
5. Accommodation and Tourism
6. Transport, and Warehousing
7. Information Media and Telecommunications
8. Financial and Insurance Services
9. Local Government
10. Higher Education
11. Health Care

The chapters identify the key 4IR technologies impacting each sector. The application and impact of the 4IR technologies is present across all sectors. Moreover, there is a 'within sector impact', where the introduction of these technologies leads to the restructuring of production and work within the sector. Sectoral boundaries are also eroded by the 4IR technologies as the divisions that were present in the past are blurred as cloud technologies, big data, new energy sources, and the internet of things transforms production, processes, employment, and skills across all sectors and generates new skill demands and new products and processes.

Chapter Summaries The first of the industry focused chapters by Cameron and Rana explores three major industries: agriculture, mining, and construction. The authors explore the major technological developments and adoptions, how they are impacting work, and those occupations most affected. They also identify how jobs are changing and the related future skills that are likely to be needed to meet these trends, the major technologies impacting each sector with key stakeholder views covered and the related policy implications. All three industry sectors have varying rates of 4IR technology uptake and adoption for reasons that are explored further in the chapter. Although the Australian and New Zealand Standard Industrial Classification (ANZSIC) includes eighteen industry sub-sectors, agriculture, mining and construction were selected as the focus for this chapter as they represent the major employers. However, the authors also provide an overview of the key trends and workforce impacts for the other fifteen industry sub-sectors in this category.

The next chapter by Rainnie and Dean addresses Australian manufacturing. The authors refer to the concept of a 'resources curse', and the implications of global 'financialisation' before examining the potential consequences of the 4IR for the sector. The authors argue that the positive implications of the 4IR are reinforced by the ramifications of deglobalisation in general and COVID-19 in particular. For example, the authors question whether the conventional wisdom which suggests that 4IR technologies (such as 3D-printing) are in fact going to help support a revival of re-shored manufacturing. Consequently, Rainnie and Dean cast doubt on just how realistic the anticipated outcomes of the 4IR are for the Australian manufacturing sector.

Chapter 3 focuses on the impact of artificial intelligence and associated technological changes on work and jobs in Australia's utility sector – electricity, gas, water and waste services. The analysis mainly concentrates on disruptive technology in a broad context which incorporates the collective effects of AI and machine learning, big data, and blockchain. The authors, Cheng, Ganganath, Lee and Fok, identify eight fundamental research gaps and business opportunities. Specifically, they conclude that the utility sector is highly applicable for digitalisation as it involves extensive physical assets that continuously generate valuable data. Further, the authors maintain that Utility 4.0 technologies can shape a utility company to become more lean and agile, which is essential for it to maintain its competitiveness for the post-pandemic era and the challenging future. However, apart from direct data usage in production control in the upstream, such as power plants and oil refineries, and in fault detections in the midstream, which cover the transmission and distribution networks, it is argued that there is a current lack of business cases that involve the massive volume of end-users. Thus, although AI can be used more extensively under human supervision to process big data collected from utility assets and therefore support improved decision making, privacy and ethical issues must be addressed whenever personal data is involved.

In Chap. 5, Larkin and Nankervis investigate the retail sector. They point out that, although retail is the largest employer in Australia, the prevalence of part-time work, casualisation and precarious work are common, as are the related low wages and low union representation. Unlike most other sectors, many retail players benefitted from the COVID-19 crisis, with the Australian Bureau of Statistics (ABS) data illustrating record increases in sales. Despite this, artificial intelligence and automation generally have had significant negative impacts on employment within the industry, particularly in relation to supply chain and distribution. The authors place emphasis on the Food Retailing and Other Store-based Retailing areas from both small-medium-enterprises (SMEs) and large business perspectives. They found that, while some predicted transformations (especially those in the lower-skilled entry level positions) did not bode well for future employment, there were some positive predictions offered by employers and unions, especially where future service-based leadership models are being adopted and supported by industry and government. Tourism is considered in the next chapter by Dhakal which focuses on the accommodation and food services [AFS] sector - considered to be one of the main drivers of economic growth in Australia. Specifically, tourism industries collectively contributed over $100 billion to Australia's GDP, employing nearly one million people in 2019. An emergent issue associated with tourism industries is the 4IR and the impacts of transformative digital technologies. These have advanced rapidly in recent years and are considered to be game-changers for the sector. That said, Dhakal maintains that, although the business-centric view of digital opportunities associated with the 4IR has received significant attention, the policy-centric examination of the 4IR and tourism nexus remains under the radar in Australia. The chapter aims to respond to this gap, drawing on the three pillars of the Automation Readiness Index (EIU 2018) - innovation, education and employment policy landscapes - to explore the challenges and a potential way forward for the AFS sector.

In Chap. 6, Dethridge outlines how AI is used in Australian media which includes advertising, journalism, publishing, film, and TV production. AI use covers (among other areas) data analytics in advertising and journalism and the automation of roles previously performed by people in screen, literary and arts production. As a result, it is predicted that the increased use of AI and automation will lead to concurrent job loss and job creation in the sector. AI currently constitutes a production tool which has led stakeholders to propose that, in future, media production companies may work in collaboration with software and interface designers to ensure that a sustainable, human-centred approach is taken when using technology. In this way AI may augment the creative, knowledge-based work undertaken by higher-skilled workers in media industries, improving their productivity and subsequently the demand for such workers. The Australian Consumer and Competition Commission (ACCC) emphasised the need for transparency in its 2020 inquiry into the impact of Google and Facebook and their use of AI and user data for commercial purposes. Dethridge proposes that similar investigations will highlight the use of AI and data analytics in the Australian and global media industries, particularly with regard to the supply of news and the implications for media content providers, advertisers and consumers.

The next chapter provides an overview of the impact of the 4IR on the transport and logistics sector in Australia. Tay, Gekara and Ghalebeigi use several case studies to provide insights into how Australia is addressing these technological challenges. The authors conclude that the sector has undergone a complex transformation in its workforce skills requirement such that it now requires new job configurations, new skills and workforce development and training to be able to address the requirements of the 4IR. Notably, the authors argue that employer responses to the changing skill needs of the sector has been varied to date, with the majority of organisations making little effort and investment in training. That said, they argue that the greater burden for training currently rests with employers, largely because the push to drive technological changes for enhanced productivity is mainly coming from that stakeholder group. Consequently, while a comprehensive government policy on workforce digital transformation in Australia is lacking, it is proposed that employers need to not only implement extensive in-house re-skilling and up-skilling for their workers but they also need to actively participate in developing a sustainable pool of workers for the sector due to the 4IR.

As in other chapters, Australia's Financial and Insurance Services sector is explored in relation to the impact of artificial intelligence and associated technological changes on work and jobs. Montague, Svanberg, Maisano, & Fernandes examine the cumulative effects of AI, incorporating machine learning, big data, blockchain, chatbots and financial technology (fintech). The chapter primarily focuses on disruptive technology in a relatively broad context, leading the authors to offer three main conclusions. First, that jobs will most likely be substantially impacted with 15–30% of employment in the risk zone. Losses are predicted not only in relation to repetitive jobs but also in analytical and decision-making jobs that may currently be well-paid and highly regarded. Second, the authors propose that most of the potential for AI in banks and insurance companies is in places where it is invisible, leading them to assert that the myriad of tasks that are relegated to the "back-office" are more at risk of being automated than those that are not. Such tasks include lending decisions, insurance policy agreements, deposits and payments and those related to internal controls such as loss prevention and fraud detection. The authors' third point concerns the Hayne (2019) Royal Commission into Misconduct in the Banking, Superannuation and Financial Services Industry which, following the malpractices uncovered due to the relentless quest for profit and bonuses, requires a culture change in the sector.

The Australian public sector incorporates federal, state, and local government agencies and is one of the largest employment sectors in the economy incorporating a range of different occupations. However, this chapter by Burgess and Shaikh specifically examines AI and technological developments in local government, as the public sector as a whole is too large and diverse to capture comprehensively. Technology is key to the development of many areas of the public sector with for example, defence, being driven by technological developments in hardware and software. In common with much of the public sector, local government has been subject to the reforms and pressures of new public sector management to improve service delivery and achieve cost reductions and efficiencies. The authors point out that, while Information Technology (IT) and automation have the potential to support both the quality and efficiency objectives of local government, there are challenges related to the impact of structural and technological change on employment, especially in the regions. The chapter considers a range of these challenges, including the potential impact of COVID-19 on finances and the demand for services which it is proposed is likely to increase the demand for technological solutions and skills development.

Next, Connell and Malik explore the impact and influence of the 4IR and artificial intelligence applications on the Australian Higher Education (HE) sector. The chapter focus is on the potential impact of new technologies and their anticipated effects on the sector, its educators, and students. The authors set out to provide a broad understanding of the potential challenges and changes within the context of the recent coronavirus global pandemic. They point out that the restructuring of employment caused by technological disruption and the 4IR followed by COVID-19 brought some areas of HE to a grinding halt. This in turn has led to huge downturns in student enrolments and job losses in the sector. Consequently, the challenges due to both the technological and health crises for the Australian and global HE sector are explored from early 2020. The authors conclude that the role of HE in society and the economy will have to transform to offer best practices in online teaching and high-quality online materials and access appropriate for all student contexts.

The final concluding chapter, by the editors, summarises the key comparative findings across the eleven sectors included in the book. A brief sector overview of the new technologies and the related impact on jobs and workers, as well as the potential challenges and opportunities is provided. With regard to the implications for government, industry, employers and unions it is pointed out that, although there is not yet a dedicated national AI strategy, the government did recently publish Australia's Tech Future, the implications of which are outlined. The editors also refer to the current Prime Minister, Scott Morrison's roadmap for Australian manufacturing which is intended to drive the uptake of digital technologies across businesses and subsequently lead to increases in productivity and innovation. As yet, the effectiveness of such strategies is, of course, unknown.

References

Acemoglu, D., & Restrepo, P. (2017). *The race between man and machine: Implications of technology for growth, factor shares and employment* (Working paper 22252). Cambridge, MA: National Bureau of Economic Research (NBER).

Adeney, R. (2018). Structural change in the Australian economy. Reserve Bank of Australia Bulletin. March 1–18.

Arnold, D., Arntz, M., Gregory, T., Steffes, S., & Zierahn, U. (2018). No need for automation angst but automation policies. In M. Neufeind, J. OReilly, & F. Ranft (Eds.), *Work in the digital age, challenges of the fourth industrial revolution*. London: Rowman & Littlefield International.

Arntz, M., Gregory, T., & Zierahn, U. (2016). *The risk of automation for jobs in OECD countries: A comparative analysis* (OECD Social, Employment and Migration Working Papers, 189) (pp. 1–34).

Australian Bureau of Statistics. (2006). *Australia and New Zealand Industrial Classification*. Catalogue 1292.0. Canberra.

Australian Bureau of Statistics. (2020). Household Impacts of COVID-19 Survey. https://www.abs.gov.au/statistics/people/people-and-communities/household-impacts-covid-19-survey/latest-release#data-download

Australian Industry Group. (2019). *The fourth industrial revolution Australian businesses in transition*. Australian Industry Group Melbourne. Retrieved March 13, 2020, from, https://cdn.aigroup.com.au/Reports/2019/AiGroup_Fourth_Industrial_Revolution_Report.pdf

Ayentimi, D. T., & Burgess, J. (2018). Is the fourth industrial revolution relevant to sub-Sahara Africa? *Technology Analysis & Strategic Management*. https://doi.org/10.1080/09537325.2018.1542129.

Bandura, R., & Hammond, M. (2018). *Volume 2: Developing country trends and insights from four country case studies, policy file*. Washington DC: Center for Strategic & International Studies.

Bryman, A., & Bell, E. (2011). *Business research methods* (3rd ed.). Oxford: Oxford University Press.

Brynjolfsson, E., & McAfee, A. (2017). The second machine age. In *Work, progress, and prosperity in a time of brilliant technologies*. New York: W.W. Norton & Company.

Cedefop, K. (2019). *Artificial or human intelligence? Digitalisation and the future of jobs and skills: Opportunities and risks*. Briefing Note, June. ISSN 1831-2411. Available at: www.cedefop.europa.eu/files/9140_en.pdf. Accessed 1 July 2019.

Cisco and Oxford Economics. (2019). Technology and the future of Australian jobs, what will be the impact of AI on workers in every sector? www.cisco.com/c/dam/m/en_au/cda/cisco-future-of-australian-jobs-report2019.pdf. Accessed 30 Oct 2020.

Connolly, E. & Lewis, C. (2010). Structural change in the Australian economy. *Reserve Bank of Australia Bulletin,* September 1–10.

Department of Employment, Skills, Small and Family Business. Labour Market Research and Analysis Branch. (2019). *Changes in the Australian labour market: a 30-year perspective*. Retrieved March 13, 2020, from http://lmip.gov.au/default.aspx?LMIP/GainInsights/SpecialTopicReports

Devasahayam, T., Higo, M., Dhirathiti, N., & Klassen, T. (2018). *Ageing in Asia-Pacific: Interdisciplinary and comparative perspectives* (1st ed.). New York: Routledge.

Dilsizian, S. E., & Siegel, E. L. (2014). Artificial intelligence in medicine and cardiac imaging: Harnessing big data and advanced computing to provide personalized medical diagnosis and treatment. *Current Cardiology Reports, 16*(1), 441.

Economist Intelligence Unit (EIU) Ltd. (2018). *The automation readiness index: Who is ready for the coming wave of automation?* Commissioned by the ABB (ASEA Brown Boveri). Available at: www.automationreadiness.eiu.com/. Accessed 1 July 2019.

Federal Treasury. (2010). *Australia to 2050: Future challenges*. Canberra: Commonwealth of Australia, The Treasury.

Finextra and Intel. (2017). *The next big wave: How financial institutions can stay ahead of the AI revolution.* Retrieved from http://www.catalina-consulting.com/wp-content/uploads/2017/07/intel_finextra_0517.pdf

Fluss, D. (2017). *The AI revolution in customer service.* Retrieved from https://www.destination-crm.com/Articles/Columns-Departments/Scouting-Report/The-AI-Revolution-in-Customer-Service-115528.aspx

Hayne, K. (2019). Final report: The Royal Commission into misconduct in the banking, *Superannuation and Financial Services Industry. Volume 1.* Commonwealth of Australia, Canberra https://financialservices.royalcommission.gov.au/Pages/reports.aspx. Accessed 12 July 2020.

Heath, A. (2016), 'The changing nature of the Australian workforce', speech at CEDA – Future skills: The education and training pipeline, Brisbane, 21 September.

Lu, S., & Burton, S. L. (2017). *Man vs robots? Future challenges and opportunities within artificial intelligence (AI) health care education model.* Proceedings of the RAIS Conference: Human Development – A Multidisciplinary Research, November 6–7, 2017, Montgomery County Campus, Rockville, MD.

Marrengo, L. (2019). Is this time different? A note on automation and labour in the fourth industrial revolution. *Economia E Politica Industriale, 46*(3), 323–331.

Nankervis, A., Connell, J., Cameron, R., Montague, A., & Prikshat, V. (2019). 'Are we there yet? 'Australian HR professionals and the Fourth Industrial Revolution. *Asia Pacific Journal of Human Resources*. 31 August. https://doi.org/10.1111/1744-7941.12245.

Rainnie, A., & Dean, M. (2019). Industry 4.0 and the quality of work in the global digital economy, Labour & Industry. *A Journal of the Social and Economic Relations of Work, 30*(1), 16–33.

Renjen, P., (2020). *Industry 4.0: At the intersection of readiness and responsibility Deloitte Global's annual survey on business's preparedness for a connected era*, issue 26 https://www2.deloitte.com/us/en/insights/deloitte-review/issue-22/industry-4-0-technology-manufacturing-revolution.html. Accessed 17 Feb 2020.

Ross, P., & Maynard, K. (2021). *Towards a 4th Industrial Revolution, Intelligent Building International*. https://doi.org/10.1080/17508975.2021.1873625.

Scarpetta, S. (2017). *What future for work?*. Retrieved from http://oecdobserver.org/news/fullstory.php/aid/5433/What_future_for_work_.html

Schwab, K. (2016). *The fourth industrial revolution: What it means, how to respond.* In *WEF Switzerland.* Retrieved March 13, 2020 https://www.weforum.org/agenda/2016/01/the-fourth-industrial-revolution-what-it-means-and-how-to-respond/.

Susskind, K. (2020). *A world without work technology, automation, and how we should respond.* UK: Penguin Books.

World Economic Forum (WEF). (2016). The future of jobs: Employment, skills and workforce strategy for the fourth industrial revolution (Geneva). Available at: http://www3.weforum.org/docs/WEF_Future_of_Jobs.pdf

Chapter 2
Agriculture, Construction & Mining

Roslyn Cameron and Vishal Rana

Abstract This chapter explores three major industries in the Australian economy: agriculture, mining and construction. Due to the size and coverage of these industry sectors we have provided an overview of key trends and workforce impacts. The chapter treats each of these industry sectors separately analysing the major technological developments and adoptions, how this is impacting work and those occupations most impacted, what skill sets are needed and how are jobs changing and being re designed. What future skilling is needed to meet these trends with key stakeholder views covered as well as policy implications before concluding the chapter.

Keywords Agriculture · Construction · Mining

Introduction

The Fourth Industrial Revolution (4IR) is heralding an epoch of unprecedented transformations and is characterised by a ground breaking era in scientific knowledge creation accompanied by an unparalleled rate of technological developments, innovations and applications across all sectors in economy. Previous industrial revolutions had profound effects on society, created opportunities and economic advancements however what characterises 4IR is that the transformations are unique in terms of the almost sonic speed at which these ideas and technologies are spreading and pervading all aspects of our lives. Schwab (2017) asserts that this revolution is distinct from preceding revolutions for 3 reasons: the **velocity** of change; the

R. Cameron (✉)
Director of the Centre for Organisational Change and Agility (COCA), Torrens University, Adelaide, Australia
e-mail: Ros.cameron@torrens.edu.au

V. Rana
Australian Institute of Business, Adelaide, SA, Australia
e-mail: Vishal.rana@aib.edu.au

A. Nankervis et al. (eds.), *The Fourth Industrial Revolution*,
https://doi.org/10.1007/978-981-16-1614-3_2

breadth and depth of the digital revolution and; **systems impact** (transformations across countries, companies, industries & society as a whole).

> "We are seeing a fusion of technologies across physical, digital and biological worlds" (Schwab 2017:1).

This chapter explores three major industry sectors in the Australian economy: agriculture, mining and construction. The characteristics of each sector are discussed, with reference to the the key new technologies employed, and the predicted impacts on employment trends, and finally, the challenges and opportunities they provide.

Industry Overview, Key Technologies & Employment Impacts

The Australian and New Zealand Standard Industrial Classification (ANZSIC) includes eighteen industry sectors. The focus of this chapter are the following three sectors: agriculture, mining and construction. The coverage of these industries is summarised below (Table 2.1).

Recent statistics from the Australian Bureau of Statistics (2020) reported on the economic performance of these three sectors. The report compared the 2018–2019 financial period to the previous period (2017–2018) and found substantial growth for the mining industry which grew 32.2% in that period in Earnings before interest, tax, depreciation and amortisation (EBITDA). In contrast the construction sector although positive EBITDA growth of 5.4%, this did not match the 8% in the previous year. The Agriculture sector also saw a decrease in EBITDA. The effects of climate change are impacting this sector which fluctuates in economic performance but generally is in slight decline.

In terms of employment movement for each sector, mining experienced a growth of 10,000 employees (5.9%) a direct result of large export growth and growth in metal or mining sub division. There has been a slow decline in employment on agriculture and a slight increase in employment in construction. According to AISC (2020a, b, c, d, e, website) 'employment in the construction industry increased between 2000 and 2019, with a slight fall in 2012 that has been recovered. Employment reached over 1,183,000 in 2019 and is projected to exceed 1,282,000

Table 2.1 Agriculture, Forestry & Fishing, Mining and Construction Industries

Agriculture, Forestry & Fishing	Mining	Construction
Agriculture Aquaculture Forestry and Logging Fishing, Hunting and Trapping Agriculture, Forestry and Fishing Support Services	Coal Mining Oil and Gas Extraction Metal Ore Mining Non-Metallic Mineral Mining and Quarrying Exploration and Other Mining Support Services	Building Construction Heavy and Civil Engineering Construction Construction Services

by 2024'. For agriculture there were 451, 000 people employed, for the mining sector employees in this sector was 179,000 and for construction the numbers were at 1,117,000 for the 2018–2019 financial year (ABS 2020).

Different 4IR technologies are affecting these sectors. For example, driverless vehicles/trains have been utilised by the mining industry for some time. Rio Tinto, the WA based iron ore company first used Komatsu autonomous haulage vehicles in the Pilbara region in 2008. The mining industry utilises robotic technologies for several purposes and these have positive workplace health and safety benefits. The agriculture sector is increasingly utilising a variety of cropping technologies and drones to monitor livestock. Blockchain in food production is also becoming widely used tracking food supply chains. In construction new technologies are impacting the industry and include developments related to: building information modelling (IBM), 3D printing, automatisation and robotics, prefabrication and offsite manufacturing, materials technology, structural analysis and design procedures and survey.

We have reviewed both grey and academic literature and statistics to provide an overview of each of these three sectors and the respective adoption and uptake of 4IR technologies across these sectors. We have analysed the impacts this is having on the nature of work and associated skills gaps and skilling requirements for 4IR readiness and adoption. The remainder of the chapter is structured around these three sectors and concludes with a summary of 4IR technology adoption and the policy and associated strategies needed between key stakeholders to support these sectors and sector workforces as we all proceed into this new unprecedented era of sonic speed technological innovation.

Construction

The World Economic Forum (2018) created the Shaping the Future of Construction initiative to guide the industry through transformation. They refer to this industry as Infrastructure and Urban Development industry (IU). The WEF devised three extreme but plausible scenarios of a possible future to frame and scope a range of possible futures for the industry. On one hand they posit the *Building in a virtual world* scenario where intelligent systems and robotics run the world. Another is *Factories run the world* scenario (involves a corporate driven society which maximises prefabrication and modularisation for efficiencies) and the third *Green Reboot* scenario. This is essentially a response to climate change and scarce resources that would see greater use of sustainable materials and eco-friendly construction methods (WEF 2018). It is likely the future will contain dimensions of all three scenarios. This scenario framework enabled the WEF in consultation with CEOs of construction companies and government ministers to come up with six industry transformational imperatives: 'attract new talent and build up required skills; integrate and collaborate across the IU value chain; and adopt advanced technologies at scale'. The remaining three were: 'maximize the use of data and digital models throughout processes; review existing product portfolios and embrace new business opportunities; and enable change management and adaptiveness' (WEF 2018: 7).

The construction industry worldwide contributes to 13% of global GDP Bartlett et al. (2019) and is facing a combination of broader macro trends such as skill shortages, rapidly evolving customer demands for flexible spaces, smart and carbon neutral construction, pressures on existing business models that are out of sync with current demands and slowing economic growth exacerbated by the recent Covid 19 pandemic. The report identified 5 big technology disruptors for the sector: unparalleled investment in engineering and construction technologies; new technology start-ups; large scale M&A; demand for technology adoption and 4-D and 5-D building information modelling (BIM) (Bartlett et al. 2019).

Key Technologies

Blanco et al. (2018) found that despite a relatively underutilised employment of AI in the engineering and construction sector there is a slow shift to technological solutions through applying AI and algorithm applications. These are primarily used to address schedule and cost overruns and safety concerns. Blanco et al. (2018) follow the construction cycle to analyse what technologies were being utilised in the sector: starting with design, preconstruction, construction and then operations and asset management. They found that the use of AI in the construction sector is relatively embryonic but hopeful identifying a few early stage examples of AI applications:

> Project schedule optimizers can consider millions of alternatives for project delivery and continuously enhance overall project planning. Image recognition and classification can assess video data collected on work sites to identify unsafe worker behavior and aggregate this data to inform future training and education priorities. Enhanced analytics platforms can collect and analyze data from sensors to understand signals and patterns to deploy real-time solutions, cut costs, prioritize preventative maintenance, and prevent unplanned down-time (Blanco et al. 2018).

Similarly, Koeleman et al. (2019:.2) also found the uptake of digital technologies to be slow in the construction industry especially on large scale projects and claimed construction is "stuck in an analog era" due to the following reasons: Fragmentation of construction projects along a value chain of smaller disciplines and layers of contractors and subcontractors; lack of replication due to relative uniqueness of each build, tailored or customised design and delivery stages; transience of project teams that come together for a project and then dissipate to the next project compounded by high employee turnover rates and lastly the decentralisation of construction activity from offices and therefore ability to teach workers how to use advanced technologies (Koeleman et al. 2019).

The Australian construction industry operates in across three main areas of construction activity:

- engineering construction (major infrastructure, mining and heavy industrial resource-based projects);
- non-residential building (including offices, shops, hotels, industrial premises, hospitals, entertainment facilities) and;
- residential building (houses, flats, home units, townhouses) (Ai Group 2020: 5).

The majority of businesses in this sector are SME or sole traders or very small and mostly Australian owned however the supply chains for this industry are becoming more and more dependent on overseas sourced materials. Although the large majority of businesses are SMEs the sector is dominated by large players. "While sector overall is made up of 345,480 businesses, the top 20 firms account for 68% of contracts won" Gruszka et al. (2017: 6) which provides a greater openness to adopting 4IR technologies as these large players have more access to resources to fund technological adoption in the name of efficiencies and productivity.

The construction workforce is predominantly male, works full time, is younger and mostly self-employed: '84.7% of construction workers are full-time, compared with 68.3% across all industries, and 15.3% part-time, compared to 31.7% for all industries and 88.2% of construction workers are male, compared with 52.9% across all industries (original data, February 2019)' (Ai Group 2019: 6). According to the Australian Industry Skills Committee 'There is a lack of gender diversity, with the percentage of women in the workforce declining from 17% in 2006 to 11.6% in 2018 and leaving the industry almost 39% faster than men' (AISC 2020c: webpage).

The vocational education and training (VET) sector plays a very important role for this sector in terms of the trades and occupations that dominate the sector. The VET sector also plays a role in licensing these occupations. The top 5 occupations in demand for the sector include: Architectural, Building and Surveying Technicians Contract, Program and Project Administrators; Civil Engineering Professionals; Electricians; Carpenters and Joiners (AISC 2020c). According to projections by PwC (2015) lower skilled construction occupations (plasterers and tilers) have a high probability of becoming automated in the next 20 years. However, construction occupations in demand and least likely to be affected by automation and or optimisation technologies include: construction project manager and site supervisors (Artibus Innovation 2019).

Employment Impacts

There is a skills replacement gap emerging for the sector due to an ageing workforce which has further ramifications: "an increase in older people in the workforce is likely to create a demand for less physically demanding jobs. Automation and new technology may provide a solution but with this comes the need to upskill and re-skill the older population of construction workers to use new technologies and automated processes" (Artibus Innovation 2019:17). There are three main drivers for workforce upskilling and training: introduction of 4IR technologies such as (automation of low skilled jobs, BIM and prefabrication); levels of regulation and compliance and; demand for green and smart buildings. Building information modelling (BIM) will assist those senior managerial construction and project management roles however the adoption of this has variety across the sector and is usually employed by larger construction companies on complex construction sites.

> BIM is projected to completely replace current computer-aided design (CAD) systems. This is helped by smartphone and tablet technologies, which allow project workers and stakeholders to quickly access building information through BIM, virtually everywhere. Governments in Australia have been slow to mandate BIM for public works, however, in late 2018 the Queensland government mandated that all major government construction projects with an estimated capital cost of $50 million or more will be required to use BIM (Artibus Innovation 2019: 20).

The issue will be the need for subcontractors to buy into the connective digital technologies and may see many of these paper based/static data process subcontractors unable to be compete with those that do. The Australian construction industry has had a slow take up of prefabrication when compared to global markets elsewhere however it is slowly becoming more common place and will require different skill sets from workers in this industry particularly manufacturing skill sets. According to Gruszka et al. (2017: 40):

> The spectrum of digital and IT maturity in the construction industry and value chain varies from those who continue to rely largely on people and paper-based processes to those who have sophisticated IT environments and have actively engaged in capitalising on digital solutions.

The Australian Construction Industry forum (ACIF) has developed resources to assist the industry with guiding principles, practises, curriculum content and professional development to build skills and knowledge for BIM technologies: *Building information modelling (BIM) Knowledge and Skills Framework*. Despite a general feeling about the inevitability of digital adoption across the sector Gruszka et al. (2017) report six major barriers to the uptake: sector dynamics, financial constraints, corporate culture barriers, solution limitations, change fatigue and lack of regulation and standards. The COVID 19 pandemic and flow on economic impact to construction growth and supply chains is also having profound effects on the sector. Reliance on overseas produced materials especially from China, social distancing of employees on site along with business closures of smaller companies and subcontractors which could future skill shortages and impacts on large projects reliant on sub-contractors are having major impacts on the sector. Consumer confidence in housing sales is also a factor in a highly probable pandemic induced economic downturn.

Mining

The mining sector covers the following: Coal Mining; Oil and Gas Extraction; Metal Ore Mining; Non-Metallic Mineral Mining and Quarrying, Exploration and Other Mining Support Services. The sector is undergoing some major structural changes and impacts which is questioning its very nature and future given the growing impetus of climate change and extreme weather events. PwC (2019b) reported that of those mining companies they surveyed some had adopted climate change strategies whilst others had not. Investors are concerned at the lack of attention to reducing emissions, lack of investment in digital technologies and unresponsiveness to consumers and the wider community through building brand (PwC 2019b). The report concluding "Technology is becoming a critical differentiator for the world's leading miners. Automation and digitisation continue to gain momentum, as companies are focused on harnessing technology to reduce the cost of maintenance and extraction. But compared with many other industries, mining's level of technological maturity is still relatively low" (PwC 2019b: 9).

An industry skills forecast for the sector, also by PwC PwC (2019a), identified 3 key drivers that are impacting the future skilling needs of the sector: steady environment and global demand with national and state investments in large infrastructure projects (rail and road). The COVID 19 pandemic has disrupted all sectors and economies globally with the Australian government looking at a stimulus package that could involve additional large-scale infrastructure projects. The second driver is the rapid pace of new digital technologies including automation, prefabrication and AI and machine learning that could greatly impact the way the industry operates. The third driver being safety and risk management (safety and environmental threats, fatigue, highly explosive materials and social license to operate).

Key Technologies

Mining Technology (2014) identified ten key technologies that have the capacity to alter the future of mining: robotic technology; internet of things (IoTs); advanced airborne gravity gradiometer technology for mineral exploration; 3D imaging and laser scanning also for exploration; automated and tele-operated drilling solutions; autonomous haulage systems; plasma technology which boosts yields of precious metals; adoption of centralised systems for operating, monitoring and controlling the mining or the processing activities from a remote location. The latter was taken up in Australia a decade ago when Rio Tinto was one of the first mining companies in Australia to adopt these operations centres off site, the first in Perth in 2010 (Perth Operations Centre). The centre remotely controlled Rio Tinto's entire Pilbara operations and synchronised the mining operations with the rail and port transport systems. In 2013 BHP Billiton followed suit with its own Integrated Remote Operations centre in Perth. Then in the following year Rio Tinto set up a similar centre in

Brisbane to monitor and analyse data in real time from 7 based operations in Mongolia, the USA and Australia (Mining Technology 2014).

The Minerals Council of Australia commissioned Ernst & Young Australia to undertake two related reports in 2019: *The Future of Work: the economic implications of technology and digital mining. Minerals Council of Australia* and *The Future of Work: The Changing Skills Landscape for Miners.*

In the first report Ernst and Young (2019a) drew upon ten industry case studies to map the productivity improvements of digital enablers across the mining value chain: starting from exploration, then onto mining operations, processing, transportation, trading and end to end. These enablers are summarised below in Table 2.2 and the report is not suggesting that all ten case studies utilise all these digital enablers however, this mapping demonstrates where these enablers add value and potential productivity gains. The report views the need for this digital disruption and acknowledges that this is investment heavy however, advocates for industry collaboration and guidance. The three key benefits of this digital investment being increases in productivity (estimates of 9% to 23% improvements), safety (reductions in workforce health and safety risks for the workforce) and environmental benefits (reduce environmental footprint and reduced reliance on fossil fuels/lower greenhouse gas emissions).

Table 2.2 Digital enablers for the mining value chain

Exploration	Mining Operations	Processing	Transportation	Trading	Ent to End
Data enabled exploration	Integrated drill and blast Autonomous & continued mining Underground mine of future	Fully integrated mine/plant	Integrated and optimised transport	Customer integration: Forecasting, product demand & upstream integration of supply market	End to end productivity optimisation Integrated quality management Asset management
Digital enablers					
Artificial Intelligence 3D visualisation software Downhole assay Hyper-spectral core imaging Autonomous drilling	Artificial Intelligence Machine learning 3D simulation and modelling Autonomous assets Digital twin Truck-less system Electrification	Artificial Intelligence Digital twin Mobile decision support Mineral sensing/ sorting Integrated Operating Centre Renewable energy	Artificial Intelligence Autonomous assets Digital twin Machine learning Integrated Operating Centre Centre of Excellence	Artificial Intelligence Machine learning Integrated Operating Centre Blockchain Smart contracts	Digital twin Remote Operating Centre Integrated Operating Centre Centre of Excellence Integrated automation

Source: Adapted from Ernst and Young Australia (2019a: 7)

Employment Impacts

The report predicted industry implications for these digital enablers at each stage of the mining value chain. For the exploration stage there would be fewer drill operators required and a reduced need for traditional surveyors and field geologists coupled with an increased demand for data analytics. In the mining operations stage the same impacts would apply (reduced need for drill operators and traditional geologists) and a refocus away from execution to decision support (hence increased demand for data analytics). With autonomous and continued mining digitally enabled this would result in fewer on-site employees (especially truck operators) and an associated change in the relationship between people and assets. For underground mining there will be similar impacts also with a reduction of workforce however this would also see increasingly reduced environmental impacts and remoteness of operations and increased demand for geotechnical engineers and modellers. At the processing stage of the value chain the digital enablers listed would increase the need for decision support and demand for data analytics. This also applies to the transportation stage which will also see a reduced on-site workforce. In terms of trading the main impacts will be around needing to build a change in culture towards a more customer focus mindset and increased demand for market forecasting and modelling. Marketing professionals with integrated views towards production development would be needed. Overall, the end-to-end system will enable the industry to remove the value chain silos as it moves towards greater integration of systems and roles across the value chain which will be realign performance metrics and systems (Ernst and Young 2019a).

The second report also produced by Ernst and Young (2019b) *The Future of Work: the Changing Skills Landscape for Miners* for the Australian Minerals Council of Australia undertook a detailed analysis of the skill sets required for the industry against a Technology Impacts Index. The impacts across the value chain, sector occupations, skills and education were all analysed.

The following skills for occupations for the future were identified as follows: Change Management; Collaboration; Complex Stakeholder Engagement; Creativity; Data Analysis; Data and Digital Literacy; Design Thinking; Stakeholder Analysis and; Strategic Planning. The report categorised sector occupations against the following categories in relation to the Technology Impacts Index: enhanced (42% of mining occupations with the majority in the 'end to end' stage of the value chain); redesigned (35% mining occupations, majority in the 'mining operations' stage of the value chain) and; automated (23% mining occupations, many in the 'Transport' and 'Trading' stages) (Ernst and Young 2019b: 5).

Table 2.3 summarises the main results of the report's skills and occupational analysis where 52 occupations make up 85% of the sector's current workforce. There are significant percentages of occupations in mining which will be subjected to all three categories of technology impact (enhancement, redesign and automation) and will require a concerted effort in reskilling and upskilling the current workforce.

Table 2.3 Occupations across value chain: Enhanced; redesigned and automated

Value Chain	Unique Occupations	Enhanced	Redesigned	Automated
Exploration	20	45%	35%	20%
Mining Operations	29	38%	45%	17%
Processing	28	43%	43%	14%
Transport	14	36%	43%	21%
Trading	13	38.5%	23%	38.5%
End-to-End	21	57%	24%	19%

Source: (Ernst and Young 2019a: 16)

The Agriculture sector saw a recent decline in Australia due to factors such as climate change, bushfires, and now Covid-19, however, is second only to mining in terms of its importance to the national economy, contributing more than $63 billion or 2.3% to Australia's GDP (AgriFutures Australia 2019). Australia is well positioned within the growing global agricultural markets due to its reputation as a leading agricultural producer (AUSTRADE 2020). It is estimated that there are 85,681 farms in Australia which uses 372 million hectares for agricultural production, which makes Australia 2nd largest agricultural area in the world (Poole et al. 2018). Moreover, Australia is already the 12th largest exporter of agricultural products in the world (AUSTRADE 2020). In addition, Australia has captured the world's attention for its pioneering efforts in agriculture and food production, delivering savvy solutions to global challenges (Potts and Kastelle 2017). With the world population expected to reach 10 billion by 2050 (Da Silva 2017), ensuring everyone is fed is one of the major global challenges for agriculture sector. Currently, the global food and agribusiness forms a $5 trillion USD global market and is only expected to grow bigger (Goedde et al. 2015).

Australia currently exports two-thirds of the total value of agriculture, fisheries and forestry production (Jackson et al. 2019). The National Farmer's Federation aims to increase Australia's agriculture output to $100 billion by 2030 (Poole et al. 2018). As Australian farmers increase their scale to maintain profitability, farmers lose the ability to observe their properties at close range (Potts & Kastelle 2017). In addition, Australian farmers face many challenges on a daily basis such as water challenge, crop disease infections, lack of storage management, pesticide control, weed management, lack of irrigation and drainage facilities, drought, aging farmers to name a few (Keating and Carberry 2010). In addition to the already existing challenges, Australia recently faced one of the worst droughts (in terms of rainfall) in over 100 years (Howden et al. 2020). If that wasn't enough, the more recent Covid-19 pandemic has and will continue to present growing challenges for Australia's agriculture sector, specifically related to supply chain restrictions (ABARES 2020).

Despite the challenges that the Australian farmers face on a daily basis, the continuous growth in technology is helping farmers deal with the challenges head on. A 2017 survey of Australian farmers found that 96% of farmers owned and used information and communications technology assets (Dufty and Jackson 2018). If

Australia has to achieve the aim of increasing agricultural output to $100 billion by 2030, the farmers have to adapt and adopt the emerging technologies and upskill themselves at a rapid pace to keep up (Dufty and Jackson 2018). Emerging technologies and new industries have the potential to transform Australian agriculture.

Key Technologies

A recent industry report by AgriFutures Australia called, "*Horizon Scanning, Opportunities for New Technologies and Industries*" identified 39 different emerging technologies from the technology domains of robotics and artificial intelligence, big data, biotechnology and genomics, business and logistics, renewable energy, and material science (Hamilton et al. 2019). In addition, the report further identified 24 potential emerging agriculture industries, where each of the identified industries represent a direct response to key contextual factors posing significant challenges to the Australian agriculture, as well as opportunities presented by emerging technologies (Hamilton et al. 2019). Some of the potential emerging agriculture industries identified were:

- Cell cultured meat
- Microgrid P2P energy (direct energy trading between peers)
- A cellular agriculture (production of agricultural products from cell cultures)
- Wild camel harvesting
- Medicinal Marijuana
- Hemp milk

To ensure that these technologies can be taken advantage of, it is important to ensure that Australian agriculture sector has enough skills set to meet the growing technological needs of the industry. Currently there are approximately 309,000 people directly employed in agriculture, forestry and fishing (Poole et al. 2018). However, agricultural employment dropped by approximately 20% over the past decade and is expected to decline further over the next 5 years (Boult and Chancellor 2019). In addition, the number of people enrolled in agricultural education and training programs in the VET sector decreased from around 60,000 enrolments and 15,000 completions in 2014, to around 50,000 enrolments and 12,000 completions in 2017 (AISC 2018). Moreover, the regional workforce is impacted by outward youth migration as it reduces the number of people locally available to fill job vacancies (Wu et al. 2019). The aging demographic of Australian farmers is concerning, particularly in terms of their ability to innovate and adopt new technologies to improve productivity (Keogh 2016). Furthermore, there is a sector-wide outcry for quality agriculture graduates with certificates and degrees from reputable universities and colleges (AgriFutures 2017). As, the technology advancements over the next decade are likely to see human–robot collaboration emerge and become more common across the agricultural sector, with humans performing the more complex work requiring judgment and classification, and robots filling in the simpler, more routine tasks, graduates should spend time and effort in the skills that machines won't be able to do (Wu et al. 2019).

Employment Impacts

The increasing deployment of automation is likely to result in the loss of some agricultural jobs, predominantly low-skilled positions. For example, a 2018 report from the Regional Australia Institute found that agricultural regions with more farm labourers than farm owners are more susceptible to job loss from automation (RAI 2018). Moreover, continual investment in skills development, which may take the form of formal or informal learning, will be crucial in ensuring that low-skilled employees facing job loss from automation are able to reskill for higher level positions (RAI 2018). Without coordinated reskilling efforts, the automation of low-skilled positions could see a large proportion of the agricultural workforce facing unemployment (Schirmer et al. 2016).

Australian state and territory governments undertake many forest conservation and forest growing and harvesting activities through large state forestry business enterprises or agencies. The Sawmilling and Timber manufacturing sub-sectors are characterised by a large number of small- and medium-size producers and a smaller number of large producers which are often vertically integrated companies. Most wood panel businesses are large-scale operations (AISC 2019). The Forest and Wood Products industry is a significant employer and contributor to rural and regional economies, and in 2017 the industry included 12,382 businesses with around 60% located in New South Wales and Victoria. (AISC 2019). The industry has developed a preference for skills development on an ad hoc basis, with many employers providing training at the outset of employment or during the course of employment when necessary (e.g. upskilling in new technology) (AISC 2019).

The Seafood industry can be described as having four main sectors:

- Aquaculture (offshore, inshore and onshore)
- Fishing (commercial)
- Seafood processing and wholesaling
- Fisheries compliance.

The industry includes more than 7000 commercial businesses that collectively employ approximately 17,000 people. Nearly 70% of these businesses focus on fishing. Over 60% of commercial businesses are non-employing operations, and over 30% employ fewer than 20 people (AISC 2019). The employment levels for 2019 and projected employment levels for 2024 are summarised below in Table 2.4. Aquaculture and fishing have downward employment trends however Seafood processing project an increase in employment numbers in 2024.

The Aquaculture and Wild Catch IRC's 2019 Skills Forecast identified a range of significant challenges that impact on the uptake and implementation of industry training (AISC 2019), including:

Table 2.4 Summary of employment levels Seafood Industry: 2019 and 2024

Seafood Industry sector	2019 employment levels	2024 employment projections
Aquaculture (offshore, inshore and onshore)	5400	5200
Fishing	6900	6000
Seafood processing	1400	2100

Source: Australian Industry and Skills Committee (AISC 2019)
Challenges & Opportunities

- Declining and ageing workforce
- Attracting and recruiting young people
- Restrictions on visa programs for skilled migration
- Limited options for subsidised training
- Geographical and regional dispersion of businesses
- Limited access to registered training organisations (RTOs)
- Competing industries
- Regulation and licensing implications.

The key priority skills identified by the Aquaculture and Wild Catch IRC that will require future projects are:

- Development of the crocodile farming market
- Increased use of FishTech and Aquabotics in operations
- Development of partnerships with traditional owners for industry operations
- Potential development of Indigenous enterprises related to aquaculture and wild catch, including customary fishing.

Conclusion

All three industry sectors have varying rates of 4IR technology uptake and adoption and there will be great variability within the sectors and sub sectors of this investment and adoption. The adoption of 4IR technology solutions is quite low in the construction industry particularly compared with other industries and this is due to several structural issues, the demographics of the sector's composition (majority of business being sole traders and SMEs) and the nature of the work (Blanco et al. 2018). There are 3 main drivers impacting the industry: introduction of 4IR technologies such as (automation of low skilled jobs, BIM and prefabrication); levels of regulation and compliance and; demand for green and smart buildings. According to the AISC (2020c) the industry is yet to experience significant digital disruption however the growing use of technologies means that lower skilled construction occupations (plasterers and tilers) have a high probability of becoming automated in the next 20 years. However, construction occupations in demand and least likely to be affected by automation and or optimisation technologies include: construction project managers and site supervisors. The increasing use of BIM by the larger industry players will have a flow on effect to subcontractors in terms of their ability to utilise technologies that integrate with these large systems.

The mining industry too has had a relatively low but increasing uptake of technologies despite some early adopters in relation to autonomous vehicles and remote operation centres. The industry is seeking to look at how technologies can improve productivity, safety, investment and brand building through a wide range of technologies across the whole value chain as they move towards more integrated systems and operations. Occupations to be most affected by these technological adoptions through automation will be truck operators, traditional geologists and surveyors, general clerks, drill operators, miners, shot firers and earth moving operators. According to the analysis undertaken by Enrst and Young (2019b) the occupations impacted the most by automation will be those in the Transport and Trading stages of the value chain however, at the mining operations stage there will be the greatest amount of job redesign with optimisation technologies being integrated into operations, such as drones, integrated information systems and geospatial technologies. This will see an increased demand for geotechnical engineers and modellers, data analysists and marketing professionals. The education/qualification requirements for the five largest occupations requires AQF level qualifications ranging from Certificate II or III to Advanced Diploma level and other occupations requiring a degree. The industry argues for large scale revisions of the training packages and qualifications from tertiary education providers (VET and HE) to keep pace with the technological advancements in the industry.

Only very recently, the BHP Mitsubishi Alliance (BMA) announced it is investing \$100 m on 34 autonomous haulage trucks for the Daunia coal mine in central Queensland and these will commence operations in February 2021. BMA also introduced autonomous haulage at its Goonyella Riverside mine in 2020 and will expand this into 2021 with up to 86 Komatsu trucks over a two year period (https://www.australianmining.com.au/news/bma-to-invest-100m-in-daunia-autonomous-haulage/ 1st July, 2020).

The agriculture sector is experiencing some major workforce demographic trends characterised by ageing workforces and youth migration out of rural and regional areas. The increasing deployment of automation is likely to result in the loss of some agricultural jobs, predominantly low-skilled positions (farm labourers). Moreover, continual investment in skills development, which may take the form of formal or informal learning, will be crucial in ensuring that low-skilled employees facing job loss from automation are able to reskill for higher level positions (RAI 2018). Without coordinated reskilling efforts, the automation of low-skilled positions could see a large proportion of the agricultural workforce facing unemployment. Nonetheless, there are some interesting new industries emerging in some of the sub sectors such as crocodile farming, medicinal marijuana, acelluar and celluar agriculture and Indigenous enterprise activities.

Table 2.5 below provides a summary of the key technologies being utilised by the three sectors in Australia. This does not attempt to indicate the rates of uptake and adoption of these technologies across the sectors as these sectors are wide

Table 2.5 Main 4IR technologies currently being utilised across the three sectors in Australia

4IR Technologies	Agriculture	Construction	Mining
AI	√	√	√
Machine Learning	√		√
Blockchain	√		√
Big data	√		√
Data mining	√		√
Expert systems			
Chatbots			√
IoT	√	√	√
3D Printing	√	√	√
Drones	√	√	√
Automation	V		√
Robotics	√		√
Autonomous vehicles	√		√
Laser sensors	√		√
Virtual Reality/ Augmented		√	√
Electronic Logging Devices (ELDs)			√
Sector Specific	Smart Dust Acellular & cellular agriculture	4-D and 5-D building information modelling (BIM) Prefabrication Project Schedule Optimisers	SADA Supervisory control and data acquisition

ranging and businesses in each vary greatly in terms of size, workforces and ability to invest in 4IR technologies.

The Australian Industry Group (Ai Group) is a long-standing peak employer body representing traditional, innovative and emerging industry sectors with membership at 60,000 plus Australian businesses with combined employee numbers of over 1 million staff. These businesses are across the following sectors: manufacturing, construction, engineering, transport & logistics, labour hire, mining services, the defence industry, civil airlines and ICT. In 2019 the Ai Group published a report on the fourth industrial revolution and listed 9 key areas for private and public policy development needed in order for the optimisation of 4IR technologies for their members. These key areas include: Cyber secure, resilient and trusted businesses; Business and technology investment; Innovation ecosystem; legal and regulatory framework; Standards; Sustainability; Trade; Workforce skills and Workplace relations. For the purposes of this chapter and edited collection we focus on the Ai Group's position on Workforce skills.

Based on data collected through CEO surveys, the Ai Group (2019) make nine recommendations to government in terms of supporting businesses with 4IR technologies by playing a stronger role with key stakeholders (businesses, industry skills bodies, VET and HE providers). The essence of these recommendations relates to more regular and responsive skills forecasting and supporting business and industry-based workforce planning, STEM and digital literacy strategies with education and training providers, support and investment in work based and work integrated education models and more flexible and responsive education and training offerings, delivery models and partnerships to meet skills demands and structural change and reform to tertiary education.

References

ABARES. (2020). *Food security and agriculture and COVID-19*. Retrieved from Canberra, Australia: https://www.agriculture.gov.au/coronavirus

ABS. (2020). *Australian Industry, 2018–19*. Retrieved from https://www.abs.gov.au/ausstats/abs@.nsf/Latestproducts/8155.0Main%20Features12018-19?opendocument&tabname=Summary&prodno=8155.0&issue=2018-19&num=&view=

AgriFutures. (2017). *Overcoming the agriculturals ector skills shortage*. Retrieved from Wagga Wagga, Australia: https://www.agrifutures.com.au/news/overcoming-the-agriculture-sector-skills-shortage/

AgriFutures Australia. (2019). Available at http://agrifutures.com.au/wp-content/uploads/2019/08/19-025.pdf

AiGroup. (2019). *The fourth industrial revolution: Australian businesses in transition*. Retrieved from North Sydney, Australia: https://cdn.aigroup.com.au/Reports/2019/AiGroup_Fourth_Industrial_Revolution_Report.pdf

AiGroup. (2020). *National CEO survey business projects in 2020: Construction in 2020*. Retrieved from North Sydney, Australia: https://www.aigroup.com.au/policy-and-research/mediacentre/reports/

AISC. (2018). *Agriculture: Industry cluster snapshot*. Retrieved from Canberra, Australia: https://nationalindustryinsights.aisc.net.au/industries/agriculture

AISC. (2019). *Aquaculture and wild catch*. Retrieved from https://nationalindustryinsights.aisc.net.au/industries/aquaculture-and-wild-catch

AISC. (2020a). *Agriculture*. Retrieved from https://nationalindustryinsights.aisc.net.au/industries/agriculture

AISC. (2020b). *Aquaculture and wild catch*. Retrieved from https://nationalindustryinsights.aisc.net.au/industries/aquaculture-and-wild-catch

AISC. (2020c). *Construction*. Retrieved from https://nationalindustryinsights.aisc.net.au/industries/construction

AISC. (2020d). *Forest and wood products*. Retrieved from https://nationalindustryinsights.aisc.net.au/industries/forest-and-wood-products

AISC. (2020e). *Mining, drilling and civil infrastructure*. Retrieved from https://nationalindustry-insights.aisc.net.au/industries/mining-drilling-and-civil-infrastructure

AUSTRADE. (2020). *Australia: Shaping the future of food and agriculture: Opportunities for investment and partnership in agriculture 4.0*. Commonwealth of Australia Retrieved from https://www.austrade.gov.au/agriculture40/why-australia

Bartlett, K., Blanco, J. L., Rockhill, D., & Strube, G. (2019). *Breaking the mold: The construction players of the future* Retrieved from https://www.mckinsey.com/~/media/McKinsey/Industries/Capital%20Projects%20and%20Infrastructure/Our%20Insights/Breaking%20the%20mold%20The%20construction%20players%20of%20the%20future/Breaking-the-mold-The-construction-players-of-the-future.ashx

Blanco, J. L., Fuchs, S., Parsons, M., & Ribeirinho, M. R. (2018). *Artificial intelligence: Construction technology's next frontier*. Retrieved from https://www.mckinsey.com/~/media/McKinsey/Industries/Capital%20Projects%20and%20Infrastructure/Our%20Insights/Artificial%20intelligence%20Construction%20technologys%20next%20frontier/Artificial%20intelligence-Construction-technologys-next-frontier.ashx

Boult, C., & Chancellor, W. (2019). *Agricultural productivity estimates*. Retrieved from Canberra, Australia: https://www.agriculture.gov.au/abares/research-topics/productivity/agricultural-productivity-estimates

Da Silva, J. G. (2017). *The state of food and agriculture leveraging food systems for inclusive rural transformation* (9789251098738). Retrieved from Rome, Italy: http://www.fao.org/3/a--i7658e.pdf

Dufty, N., & Jackson, T. (2018). *Information and communication technology use in Australian agriculture: A survey of broadacre, dairy and vegetable farms* (18.15). Retrieved from Canberra, Australia: https://www.agriculture.gov.au/sites/default/files/sitecollectiondocuments/abares/ict-use-australian-agriculture.pdf

EY. (2019a). *The future of work: The changing skills landscape for miners: A report for the Minerals Council of Australia*. Retrieved from https://minerals.org.au/sites/default/files/190214%20The%20Future%20of%20Work%20the%20Changing%20Skills%20Landscape%20for%20Miners.pdf

EY. (2019b). *Future of work: The economic implications of technology and digital mining A Report for the Minerals Council of Australia*. Retrieved from https://minerals.org.au/sites/default/files/190214%20The%20Future%20of%20Work%20The%20economic%20implications%20of%20technology%20and%20digital%20mining.pdf

Goedde, L., Horii, M., & Sanghvi, S. (2015). *Pursuing the global opportunity in food and agribusiness*. Retrieved from https://www.mckinsey.com/industries/chemicals/our-insights/pursuing-the-global-opportunity-in-food-and-agribusiness

Gruszka, A., Jupp, J. R., & De Valence, G. (2017). *Digital foundations: How technology is transforming Australia's construction sector*. Retrieved from https://opus.lib.uts.edu.au/handle/10453/124861

Hamilton, G., Swann, L., Pandey, V., Moyle, C.-L., Opie, J., & Dawson, A. (2019). *Horizon scanning: Opportunities for new technologies and industries* (9781760530495). Retrieved from Brisbane, Australia: https://www.agrifutures.com.au/product/horizon-scanning-opportunities-for-new-technologies-and-industries/

Howden, M., Nelson, R., & Cameron, A. (2020). *Agricultural overview: June Quarter 2020*. Retrieved from https://www.agriculture.gov.au/abares/research-topics/agricultural-outlook/agriculture-overview

Innovation, A. (2019). *Construction, plumbing and services: IRC skills forecast and proposed schedule of work*. Retrieved from North Hobart, Tasmania: https://artibus.com.au/wp-content/uploads/2019/03/ConstructionPlumbingServices_SkillsForecast_2019.pdf

Jackson, T., Hatfield-Dodds, S., & Zammit, K. (2019). *Sanpshot of Australian agriculture*. Retrieved from Canberra, Australia: https://www.agriculture.gov.au/sites/default/files/abares/documents/snapshot-australian-agriculture.pdf

Keating, B. A., & Carberry, P. S. (2010). Emerging opportunities and challenges for Australian broadacre agriculture. *Crop and Pasture Science, 61*(4), 269–278. https://doi.org/10.1071/CP09282.

Keogh, M. (2016). *Will ageing farmers limit future farm productivity?* Retrieved from Sydney, Australia: http://farminstitute.org.au/ag-forum/ageing-farmers-and-productivity

Koeleman, J., Ribeirinho, M. J., Rockhill, D., Sjödin, E., & Strube, G. (2019). *Decoding digital transformation in construction*. Retrieved from https://www.mckinsey.com/industries/capital-projects-and-infrastructure/our-insights/decoding-digital-transformation-in-construction#

Poole, R., van Deldon, B., & Liddell, P. (2018). *Talking 2030: Growing Agriculture into a $100 billion Industry.* Retrieved from https://assets.kpmg/content/dam/kpmg/au/pdf/2018/talking-2030-growing-australian-agriculture.pdf

Potts, J., & Kastelle, T. (2017). Economics of innovation in Australian agricultural economics and policy. *Economic Analysis and Policy, 54*, 96–104. https://doi.org/10.1016/j.eap.2017.03.003.

PwC. (2015). *Future-proofing Australia's workforce by growing skills in science, technology, engineering and maths (STEM): A smart move*. Retrieved from https://www.pwc.com.au/pdf/a--smart-move-pwc-stem-report-april-2015.pdf

PwC. (2019a). *Industry skills forecast and proposed schedule of work mining, drilling and civil infrastructure*. Retrieved from https://s3-ap-southeast-2.amazonaws.com/pwcau.prod.s4aprod.assets/wp-content/uploads/20190918164118/MDCI-ISF-2019-26-April-FINAL-SIGNED.pdf

PwC. (2019b). *Mine 2019: Resourcing the future*. Retrieved from https://www.pwc.com/gx/en/energy-utilities-mining/publications/pdf/mine-report-2019.pdf

RAI. (2018). *Riding the next wave of automation in rural Australia*. Retrieved from Canberra, Australia: http://www.regionalaustralia.org.au/home/wp-content/uploads/2018/06/RAI_Riding-the-next-wave-of-automation-in-rural-Australia.pdf

Schirmer, J., Yabsley, B., Mylek, M., & Peel, D. (2016). *The 2015 regional wellbeing survey: Wellbeing, resilience and liveability in regional Australia*. Retrieved from Canberra, Australia: https://apo.org.au/sites/default/files/resource-files/2016-06/apo-nid64962.pdf

Schwab, K. (2017). *The fourth industrial revolution*. World Economic Forum.

Technology, M. (2014). *Ten technologies with the power to transform mining*. Retrieved from https://www.mining-technology.com/features/featureten-technologies-with-the-power-to-transform-mining-4211240/

WEF. (2018). *Shaping the future of construction: Future scenarios and implications for the industry*. Retrieved from Geneva, Switzerland: http://www3.weforum.org/docs/Future_Scenarios_Implications_Industry_report_2018.pdf

Wu, W., Dawson, D., Fleming-Munoz, D., Schleiger, E., & Horton, J. (2019). *The future of Australia's agricultural workforce*. Retrieved from Canberra, Australia: https://www.qff.org.au/blog/future-australias-agricultural-workforce-report/

Chapter 3
Manufacturing

Al Rainnie and Mark Dean

Abstract In this chapter, we track and critically evaluate, the decline of Australian manufacturing. We look to explanations rooted in the idea of a 'resources curse', and, more recently, the far from benign implications of global financialisation. We then examine the implications for Australian manufacturing of the supposed Fourth Industrial Revolution (4IR). The positive implications are being reinforced, it is suggested, by the ramifications of deglobalisation in general and Covid-19 in particular. The last major section of the chapter considers the way that apprenticeships, training in particular, and the training sector, in general have echoed the decline in the manufacturing industry. We conclude by questioning how realistic the anticipated outcomes of the Fourth Industrial Revolution are for the Australian manufacturing industry.

Keywords Decline · Industry policy · Manufacturing · Training

Introduction

In July 2019, the Australian Parliamentary Library published a Briefing entitled '27 years and counting since Australia's last recession'(O'Brien 2019: 1). The Briefing claimed an unprecedented stretch of economic growth since the 'recession we had to have' in 1991. This period of economic stability, it was claimed, distinguished Australia from other similar developed economies. Economic stability had translated to relatively high levels of average economic growth compared to other

A. Rainnie (✉)
UniSA Business, University of South Australia, Adelaide, SA, Australia
e-mail: al.f.rainnie@gmail.com

M. Dean
UniSA Business, University of South Australia, Adelaide, SA, Australia

Carmichael Centre - Centre for Future Work, The Australia Institute,
Canberra, ACT, Australia

A. Nankervis et al. (eds.), *The Fourth Industrial Revolution*,
https://doi.org/10.1007/978-981-16-1614-3_3

developed economies over the period. However, it was acknowledged that population growth had been important when accounting for the resilience of the Australian economy. Gross Domestic Product (GDP) growth bore out some widely recognised industry trends: the relative decline of manufacturing; the increased importance of services; the continuing importance of mining and construction. A notable outcome was that women had come to dominate employment growth overall (both full time and part time). Women's jobs were growing at a rate nine times faster than the rate for men. However, many of these jobs were low paying and in female-dominated service industries (Catalyst 2020).

How Did We Get Here?

During the 1980s and early 1990s, the Hawke-Keating Government significantly reformed normative policy commitments to full employment and demand management, turning increasingly to fiscal policy responses that would emphasise global market determinations of employment and economic growth (Wilson and Spies-Butcher 2016). A raft of deregulations and privatisations occurred to open the way for foreign capital investment at the expense of policy to develop sovereign manufacturing capabilities and tertiary service industries. As the decade progressed, a new "competition policy" pulled any safety net out from under industry, exposing it to pressures of Asian competition prematurely after decades of protection; and the implementation of the Prices and Incomes Accord YEAR?, despite increases to the social wage, restrained the labour movement at the industrial level in very important ways that would later have enormous ramifications for industrial relations in Australia and negotiations on industrial transformation (Bell 1997; Stilwell 2000).

Australian markets increased the amount of money being lent to speculative financial investors without making any productive investments in Australian industry. Their profits were not reinvested in job creation and "instead went to finance property or stockmarket speculation, increased dividends, increased executive salaries, increased investments off-shore, increased profit repatriation overseas or into the foreign exchange market 'gambling pit'" (Broomhill 1991: 5–6). Growth in productivity was supported by a boom in Australia's commodity prices, which undermined the productivity of Australia's manufacturing industries (Bell 1993: 131–132).

Finance, industry, and labour deregulation helped accelerate the restructuring of Australian capital and its integration into global markets. This damaged Australia's opportunities for long-term productivity. The lack of a macroeconomic strategy in policy responses was indicative of the government's broader neoliberal agenda, and lack of full commitment to an active intervention to advance Australia's industrial transformation.

Over the decade from 1998 to 2008, Australia's economic complexity deteriorated significantly as national exports became dominated by minerals including coal and iron ore (Hausmann et al. 2017). By 2001, total employment in the 'extractive industries' reached 83,000 (1% of Australia's total employment) and then rose to 136,000 by 2007; but employment in manufacturing fell from 1.87 million to 1.63 million in just 3 years between 2004 and 2007, despite increased output in the sector (Goodman and Worth 2008: 208).

Other policy responses had the effect of providing industry protection without a strong focus on the innovation intended to help the sector adjust to global pressures and new competitive demands. The *New Car Plan for a Greener Future* policy for the automotive industry was launched during the Global Financial Crisis (GFC) and was designed to not just create conditions for industry to build a 'green car', but to also establish the conditions for a 'green car industry' that could respond to growing environmental sustainability trends (Goods et al. 2015). However, the impact of the GFC was soon felt by Australian automotive manufacturers. It forced Ford and Holden to cut production and workforces, so the Rudd Government shifted the focus of its plan to responding to the economic crisis the GFC represented (ibid.: 104–105).

Industry Overview

Since 2015, the Coalition Government has undergone two changes in leadership – the first in 2015 from Tony Abbott to Malcolm Turnbull; the second in 2018 from Turnbull to Scott Morrison – the incumbent Prime Minister. In this period, manufacturing's share of GDP has fallen further still, eclipsed by resource extraction at the tail-end of the nation's mining boom. The decline in manufacturing, it was stressed, was relative although a long-term trend. The share of manufacturing in GDP fell from 10.7% in 1991–92 to 5.8% in 2017–18. The manufacturing industry had actually grown at 0.9% per annum over the same period, but this rate of growth was much smaller than the economy as a whole.

Growth in the mining sector, 4.3% per annum over the period as a whole, was very uneven though much higher than manufacturing. Coal mining grew at 4.8% per annum and iron ore mining grew at an annual average rate of 9% p.a. This represents a seven-fold increase in the real value of iron ore mining between 1991–92 and 2017–8 (O'Brien 2019: 4). This, we shall see, led some commentators to suggest that, in both sectoral and geographic terms, Australia had a two-speed economy (the resources curse) – the resources sector and everyone else. Writing in 2019, the Guardian Australia economist Greg Jericho commented that:

> Unlike in previous years when we had a two-speed economy, with the mining and non-mining states taking it in turns being the ones to grow fast, we now mostly have a one-speed economy – and that speed is slow … the weakness of the private sector across all states and the need for government spending – both state and federal – to do more than its share highlights how fragile the economy across the nation remains (Jericho 2019).

Key Technologies

However, not everything was gloomy. The Fourth Industrial Revolution (4IR), or 'Industry 4.0 (i4.0) was apparently poised to come to the rescue of the Australian manufacturing industry. Representing the "digitalisation" of just about everything, the 4IR is premised on the integration of "key enabling technologies" in production processes, which includes but is not limited to artificial intelligence (AI), digital sensors, big data analytics, additive manufacturing (i.e. 3D-printing), virtual reality (VR), augmented reality (AR) and machine learning. Given the innovative technology focus of i4.0 transformations, the employment implications of the 4IR for Australian manufacturing are manifold. Fundamentally, however, it implies that high-value employment in the digital future of work will be work that requires the integration of technical skills with personal skills. Payton and Knight (2018) have identified 'soft' skills relating to adaptability, collaboration and problem-solving as having increased in value with the growth of digitalisation, and demand for these skills now accompanies the demand for technical skills. The implications for future generations are outlined by the Foundation for Young Australians (FYA 2016), which has identified seven unique skills 'clusters' that will underpin 'portfolio careers' in which young people transfer a mix of soft and technical skills across occupations, industries and sectors drawing on their experience and deploying it in new and challenging settings. Industry insights state that Australian workers in the digital age will need to exhibit flexibility and responsiveness to move between a range of skillsets and carry out emerging tasks with the assistance of digital technologies (Avogaro 2019; AiGroup 2018).

Industry 4.0 and Resurgent Manufacturing

According to the Department of Industry, Science, Energy and Resources (2020), Industry 4.0 technologies have the potential to provide a major boost to Australia's economic competitiveness and could create an environment that would allow businesses to grow, explore new models, and embrace technologies (DIESR 2020). The background to the Australian federal government's identification of 4IR-driven opportunities was a growing discussion of 'deglobalisation' (Pegoraro et al. 2019). This was evidenced, firstly, by the rise of nationalist and increasingly protectionist governments across the world; and, secondly, by a restructuring of the seemingly all-encompassing Global Value Chains (GVCs). GVCs have been accepted by the major institutions of the world economy (IMF, World Bank, ILO, WEF) as the main drivers of economic activity. Furthermore, it was argued that the rise to predominance of GVCs had driven a particular pattern to the spatial division of labour at a global level. Increasingly however, voices argued that these chains had become overstretched, and, for a number of reasons, were undertaking a relocation process (near- or re-shoring) that brought production processes back to being closer to major markets (Kinkel et al. 2020). It was argued that this process was accelerated by the increasing adoption of new technologies (artificial intelligence, advanced robotics and 3D-printing) that had important implications for the number and nature of jobs in the new units (Pittarello et al. 2020).

Proponents of the 4IR also suggested that this process, particularly in manufacturing, would promote the re-emergence of patterns of industrial clustering, similar to those supposedly exhibited in post-Fordist industrial structures (Götz and Jankowska 2017). Developments in advanced manufacturing, particularly in 3D-printing, would accelerate and reinforce these tendencies. The problems that Jericho (2019) pointed to were all evident before the Covid-19 pandemic hit the Australian population and the economy with devastating effect during 2020. So how had the two-speed economy waxed and waned, and how would the 4IR and Covid-19 affect the outlook for the Australian manufacturing industry?

Employment Impact

Pre-COVID

Between 1988 and 2018, the Australian economy moved from being reliant on agricultural products and manufactured goods to a position in 2018 where service industries were increasingly important for employment. In 1988, manufacturing accounted for around 15% of total employment, a figure which had fallen to around 8% in 2018, leaving manufacturing as the sixth largest industry in employment terms. By 2018, around three out of every four Australian workers were employed in the service sector.

In May 2020, the ABS reported that manufacturing employed approximately 852,8000 persons, around 7% of the labour force (see Fig. 3.1), in a range of distinct manufacturing industries (see Fig. 3.2). Over the past 5 years, employment in the industry decreased by 6.7% (see Table 3.1). The median age of workers was 42 and median weekly earnings were around $1125 per week (Fig. 3.1).

The following Figure (Fig. 3.2) shows the employment proportions in each component of the Australian manufacturing sector.

Employment level ('000)	**852.8**
Employment growth – Five years to May 2020, ('000)	-61.3
Employment Growth – Five years to May 2020 (%)	-6.7
Male share of employment – year to May 2020 (%)	71.7
Female share of employment – year to May 2020 (%)	28.3
Full-time share of employment – year to May 2020 (%)	84.0

Fig. 3.1 Australian manufacturing sector employment (May 2020). Source: Australian Bureau of Statistics (2020)

Fig. 3.2 Australian manufacturing sector employment by industry (May 2020). Source: Australian Bureau of Statistics (2020)

Manufacturing sector employment by industry ('000)	
Food, beverage & tobacco products manufacturing	**213.6**
Food products	182.6
Beverage & tobacco products	31
Transport equipment manufacturing*	**190.3**
Transport equipment	71.5
Machinery & equipment	118.8
Metal products manufacturing	**132.3**
Primary metal & metal products	69.3
Fabricated metal products	63
Chemicals, petroleum and rubber manufacturing	**90.6**
Petroleum & coal products	6.7
Basic chemical and chemical products	54.3
Polymer products & rubber products	29.6
Building, wood, furniture & other manufacturing	**154.5**
Non-metallic mineral products	41.5
Wood products	43.7
Furniture & other manufacturing	69.3
Textile, clothing & footwear manufacturing	**80.2**
Textile, leather, clothing & footwear	31.6
Pulp, paper & converted paper products	18.6
Printing (including recorded media)	30
Other manufacturing	**3.1**
Manufacturing nfd	3.1

The Top Ten occupations in manufacturing present an image that is somewhat removed from the common perception:

- Structural steel and welding trades workers
- Metal fitters and machinists
- Production managers
- Packers
- Food and drink factory workers
- Product assemblers
- Advertising, public relations and sales managers
- Cabinet makers
- Store persons
- Bakers and pastrycooks

Source: ABS Labour Market Information – Manufacturing (Labour Market Information Portal 2020)

The Australian Manufacturing Forum (Roberts 2019: 2) painted a gloomy picture, arguing that Australia now had the economic diversity and export profile of a typical developing nation:

> Our antipathy to value-adding activities such as manufacturing in favour of industries that require little more than digging it up and shipping it out, has left us dangerously dependent on quarrying.

Manufacturing represents the major expression of production by multiple individuals that possess distinct fragments – or 'modules' – of knowledge. Knowledge takes two forms: explicit – the kind that can be easily written down or explained and interpreted; and tacit – the specialised kind that is embedded in the knowledge held by individuals, organisations and networks which is harder to capture or learn in conventional processes (ibid.: 16).

In 2017, Australia ranked 93rd in Harvard University's ranking of economic complexity. In 2019, Australia ranked 14th out of 63 countries in the World Competitiveness Digital Ranking, a situation that had not improved over the previous 5 years. Australia was ranked 34th overall for investment and development and 44th for both apprenticeships and employee training (Institute for Management Development 2020). Australia was reportedly poorly connected into Global Value Chains (with the exception of the resources sector) and even Australian small businesses did not have a great record of innovation (Cunningham et al. 2016). Before Covid-19 erupted onto the global stage, Roberts (2019: 2) was already arguing that:

> Rather than a smart nation, or an innovation nation as politicians would have it, we are uniquely a land of the lotus eaters, wallowing in an undeserved economic security.

So how did Australian manufacturing get to this state?

Rise and Fall of the Two-Speed Economy – Beyond the Resources Curse?

Writing in 2008, Goodman and Worth argued that there were three elements to the Australian 'resources curse':

- Deindustrialisation and social division;
- Regulatory capture and energy security; and
- Ecological degradation and exhaustion.

More than 20 years previously, in an examination of the development of the resources sector in Western Australia and Queensland, Harman and Head (1982) argued that five factors stood out:

- the high degree of foreign ownership, particularly in the mineral sector;
- acrimony between state and federal governments over resource issues;

- strong partnerships forged between state governments and development companies;
- the existence of a frontier ethos; and
- a growing debate about the relative costs and benefits of resources development.

Combined, these factors had led commentators such as Harry Perlich (2013: 107) to suggest that even before the GFC, Australia had a two-speed economy, but that after 2011 "the two-speed differential between the 'resource states' and the 'manufacturing states' was firmly established." Mining had an almost 60% share of total private investment in 2012, with Western Australia and Queensland taking about 85% of this total. Perlich argued that the period of the mining boom coincided with weakness in several employment sectors, notably manufacturing, despite the fact that, in employment terms, manufacturing had been in decline for many years:

> The Australian economy avoided the recession experienced in many advanced industrialised countries after the onset of the GFC. Yet this avoidance masked problems of distorted investment and employment activity. Mining investment held up GDP performance for the country as a whole, but it was an economy at two-speeds geographically (Ibid.: 122).

Looking forward, Perlich concluded that the Australian economy remained conflicted, narrowly focussed and vulnerable as it entered the next period of restructuring. The structural changes to Australia's economy had allowed the mining, construction, finance and property sectors to supplant manufacturing and agriculture as the dominant fractions of Australia's capital (Duck 2019: 64).

Writing in 2016, Jim Stanford of the Australia Institute argued that:

> Australian manufacturing has endured hard times for several years. So long, in fact, that Australians could be forgiven for concluding that industrial decline is a "normal" state of affairs. The manufacturing sector has been in broad decline since 2008, and real output has now contracted every single quarter since September 2011. Over 200,000 manufacturing jobs have disappeared since 2008, and the rate of job loss is accelerating: employment fell 6 per cent in 2015 alone. Announcements of factory closures and redundancies add to the gloom (Stanford 2016: 1).

As Weller and O'Neill (2014) pointed out, after the year 2000 the Australian manufacturing decline continued, but this time with a new cause, the increasingly financialised nature of the global economy. Australia's manufacturing decline was now seen as an effect of a newly spatialised and financialised global capitalism. Deindustrialisation was now attributable to the external repositioning of nations in globalised circuits of capital, rather than the internal sectoral reallocation of capital and labour:

> The further loss of manufacturing jobs seems likely to entrench high unemployment in regional areas and in the manufacturing belts of Melbourne, Sydney, and Adelaide and to retard technical skills development (Weller and O'Neill 2014: 525).

It was this situation that an already underdeveloped and vulnerable manufacturing industry, outside of the resources sector, found itself in as COVID-19 erupted.

Fourth Industrial Revolution Implications

There is a growing wave of support from industry, business and governments globally for the development of the 4IR. A report for the World Bank in 2018 argued that trends affecting the geography of production would come from changing globalisation dynamics (deglobalisation) and emerging technologies:

> …the production of these advanced manufacturing goods (such as wearable tech, autonomous vehicles, biochips and biosensors, and new materials) are most likely to collocate with R&D facilities in high-income economies … This mirrors the manufacture of certain capital goods and advanced inputs (such as semiconductors, doped wafers for semiconductors, and fibreoptic cables), which stayed in high income economies during Industry 3.0. At the same time, the assembly of high tech goods such as laptops and mobile phones did move to low- and middle-income economies with Industry 3.0. The same is unlikely to happen with the advanced manufacturing product lines associated with Industry 4.0 because of the likely skill and infrastructure requirements needed throughout the product's value chain (Hallward et al. 2017: 93–94).

The level of digital connectivity enabled by the internet has created new possibilities for innovative manufacturing processes and a so-called 4IR. As a result, manufacturing processes are on the cusp of another major disruption. The digital innovations propelled by the 4IR have significant implications for production processes, supply chains and value chains. It represents a transformation of the way manufacturing firms do business and a significant opportunity to apply innovation to firms, industries and economies.

In terms of implementation, the 4IR depends upon the development of 'smart factories.' This fusion of technical processes and business processes can provide real-time quality, resources, and cost advantages when compared with typical production systems. More important is the opportunity seen to transform work and society, as it is a system that potentially represents more than simply smart machines making things. Rather, the ability of machines to bridge the physical and virtual worlds is intrinsic to the innovative transformation of economies and societies attainable with the rapid digitalisation of production.

Critical perspectives on Industry 4.0 from the social sciences have dissected the technologically deterministic vision that occupies the debate over its development and its transformative potential. Pfeiffer (2017a) has warned that the technologically deterministic view of 4IR and its technological marvels threaten a 'digital despotism' that will make human workers subservient to integrated digital production systems that monopolise decision-making. It is in this vein that Reischauer (2018) has interpreted the 4IR as a policy driven discourse intended to embed a digitally-driven innovation system in manufacturing production, fulfilling capital's essential drive to expand in the form of a digitally-driven regime of accumulation.

These critical inroads on the human organisational dimensions of the 4IR remain on the fringe of research and policymaking. The focus of most research is on macro-level changes to manufacturing production and a technological determination of outcomes is being produced in what Morgan (2019: 14) defines as 'quasi-determinism' where 'anxiety combined with passivity and complacency are being produced.' The foundation provided by technical and business approaches to interpreting the 4IR is easily transferrable from the template that global management consulting firms mobilise to provide techno-centric solutions to manufacturing companies for implementing automation strategies and raising employee productivity. The innovations proposed by the 4IR that are commonly cited may imply significant opportunities for improving manufacturing output, market share and competitiveness, and for driving business model innovation amongst manufacturing firms. Ultimately, these drive the transfer of recommendations to the policy responses of governments throughout the world. But according to Kotynkova (2017), ultimately income and social inequality will loom large as those with the capital benefit the most from automation, whilst the millions of people dependent on manufacturing work are dispossessed of their livelihoods by smart machines. Pfeiffer (2017b) has also interpreted the 4IR as a marketing exercise that provides an imaginary vision of a future in which none of the sociological implications have been given much detail. Fuchs (2018) has echoed this sentiment, arguing that it acts as a 'capitalist panacea' to economic and social problems that ignore the existing social and economic inequalities being created by the 'disruptive' nature of digital capitalism.

Fourth Industrial Revolution and Advanced Manufacturing in Australia

In Australia, the Government was an enthusiastic, if uncritical, supporter of the 4IR, arguing that it was affecting almost every industry worldwide, rapidly transforming how businesses operate (DIESR 2020). Industry 4.0 technologies, it was suggested, could help overcome traditional challenges such as high labour costs and distance to markets. Benefits and opportunities included:

- Better connectivity between customers and supply chains through real-time access to production information, logistics and monitoring;
- Greater flexibility for businesses to produce differentiated products and services to tap unmet consumer demands, compete in global markets, and capture emerging opportunities;
- Enhanced workplace safety, production and improvements across the entire value chain (DIESR 2020).

Furthermore, the Advanced Manufacturing Growth Centre (AMGC) bought in to the new narrative – totally and uncritically:

> …the traditional assembly line is becoming disaggregated as global systems integrators outsource key functions and individual firms move to specialise along different parts of the manufacturing process. In this fast changing landscape, the key opportunity for manufacturers is to offer differentiated value propositions both before and after goods are produced – and to feed distinctive products, components and services into global supply chains.

> Digital innovations such as 3D printing, which allows goods to be produced anywhere, at any time, overlay the new manufacturing value chain and are accelerating the reinvention of the assembly line. Industry 4.0 technologies denote a broader paradigm shift in which intelligence and machine learning are embedded across the entire manufacturing cycle (AMGC nd(a): 8).

In a submission to the Australian Government's Department of Industry, Innovation and Science, the AMGC argued that for Australian manufacturers, building relationships with global systems integrators or primes was worth the costs of investing in new equipment or becoming compatible with the latter's business software (including complying with cybersecurity requirements) because in so doing, the company was 'pulled up' or 'dragged on the journey'. Furthermore:

> By embracing Industry 4.0, Australia can even begin to 'reshore' some production from countries with low labour and electricity costs, such as China. This will help bring back jobs to regional areas … In particular, capabilities such as 3D printing … have the potential to help Australian manufacturers meet demand for highly customised products and materials that can be quickly replicated anywhere in the world. According to one local manufacturing expert: "*Whereas previously you may have been a manufacturer of toys, bikes or weapons, 3D printing capabilities mean that on Monday you print toys, on Tuesdays, it's bikes and on Wednesday its weapons.*" (AMGC nd(b): 10).

3D-printing has been identified as a key enabling technology considered essential to helping relocate, and thus to aid, the restoration of Australian manufacturing. Lacking any semblance of coordinated industry policy, the 'nearby' technology and production possibilities for many firms in Australia have centred on such digitally enabled and cost-effective technologies and their ability to make some more sophisticated use of the vast resources otherwise dug out of the ground in Australia and promptly shipped overseas for use in the elaborately transformed manufacturing capabilities of other nations. At once overcoming both digital and geographic barriers, whilst helping Australian manufacturers to quickly and relatively cheaply upgrade their technological capabilities, 3D-printing has represented an achievable goal for a nation with the narrow economic structure but skilled workforce, technological know-how and investment potential that Australia possesses.

Post-COVID

The advent of COVID-19 had some immediate and far-reaching consequences. For example, the resulting, almost complete shutdown of China had a dramatic effect. Across the world the fragility of Just-In-Time driven supply chains has been vividly exposed. The impact on Australia was significant, as John L Hopkins pointed out in the Conversation (2020):

> Moreover, 90% of all Australia's merchandise imports are from China and half of these are engineering products such as office and telecommunications equipment.

> Besides the well-publicised impact on airlines, universities and tourism, Australian construction companies are warning clients of upcoming project delays as a result of forecast disruptions in materials sourced from China. Aurizon, Australia's largest rail operator, has said that coronavirus will delay the arrival of 66 new rail wagons being made in Wuhan, the city at the epicentre of the outbreak.

Writing in *The Guardian* (2020), Nouriel Roubini gave as one of ten reasons that a Greater Recession was inevitable that:

> To guard against future supply shocks, companies in advanced economies will reshore production from low-cost regions to higher-cost domestic markets. This trend will accelerate the pace of automation, putting downward pressure on wages and further fanning the flames of populism, nationalism and xenophobia.

This has caused a rethink in some quarters as the *Australian Financial Review* outlined, advocating more resilient supply chains that are insulated from the prospect of global disruption and a rebuilding of domestic manufacturing capacity for critical goods:

> The health and well-being of Australians is a national security-resilience issue and one that has to be assessed for risks and vulnerabilities just like every other aspect of national security from energy to the economy to the environment to the military (Coorey 2020).

Echoing Roubini, Joseph Stiglitz (2020) suggested that developed economies might recall some manufacturing activities onshore to be less exposed to future disasters. Former Labor Treasurer Wayne Swann argued that Australia's industrial base had been hollowed out. There was, he suggested, a new debate to be had in Australia about re-industrialisation (quoted in Hutchens 2020).

Andrew Liveris, a special advisor to the Australian National Covid-19 Commission and former CEO of Dow Chemicals had also bought into the new conventional wisdom (Stott and Aedy 2020). He argued that the domestic shortage of all PPE items had brought Australian manufacturing, or the lack of it, to national attention. Pointing to Australia's current standing of 87th in the Harvard Economic Complexity Index, he suggested that the country needed onshore access to the basics of healthcare, energy, defence, technology, food and water. He was quoted as arguing that 'we are connected to the world through technology these days, and that means we can have new opportunities to scale, in areas we could not scale before'. Lightweight materials, advanced sensors and 3D printing would help produce the technologies and goods needed for the twenty-first century. The market itself would not be capable of driving this innovation; top down control would be needed to balance bottom-up innovation. Workers in this new world would have to be 'new collar', that is very technologically proficient with the human-machine interface (Stott and Aedy 2020).

Challenges & Opportunities

A significant challenge to any form of re-industrialisation in Australia over the next decade driven by newly skilled and upskilled workers exists on the supply-side of industrial training and skills development. The COVID-19 pandemic has dealt an enormous blow to Australia's Vocational Education and Training (VET) sector, with a downturn in apprenticeship commencements and suspensions. The Mitchell Institute predicted a forecasted drop of 20,000 in apprenticeship commencements to June 2020, with an estimated 45,000 less in both 2021 and 2022 when compared to pre-COVID-19 levels (Hurley 2020). The bulk of these commencement losses have been in construction, electrotechnology and automotive skills areas (Business NSW 2020: 11). In "last in, first out" dynamics, very high rates of cancellations or suspensions of 1st and 2nd year apprenticeships have occurred in response to economic recession in Australia. The Mitchell Institute has indicated that apprenticeship commencements would not return to pre-COVID-19 levels until at least 2024 and that subsequently, "the supply of trained tradespeople could be diminished by up to eight years" (Hurley 2020: 5). This research has also warned that the impact of this will not be felt fully until 2024, at which time a much shallower pool of graduating apprentices will be available in the labour market. A concomitant cause of this is the marked increase of university applications for 2021 intakes that Business NSW (2020: 16) argues include scores of young people that "would have sought an apprenticeship if training positions were available."

In combination, these shifts in the education system will be seismic and compound existing weaknesses in what is likely to be a fragile and tentative economic recovery. In just New South Wales alone, the commerce peak body has surveyed businesses that employ apprentices and trainees and, on the basis of its findings warns, "it is entirely possible that 30–40 per cent of in-training apprentices will lose employment before the end of 2020 without significant recovery in the economy and extension of existing employer supports" (Business NSW 2020: 12). Further, in their report, Business NSW stressed that there will be no recovery without policy intervention.

What has the Morrison Government done to address this? Beyond short-term, passive JobKeeper payments to employers and JobSeeker payments to workers laid off as a result of the pandemic, the Coalition Government has signalled supply-side only economic policy responses over the long-term that will see its only structural interventions pursue a hardline neoliberal position of austerity (Seccombe 2020). This runs in contradiction to growing evidence from advanced industrial countries which have, in the post-GFC global economy, adopted demand-side industry policies that seek to focus strengths in areas of "smart specialisation". To confront the consequences of COVID-19 for skills and education in Australia, the Morrison Government has offered heavy-handed price signalling of degrees it considers "unproductive" (in other words, those in the Arts and Humanities). At the same time it has ignored or delayed many of the recommendations in the Joyce Review of the VET sector that would bolster the positions of public TAFE institutions which would be instrumental in a coordinated skills-and training-led recovery. This applies particularly to investment in those areas of a range of Training Packages that contain low-level digital skills and which have been identified by industry as in need of augmentation if Australia is to remain competitive in the global digital economy (AiGroup 2018).

An evident shortcoming in the resources available for VET with which to train apprentices and industrial workforces for the 4IR can be explained by a history of VET's under-funding, relative to tertiary education and schooling. The Mitchell Institute has analysed education funding data to report that VET had reached its lowest point in 2018, in real terms, since 2008 (Hurley and Van Dyke 2019). It has also recently argued in support of the VET sector's primary role in any recovery that would help Australia's economy transition out of the pandemic and into future-oriented employment and industrial transformation:

> Many parts of the VET system are succeeding despite, rather than because of, the policy environment. There is a clear need to build on the sector's strengths and successes, while eliminating practices that have posed the greatest threats to the quality of learning students receive. This requires policymakers to recognise the value that VET delivers to the economy, and create policy settings that reward and grow that value, rather than undermine it (Pilcher and Hurley 2020: 3).

The direction forward for Australian manufacturing in a post-COVID-19 economy will be characterised by intersecting trends. It will be much narrower in terms of what advanced, complex manufacturing capabilities Australian industry possesses because decades of adherence to comparative advantage in resource exports has undermined any sophisticated form of specialisation in elaborately manufactured goods (Leigh 2018). This reflects long-term trends in the sector's fate being left to market dynamics with no semblance of any industry policy that is a prerequisite for the coordination of advanced, complex economies throughout the world. Via sophisticated industry policy formations, many nations are able to identify opportunities for advanced industrial transformations that leverage the knowledge of the economy and labour market. A similar industry policy in Australia would have identified opportunities to leverage both the capital and labour remnants of Australia's automotive manufacturing supply chain.

As it stands, a range of initiatives in Australia aimed at bridging the gap between Australia's industrial history and the great leaps in innovation required to benefit from the 4IR have either been short-lived, under-funded, or have embedded within them market-based principles for transformation (for an overview, see Dean and Spoehr 2018). Such policy initiatives are not suited to economies like Australia's which is highly dependent on global value chains for high-quality jobs (see Rainnie and Dean 2019) and as outlined previously, which lack the economic complexity that can form the basis of new industrial innovations. To date, such policy responses have proved too shallow to capture opportunities for innovation in the significantly narrowed advanced manufacturing base characterising Australian industry. The lacklustre response to the economic effects of COVID-19 evident in numerous instances of the Australian industry's ineffective response to demand bares this reality of having no industry policy to coordinate a recovery and set in motion the necessary reforms to training and education that can sustain it.

For many nominally pro-market institutions in Australia, recommended responses to the impact of the pandemic now commonly reflect the clear and present reality of Australia's bleak economic outlook – policy intervention is necessary to overcome apparent market failures. Thus, all talk of economic recovery continues to skirt around the issue of an overarching, coordinated industry policy.

Such a policy would need to include incentives to not only encourage manufacturing in Australia but also deter contracting from overseas if products and equipment can be made in Australia. A recent debacle concerned three new ferries bound for Sydney, which after arriving from Indonesia in August 2020 (where the building work was outsourced) were declared 'off-limits' by the Maritime Union of Australia (MUA). The MUA criticised the NSW government for allowing Sydney's new ferries to be built overseas after three of four vessels were found to contain asbestos. In addition, the ferries were too tall to fit under bridges when travelling to Parramatta, so any passengers on that route have to move to lower decks. There are still another six ferries to be delivered as part of a $1.3 billion dollar contract leading the opposition to demand the contract be ripped up. Newcastle state MP Tim Crakanthorp compared the situation to the trains the government ordered from South Korea in recent years "that didn't fit our tracks" (McKinney 2020). NSW State Premier Gladys Berejiklian spoke to a media press conference saying "Australia and New South Wales are not good at building trains, that's why we have to purchase them from overseas" (Carr 2020) leading to outcries from the opposition regarding need to bolster jobs by relying on Australia's proud history of train building and more in future.

Conclusion

In this chapter, we traced the seemingly inexorable decline of the Australian manufacturing industry, firstly at the hands of a 'resources curse', and then through suffering the localised effects of globalised financialisation. As we pointed out, manufacturing decline was echoed in the experience of apprenticeships and training in particular and vocational education in general. However, the Fourth Industrial Revolution appears to hold hope for a resurgence in the manufacturing sector, reinforced by the deglobalisation implications of Covid-19.

As we have seen, a new conventional wisdom suggests that 4IR technologies, in particular additive manufacturing technologies like 3D-printing, are going to help support a revival of clustered firms producing a new geography of re-shored manufacturing industry. This process of deglobalisation is going to have implications for the nature and location of employment into the future. The deglobalisation thesis has been widely, and usually uncritically, accepted, including in Australia. However, as we have argued here, and at length elsewhere (Rainnie 2021 forthcoming), it is unlikely to materialise.

The case of the Australian defence industries would seem to support our more critical argument, with the suggestion being that the Australian part of Australia's defence industry is small and getting smaller (see Dunk 2020). A survey for the Australian Defence Magazine reported that, although the amount of work conducted by Australian-controlled companies has held up since 2015, it has been increasingly subcontracted to foreign-owned prime contractors. Dunk (2020) argues that this means that Australia is denied the full economic benefits that would come from designing and running projects and owning the intellectual property. Hence, the need for a movement to bring manufacturing back to Australia and strengthen and support the brand 'Australian Made'.

References

AiGroup. (2018). *Developing the workforce for a digital future: Addressing critical issues and planning for action*. Sydney: Australian Industry Group.

Australian Bureau of Statistics. (2020). *Labour force, Australia, detailed quarterly: Manufacturing* (Australia Cat No 6291.0.55.003). Canberra: Government of Australia.

Avogaro, M. (2019). The highest skilled workers of industry 4.0: New forms of work organization for new professions: A comparative study. *E-Journal of International and Comparative Labour Studies, 8*, 29–50.

Bell, S. (1993). *Australian manufacturing and the state: The politics of industry policy in the post-war era*. Melbourne: Cambridge University Press.

Bell, S. (1997). *Ungoverning the economy – The political economy of Australian economic policy*. Melbourne: Oxford University Press.

Broomhill, R. (Ed.). (1991). *The Banana Republic? Australia's current economic problems*. Sydney: Left Book Club.

Business, N. S. W. (2020). *Skilling Australia for a better future: Supporting apprenticeships through COVID-19*. Sydney.

Carr, M. (2020) *Labor blasts Premier Gladys Berejiklian for claims NSW 'not good at making trains'*. Accessed 8/9/20 https://www.newcastleherald.com.au/story/6898914/not-good-labor-slams-berejiklian-over-insult-to-nsw-made-trains/

Catalyst. (2020). *Women in the workforce – Australia quick take*. Catalyst, 18 February.

Coorey, P. (2020). 'Australia dangerously dependent on medical imports', *Australian Financial Review*, 18 February.

Cunningham, S., Theilacker, M., Gahan, P., Callan, V., & Rainnie, A. (2016). *Skills and capabilities for Australian enterprise innovation*. Report for Australian Council of the Learned Academies (ACOLA).

Dean, M., & Spoehr, J. (2018). The fourth industrial revolution and the future of manufacturing work in Australia: Challenges and opportunities. *Labour and Industry: A Journal of the Social and Economic Relations of Work, 28*(3), 166–181.

DIESR. (2020). *Industry 4.0*. https://www.industry.gov.au/funding-and-incentives/industry-40

Duck, M. (2019). The Australian resources boom: Consolidating neoliberal hegemony. *Journal of Australian Political Economy, 83*, 60–85.

Dunk, G. (2020). It's one thing to build war fighting capability, it's another to build industrial capability. *The Conversation*, 6 July.

Foundation for Young Australians. (2016). *The new work mindset: 7 new job clusters to help young people to navigate the new work order*. Melbourne: Foundation for Young Australias.

Fuchs, C. (2018). 'Industry 4.0: The Digital German Ideology' *Triple* C, No. 16, 280-289.

Goodman, J., & Worth, D. (2008). The mineral boom and Australia's resources curse. *Journal of Australian Political Economy, 61*, 201–219.

Goods, C., Rainnie, A., & Fitzgerald, S. (2015). Ecological modernisation, industry policy and the Australian automotive industry, 2007-13. *Australian Journal of Political Science, 50*(1), 93–113.

Götz, M., & Jankowska, B. (2017). Clusters and industry 4.0 – Do they fit together? *European Planning Studies, 25*(9), 1633–1653.

Hallward-Driemeier, M., & Nayyar, G. (2017). *Trouble in the making? The future of manufacturing led development*. Washington, DC: World Bank Group.

Harman, E., & Head, B. (Eds.). (1982). *State, capital and labour in the north and west of Australia*. Perth: UWA Press.

Hausmann, R., Hidalgo, C. A., Bustos, S., Coscia, M., Chung, S., Jimenez, J., Simoes, A., & Yildirim, M. A. (2017). *What did Australia export between 1998 and 2008?* Cambridge: Centre for International Development, Harvard University.

Hopkins, J. L. (2020). 'High-tech shortages loom as coronavirus shutdowns hit manufacturers', *The Conversation*, 13 February.

Hurley, P. (2020). *The impact of coronavirus on apprentices and trainees*. Melbourne: Mitchell Institute for Education and Health Policy, Victoria University.

Hurley, P., & Van Dyke, N. (2019). *Australian investment in education: Vocational education and training*. Melbourne: Mitchell Institute, Victoria University.

Hutchens, G. (2020, May 3). Coronavirus is focusing attention on how fragile global supply chains can be, so how will Australia respond? *ABC News*. https://www.abc.net.au/news/2020-05-03/coronavirus-global-supply-chains-and-essential-services-exposed/12209246

Institute for Management Development. (2020). *World competitiveness yearbook, Talent & Digital 2019: Summaries*. Lausanne: IMD World Competitiveness Center.

Jericho, G. (2019). *Australia now has a one-speed economy – and that speed is slow*. Guardian Australia, 19 November.

Kinkel, S. (2020). Industry 4.0 and reshoring. In L. De Propris & D. Bailey (Eds.), *Industry 4.0 and regional transformations*. London: Routledge.

Kotynkova, M. (2017). Re-industrialization of Europe: Industry 4.0 and the future of work. *European Scientific Journal, 13*(12)., (e-journal).

Labour Market Information Portal. (2020). *Industry information – Manufacturing*, Australian Government, Commonwealth of Australia. https://lmip.gov.au/default.aspx?LMIP/GainInsights/IndustryInformation/Manufacturing.

Leigh, A. (2018). 'Is the Australian economy too simple?', *Policy Forum*, 16 March.

McKinney, M. (2020). *Labor, union slam offshore build of ferries after asbestos found in new vessels docked at Carrington*. Accessed 8/9/20 https://www.newcastleherald.com.au/story/6891013/asbestos-found-in-new-sydney-ferries-docked-at-carrington/.

Morgan, J. (2019). Will we work in twenty-first century capitalism? A critique of the fourth industrial revolution literature. *Economy and Society, 48*, 1–28.

O'Brien, G. (2019). *27 years and counting since Australia's last recession*. Canberra: Australian Parliamentary Library Briefing Book, Parliamentary Library Research Publications.

Payton, A., & Knight, G. (2018). *Skills for a global future*. Paper presented at the 27th National VET Research Conference 'No Frills', Sydney, Australia.

Pegoraro D., De Propris, L., & Chidlow, A. (2019). Deglobalisation, value chains and reshoring. In L. De Propris & D. Bailey (Eds), (2020), *Industry 4.0 and regional transformations*, Routledge, London.

Perlich, H. (2013). Australia's 'two-speed economy'. *Journal of Australian Political Economy, 72*, 106–126.

Pfeiffer, S. (2017a). Industrie 4.0 in the making – Discourse patterns and the rise of digital despotism. In K. Briken, S. Chillas, M. Krzywdzinksi, et al. (Eds.), *The new digital workplace: How new technologies revolutionise work* (pp. 21–41). London: Springer.

Pfeiffer, S. (2017b). The vision of "Industrie 4.0" in the making – A case of future told, tamed and traded. *NanoEthics, 11*, 107–121.

Pilcher, S., & Hurley, P. (2020). *Skills for recovery: The vocational education system we need post-COVID-19*. Melbourne: Mitchell Institute for Education and Health Policy, Victoria University.

Pittarello, A., Trevisanato, A., & De Propris, L. (2020). Jobs 4.0. In L. De Propris & D. Bailey (Eds.), *Industry 4.0 and regional transformations*. London: Routledge.

Rainnie, A. (2021). i4.0, 3D printing, deglobalisation and new manufacturing clusters: the view from Australia. *Economic and Labour Relations Review, 32*(1), 115–133.

Rainnie, A., & Dean, M. (2019). Industry 4.0 and the future of quality work in the global digital economy. *Labour and Industry: A Journal of the Social and Economic Relations of Work, 30*(1), 16–33.

Reischauer, G. (2018). Industry 4.0 as policy-driven discourse to institutionalize innovation Systems in Manufacturing. *Technological Forecasting and Social Change, 132*, 26–33.

Roberts, P. (2019). *Manufacturing decline leaves Australia in the third world of exporters*. https://www.aumanufacturing.com.au/manufactruing-decline-leaves-australia-in-the-third-world-of-exporters

Roubini, N. (2020). Ten reasons why a 'Greater Depression' for the 2020s is inevitable. *Guardian Australia.* https://www.theguardian.com/business/2020/apr/29/ten-reasons-why-greater-depression-for-the-2020s-is-inevitable-covid. 29 April.

Seccombe, M. (2020). Could Frydenberg ease this crisis by printing money? *The Saturday Paper*, 1 August 2020.

Stanford, J. (2016). *Manufacturing (still) matters*. Canberra: The Australia Institute.

Stiglitz, J. (2020). We need a better balance between globalisation and self-reliance. *Australian Financial Review* 24 April.

Stilwell, F. (2000). *Changing track: A new political economic direction for Australia*. Sydney: Pluto Press.

Stott, E., & Aedy, R. (2020). Keeping the focus on Australian manufacturing after coronavirus. *ABC Radio National* 30 June. https://www.abc.net.au/news/2020-06-30/andrew-liveris-manufacturing-in-australia-after-coronavirus/12387448.

Weller, S., & O'Neill, P. (2014). De-industrialisation, financialisation and Australia's macroeconomic trap. *Cambridge Journal of Regions, Economy and Society, 7*, 509–526.

Wilson, S., & Spies-Butcher, B. (2016). After new labour: Political and policy consequences of welfare state reforms in the United Kingdom and Australia. *Policy Studies, 37*(5), 408–425.

Chapter 4
Retail Sector

Roslyn Larkin and Alan Nankervis

Abstract The retail sector is the largest employer in Australia providing significant work opportunities for low and semi-skilled persons, students, and those entering or re-entering the workforce. Casualisation and precarious work arrangements are common and come with low wages and low union representation. Unlike most other industries, many retail players benefitted greatly from the COVID-19 crisis, with the Australian Bureau of Statistics (ABS) data showing record increases in sales. Even so, artificial intelligence (AI) and automation generally have already started having significant negative impacts on employment within the industry. At this time, effects are particular to supply chain and distribution, but automation-pressured change is beginning to impact front-facing operations and the employment of those in such positions. This chapter takes a closer look at the effects of automation to date and the consequences for employment that are likely to occur as further automation rolls out. In doing so it will consider the composition and structure of the sector with an emphasis on Food Retailing and Other Store-based Retailing from both small-medium-enterprises (SMEs) and large business perspectives. While some predictions of the transformation are ominous for future employment, especially those in the lower-skilled entry-level positions, there are also optimistic predictions made by both employers and unions mostly where future service-based leadership models are adopted and supported by industry and government.

Keywords Artificial intelligence · Automation · Distribution · Retail · Supply chain

---

R. Larkin (✉)
School of Management, University of Newcastle, Newcastle, NSW, Australia
e-mail: Roslyn.larkin@newcastle.edu.au

A. Nankervis
Centre for Organisational Change and Agility (COCA), Torrens University, Adelaide, SA, Australia

School of Management and Law Curtin University, Perth, NSW, Australia
e-mail: a.nankervis@curtin.edu.au

A. Nankervis et al. (eds.), *The Fourth Industrial Revolution*,
https://doi.org/10.1007/978-981-16-1614-3_4

Introduction

The retail sector is a key component of Australian industry, ranking eighth of all industry sectors in terms of revenue and employment growth and first by employee numbers. According to Dwyer/SDA (2018: 1), there are in excess of 140,000 retail businesses across Australia in urban, rural and remote areas, and between 2012 and 2013 the sector contributed 4.5% or $68.5 billion to Australia's Gross Domestic Product (GDP). While the 2020 Covid-19 crisis was highly destructive to many industries, retail showed a record seasonally-adjusted rise in sales (ABS 2020). Nevertheless, Dwyer/SDA also suggest that there have been, and will continue to be, 'massive changes in the structure and organisation of Australian retail' due primarily to the internationalisation of commerce and the digital revolution (Dwyer/SDA 2018: 2; Verhoef et al. 2015). Two recent articles seem to confirm this prediction, driven by both customer and retailer imperatives. First, a 2017 KPMG report suggested that retail customers are increasingly demanding 'more informed decision-making, targeted (product and service) offers and the ability to access services in a faster manner' (Grewal et al. 2017a: 2). Second, Inman and Nikolova (2017) assert that the collection of 'large, complicated data that can be streamlined (allows) retailers to reach targeted customers at a lower cost' (p. 9).

Retail is also one of Australia's most competitive sectors, with local and increasingly global competition, facilitated through internet technology. Powell (2020), for example, suggests that large retailers such as Coles, Woolworths and JB Hi-Fi earned enormous rewards from online sales growth of between 20 to 35 during 2019 alone; with Myers reaping $292 million, and nearly 8% of David Jones' profit deriving from such activities. These statistics are only the tip of the financial iceberg for the retail sector as it explores the implementation of artificial intelligence, machine learning, and robotics technologies to ultimately replace much of its customer-facing workforce throughout Australia.

Although it is Australia's largest provider of employment, numerous retail jobs are either unskilled or semi-skilled in nature (for example, cashiers, cleaners, product stackers), with sales assistants representing more than a third of the total jobs in the sector (ABS 2019; Dwyer/SDA 2018). Not surprisingly, such workers are often school or university students, backpackers, or previously stay-at-home parents (Feller 2020) seeking entry back into the workforce. Three-quarters of the workforce is aged under 45, and a third is under 24 years of age. Females are heavily represented (56% compared with the overall industry average of 46%) and almost half of the workforce is precariously employed on a part-time or casual basis (Dwyer/SDA 2018). Consequently, wages are low and union representation through the principal representing union (Shop, Distributive and Allied Workers (SDA) covers only 12% of the retail sector's workforce (ABS 2019; Dwyer/SDA 2018).

To place the above descriptors in a global context, a recent OECD report suggested that Australian industry overall has the highest rate of casual workers amongst the OECD's thirty-four member countries and has experienced one of the largest increases in under-employment since 2007. Subsequently, union membership across all sectors has dropped from 45.6% in 1986 to only 13.7% in 2018 (Khadem 2019). Further, 36% of Australian jobs face a 'significant or high risk' of displacement through automation, 33% are likely to change dramatically, and approximately 14% are likely to disappear over a 15–20-year period. Given that the retail sector workforce is especially vulnerable within this scenario, it is timely to consider how these imminent challenges might be more effectively addressed by governments, employees and their unions, industry associations and educational institutions – the key stakeholders in the sector.

In summary, the Australian retail sector workforce is characterised by: relatively younger, mostly female employees on low incomes, with limited access to career opportunities and a significant lack of the job security or employment conditions enjoyed by employees in other sectors. Many of these employees are employed on a part-time or casual basis, including school and university students, and holiday visa holders who are transitioning through the sector towards other careers. Although the SDA claims to be Australia's largest union by membership numbers (Dwyer/SDA 2018), it only represents 12% of the associated sector workforce. Given the increasing competition in the sector from both local and global companies, the trend towards online, rather than face-to-face sales processes, and the looming threat from artificial intelligence, machine learning and robotics technologies, the retail workforce can be considered (alongside tourism and hospitality) as perhaps the most vulnerable of all Australian industry sectors from job displacement consequent on the Fourth Industrial Revolution (4IR).

This chapter explores the current and likely future of the high end of the retail sector, especially large supermarket chains, the particular new technologies which will transform workplaces, jobs and skills and their specific impacts. The views of pertinent industry stakeholders are considered before some strategies, policies and processes are proposed which might address the challenges more effectively for employers and their dwindling workforces.

Industry Overview

According to the Australian Bureau of Statistics (ABS), the retail trade sector (see Chart 4.1 below) is defined as 'the purchasing and/or on-selling, or communication-based buying and communication-based selling, of goods, without significant transformation, to the general public' (ABS 2019: webpage). A 2019 report released by the Australian government identified Small to Medium size Enterprises (SMEs) as contributing almost 60% of industry value add and approximately 52% of employment (ASBFEO 2019). The ABS report also explained that whilst retailers generally operate from traditional 'physically-accessible' premises, there are also 'non-store' (primarily online) retailers. As noted elsewhere in this chapter, the share of the latter option has increased significantly in the last decade and is expected to grow exponentially in the future, aided by the new 4IR technologies - a future recognised by the SDA who reported that 'the digital platform has become a must for retail. Retail

Key Statistics Snapshot	Total Revenue 2020	Annual Growth 2015-2020	Annual Growth 2020-2025
	$29.4bn	**15.4%**	**5.0%**
	Profit Margin 2020	**Wages as a share of Revenue 2020**	**Number of Businesses 2015-2020**
	4.2%	**13.9%**	**9.0%**

Chart 4.1 Key features of the online retail sector. (https://my-ibisworld-com.ezproxy.lib.rmit.edu.au/au/en/industry/home, p. 6)

ANZSIC Category G – Retail Trade	
39	Motor Vehicle and Motor Vehicle Parts Retailing
40	Fuel Retailing
41	Food Retailing
42	Other Store-Based Retailing
43	Non-Store Retailing and Retail Commission-Based Buying and/or Selling

Fig. 4.1 Composition of the retail sector (ANZSIC categories). (Source: ABS 2019)

and technology have become inseparable' (Dwyer/SDA 2018: 3). However, the SDA harbours serious concerns about the impact of such technologies on the retail workforce, which they represent a significant loss of jobs in some occupations and associated deskilling of the workforce. It also fears that part-time and casual employment will be extended beyond their current high proportions.

The following chart shows the scope and extent of the online retail component in Australia.

In addition, to purely store or non-store operations, a growing component of the sector is 'omnichannel retailing' which blends both physical and online stores into one seamless experience (Pentina et al. 2009; von Briel 2018). Some of these developments have been driven by retailers in an attempt to increase markets and decrease their costs; but customer preferences have also been influential– 'Retail channels are becoming blurred: consumers are demanding options such as ordering online with in-store pick-up. Endless inventory regardless of where they shop, and free returns across all channels' (Chaturvedi et al. 2018: 1). Feller (2020: 13) reinforced such predictions, suggesting that 'hybrid retail models are projected to grow in popularity, increasingly blurring the line between traditional and online retail'.

Figure 4.1 shows the current sub-categories of the overall Australian retail sector.

These sub-categories embrace a host of retailing operations, including food, clothing, books and newspapers, recreational goods, pharmaceuticals and cosmetics, toiletries, stationery, antique and used goods, flowers; cafes, restaurants and fast foods, inter alia. Retailers range across global and local retail chains; large, small and medium enterprises; public, private and not-for-profit organisations. Here it is important to note that this chapter reports only on findings from three sub-sectors of the industry, as classified by the ANZSIC categories – namely, 'food retailing', 'other store-based retailing' and 'non-store retailing', as these categories presently represent the major employers in the sector.

Changing Retail Sector Supply Chains

The retail sector is characterised by four key components – namely, wholesalers (vendors), warehouses (distribution centres), stores (or online outlets) and of course, its customers (Ge et al. 2019: 45) usually represented as a linear relationship. In order to maintain competitiveness, each retailer (chains or single entities) has to address three main challenges, and the responses to each of these challenges have implications for both the extent of technology adoption and the nature of retail workforces (Ge et al. 2019). First, there are inherently many more partners in the retail supply chain than in most other industry sectors, thus requiring retailers to constantly review the efficiency, associated costs and coordination of their integrated supply chains. As Ge et al. (2019) suggest, 'effective vendor management requires information-sharing between the retailer and the vendors, such as sharing of demand forecasts and inventory information through a vendor-managed inventory (VMI) system' (p. 46).

Second, unlike other sectors, retailing has an extensive range of customers and consumers, spread across urban, rural and remote locations in Australia, and in the case of online services, it has global spread. Customers are increasing demands for product quality and personalised service. Accordingly, many large retailers have invested heavily in artificial intelligence, machine learning, and robotics technologies to enhance their customer databases to provide desired products and services in more streamlined, efficient and cost-effective processes. In the SME space to date, resource constraints have limited responses to the take-up of automation and the digital economy challenges faced by the sector (Bennett and Brookes 2019). The final, and arguably most important, challenge for retailers is to maintain and reduce the costs of their operations to remain competitive and profitable. Whilst inventory costs (purchase of goods) represents the largest proportion of their total budget and thus inventory management is a crucial imperative; human resource costs account for a significant slice of their budgets, so workforce replacement by 4IR technologies will become more important in future years to remain cost-competitive.

According to Ge et al. (2019), Fig. 4.2 presents a more contemporary representation of the retail supply chain. Manufacturers are included in this version of the supply chain, requiring more interaction between themselves and wholesalers, and creating links between the manufacturers, the wholesalers and customers, on the one hand; and between manufacturers, wholesalers, distribution centres and stores, on the other. Given the increased complexity of these relationships, data collection,

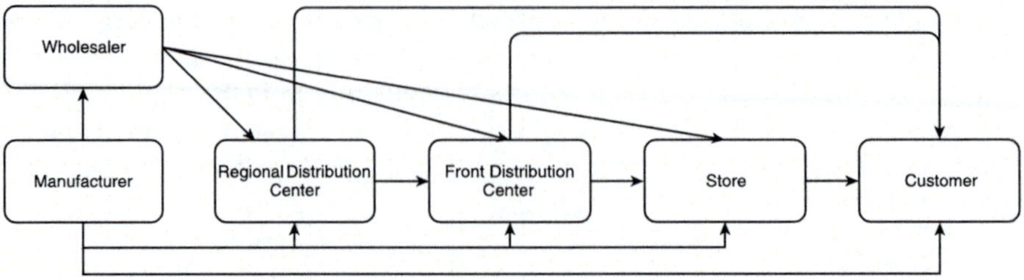

Fig. 4.2 Modern retail supply chain. (Source: Ge et al. 2019: 45)

analysis, and communication will most likely be transferred through digital technology rather than personal interactions. Customer demand in this scenario may be met through omni-channels – stores and distribution centres - or directly from the manufacturers. Communication of stores' inventory needs may be improved by direct manufacturer-distribution centre-store relationships which again will be technologically-mediated. The bottom line for retailers is, of course, 'lower cost, higher efficiency and ultimately better customer experience' (Ge et al. 2019: 4). However, as Tony Sheldon, the former Transport Workers Union (TWU) secretary, asserted, the missing link in this new form of the retail supply chain is the workforce – 'the basic rights of working people are under threat…Australia has no coordinated approach to managing the (4IR) and the future of work in Australia…a very bright red-light risk!' (cited in Taylor 2019a).

The Retail Sector Workforce

Table 1.1 in Chap. 1 illustrates employee growth in the retail sector (compared with all other industry sectors) between 1989 and 2019, indicating that the sector was fifth concerning negative employment growth (−0.90%), behind agriculture and mining, manufacturing, finance and insurance, and wholesale trade sectors. This trend is likely to escalate in subsequent decades with the confluence of the new digital technologies associated with the 4IR; the transition to increased online selling; and the anticipated significant reduction in the workforce and consequent cost reductions. It is highly likely that revenues and profits will surge in the next decade accompanied by structural changes favouring large international and domestic retailers.

Within this scenario (and unlike some other industry sectors), it is proposed that global disasters, such as COVID-19, provide unexpected but potentially desirable benefits to these corporate players. Indeed, preliminary data released by the ABS show a seasonally-adjusted estimated rise in retail sales by 8.2% between February and March 2020 when COVID first emerged in Australia – 'the strongest seasonally adjusted month-on-month rise in the history of the series' (ABS 2020). There was a 9.8% rise in retail turnover, attributed specifically to supermarkets and grocery stores, liquor retailing, and specialised food retailing, between March 2019 and March 2020 (ABS 2020).

More generally, on the conundrum of whether artificial intelligence, machine learning and robotics technologies will be able to perform more effectively and productively, Grace et al. (2018) conducted a global survey of machine learning researchers and concluded that ‘AI will outperform humans in many activities in the next ten years…(and) there is a fifty percent chance of AI outperforming humans in all tasks in forty-five years, and of automating all human jobs in a hundred and twenty years’ (p. 729). A bold prediction perhaps, but given the less complicated skills requirements required in many retail positions (as further discussed below), such projections may be realised over a much shorter period of time.

The Australian Bureau of Statistics reports that the retail sector employed more than 1,200,000 million people, or 10% of the total workforce in November 2018 (ABS 2019). Of these, approximately 2.45% (seasonally adjusted) were sales assistants on annual salaries of between $42,000 and $65,000 (ABS 2019). However, given the disproportionate number of part-time and casual positions in this job category, it is likely that very few such employees receive these salaries. According to the World Economic Forum (WEF 2016), salespersons are the most vulnerable cohort to be displaced by 4IR technologies. The WEF report also suggests that sales managers, administrative assistants, customer service representatives, retail managers, merchandisers and accountants are also in the firing line. However, marketing specialists, marketing managers, software engineers, human resource specialists, food and beverage servers, and account managers are predicted to be the least adversely affected (WEF 2016).

In terms of vulnerability, a recent study by the Australian Industry Skills Committee suggested that such jobs include office cashiers, shelf fillers, storepersons, pharmacy sales assistants, sales representatives, parts salespersons, advertising and public relations positions, sales managers and retail supervisors (AISC 2020). More optimistically, a report by the Australian Computer Society predicted that over the next 15 years an additional 455,000 jobs could be added to the Retail and Wholesale Trade Industry, comprising ‘38% or 171,000 technical jobs and 62% or 284,000 non-technical jobs…however during this period, 458,000 roles within the industry could be automated by technology’ (ACS 2020: 81). In addition, some of these jobs will inevitably be moved to logistics roles or performed in offshore call or contact centres. Examples of jobs likely to be ‘augmented’ by 4IR technologies include software developers, process improvement specialists, data engineers, data scientists, infrastructure service analysts, data integrators, strategy analysts, software quality assurance engineers and testers and security testers (AISC 2020). If these predictions prove to be correct, then the whole retail sector landscape, its infrastructure, organisational structures and skills profile will change irrevocably.

The same Australian Industry & Skills Committee report found that major challenges and opportunitesfacing human resource management produced by these developments in the future will include staff retention difficulties, a severe reduction in the options for career development, a lack of existing digital skills, and inadequate skills upgrading programs which are often ‘broad and generically based’ rather than specifically applied to the needs of the retail sector (AISC 2020: webpage).

Contrary to these gloomy perspectives, and perhaps somewhat optimistically, Priya Iyer, Chief Executive Officer of Vee24 (an AI enabled platform for live customer engagements), argued that 'while AI technology can provide efficiency and cost savings, human interaction creates value like no other. People are social beings, and ultimately nothing can ever truly replicate the experience of connecting with another person' (Szana-Hopgood 2018).

Arguably, robots, chatbots and virtual assistants (not to mention call centres) may well be perceived by both future customers and retailers to provide more efficient, knowledgeable, reliable and cost-effective customer service solutions than their human counterparts in the personalisation of service encounters. The successful implementation of automatic checkout counters at supermarkets over the past decade or so may provide a blueprint for such future technological developments.

Key New Retail Technologies

As discussed earlier in this chapter, the retail supply chain is undergoing a significant transformation, with many more interconnected players and a shift of emphasis from marketing to product development. This also relates to how customers search and buy products, as they move from traditional forms of physical purchasing to online shopping. Accordingly, all components of this new supply chain are becoming impacted by 4IR technologies. Retailers can benefit from AI through the reengineering of large complicated data that can be streamlined, thus allowing retailers to reach targeted consumers at a lower cost (Inman and Nikolova 2017).

The introduction of Amazon and eBay to the retail world shifted the way traditional forms of retail operated, giving rise to omnichannel retailing, which integrates physical and online stores into one seamless customer experience (Pentina et al. 2009; von Briel 2018). Such online forms of retail altered consumer purchasing behaviour and loyalty (Zhang et al. 2010), as it means that consumers can now browse and test products in a physical store then buy them online at a reduced cost, thus intensifying competition in the retail industry (Balakrishnan et al. 2014). This has forced many physical retailers to expand their channels into the online marketplace (Bernstein et al. 2008). Such omnichannel retailing is driven mainly by technological advancements that have given rise to augmented reality technologies, enabling retailers to be more efficient in terms of communication between channels (Brynjolfsson et al. 2013). However, as more channels become available to consumers to access products, they can also create more 'touchpoints' between retailers and customers, thus resulting in the increased management of different forms of retailer-customer interaction (Verhoef et al. 2015). As a result, many retailers have struggled to move from single or multi-channel retail to an omnichannel approach.

There are many examples of the different technologies implemented for these purposes. These include the 'continued rise of BNPL (buy now, pay later), marketplace and mobile shopping and express delivery' (Yip and Jones 2019: 8), with the global online market predicted to reach US$3.43 trillion by 2023 (or 17% total retail market). In addition, virtual assistants, augmented reality, algorithms, data-driven insights, AI-enabled chatbots and biometric payments systems are beginning to permeate some, but not all, retailers (Yip and Jones 2019). Other Australian examples include Coles working with Microsoft to improve customer data collection, and a A$950 million deal with Witron (Germany) to build fully automated distribution centres in Sydney and Brisbane; and a $4150 million partnership with Ocado's Smart Platform, a proprietary e-commerce warehousing solution, to create two 'highly automated' centres in Sydney to determine how energy is used in distribution centres (Taylor 2019a). Blockchain inventory management is also being used, as robots conduct inventory checks, meet and greet customers in retail stores, read their emotions for the purpose of analysing their product preferences, and store them for future inventory purchasing. They are also used, along with virtual assistants and chatbots, to solve customer problems and provide advice and directions to the appropriate aisles in the stores (Dwyer/SDA 2018). Taylor (2019a) reported that Woolworths, amongst other retailers, is currently trialling a Greggles robot to scan distribution centres and retail stores for potential hazards as well as robot shelf-stacking, heralding the beginning of the end of casual, transitional jobs for school and university students and part-time workers.

From the customers' perspective, examples of AI applications in current use include:

- *QueVision,* which collects and analyses data received from infrared sensors above store doors and cash registers, give retailers insight into how many registers are needed and expected wait times which assist, improvements to overall customer experiences (Inman and Nikolova 2017)
- *Amazon Go* allows customers to shop and leave without checkout;
- *Domino's Pizza* employs Facebook ordering systems;
- *Starbucks* and many other outlets provide 'order and pay before purchase' processes;
- *Aussie Farmers* offers a complete online service;
- *Amazon and Domino's* Pizza are trialling drones for product deliveries, and;
- *Uber Eats, Foodora and Deliveroo* 'bypass minimum wages for employees by classifying staff as contractors and gig workers and paying them per delivery, on individual contracts' (Dwyer 2018)

As only one illustration of how these new technologies have transformed the nature, purposes and associated workforces of many Australian retail businesses, Telstra is reportedly recruiting 1500 software specialists – data science, data analytics and cybersecurity - but cutting 18,000 direct workforce and contractor roles by 2022 (Taylor 2019a).

The following case (Case 4.1) provides a snapshot of how some large Australian retailers are managing the implementation of these new technologies in their distribution centres, supermarkets and call centres, and some of the associated industrial relations and employee challenges.

Case 4.1: Retailers' Perspectives

From discussions with representatives from the retail sector and a review of the relevant literature, it is clear that Australian retailers (like their US and European counterparts) are seriously considering the implementation of AI technologies in their associated distribution centres, supermarkets and support services. As examples, some have trialled semi- or fully-automated product distribution centres to increase productivity and reducing labour costs. A recent example from Woolworths illustrates the rationale, benefits and challenges associated with the development of automated distribution centres (Janda 2020). The company issued a press release which indicated that there would be a loss of around 700 jobs in Sydney and Melbourne as it automates these fundamental facilities. Its Chief Supply Chain Officer stated that 'cutting-edge automation will build tailored pallets for specific aisles in individual stores, helping us improve on-shelf product availability with faster restocking, reducing congestion in stores, and enabling a safer work environment for our teams with less manual handling' (Janda 2020 page number or webpage??).

However, targeted and personalised technologies, while having benefits for both the customer and retailer, could also potentially diminish customer-retailer engagement as customers might worry about personal privacy due to retailers collecting and storing their data. Therefore, retailers need to be aware of consumer concerns regarding privacy and be able to balance their knowledge about customers with how they target their products (Aguirre et al. 2015).

It is also important to acknowledge the importance of understanding and managing customer experience and engagement levels (Grewal et al. 2009; Verhoef et al. 2009). However, to date, there appears to be limited in-depth research that addresses ways in which firms can enhance customers' sense of engagement. Drawing on research into 'conscious capitalism', Grewal et al. (2017b) proposed a hierarchal model of consumer engagement that reflects customer experience, an emotional connection, and a shared identity. They report that retailers that implement this form of consciousness into their way of doing business create a deeper relationship with their customers by leveraging their values. AI will influence how consumers select where to shop, what to shop for, and how to purchase their goods and services. The offline retail sector has already begun converging with the online retail world, and retailers need to embrace the future of AI to make sure customer engagement is maintained at a high level. Through the use of data captured via customer loyalty and social data, enterprise systems, and location-based details, retailers are optimising their prices and increasing sales revenue (Bradlow et al. 2017). Therefore, large amounts of data which enable retailers to increase an understanding of consumer behaviour through AI technologies will generate greater levels of customer engagement, loyalty and profit.

According to Toby Walsh, Scientia Professor of Artificial Intelligence at the University of New South Wales, the retail sector's adoption of AI, robotics and automation is driven by the increasing competition between domestic and international retailers. Walsh stated – 'saving manpower will help them stay competitive and increase their profits' (Taylor 2019b, page number?). However, he highlighted the significant downside for the stakeholders not often included in the retail supply chain, its employees – 'they'll make promises that this will free up time for their staff to interact with customers, but in a cut-throat business like supermarkets, where the consumer is always looking for lower prices, they'll be tempted to reduce head counts and improve their margins' (Taylor 2019b, page number?), as the following case illustrates.

Case 4.2: Union Perspectives

Discussions with spokespersons from unions with membership in the Australian Retail Sector support such contentions. Job losses to automation in both distribution channels and stores will occur, and while there are concerns about ethical violations of workers' rights, it is not all doom and gloom. For example, associated unions see some opportunities for growth in other areas, and are sending clear messages to the government to drive a paradigm shift towards training tools and education to help the change. The retail sector is built on a dual leadership model. On the one hand, you can lead by price. This will be the model for businesses investing heavily in automation. On the other, you can lead by service, and it is here where jobs are most likely to grow.

Employment Impacts, Challenges & Opportunities

The literature and available evidence suggest that significant structural, sectoral, organisational and social changes are occurring across the entire Australian retail sector. These changes are boosted by both generational differences in customer preferences and the impact of 4IR technologies; the latter being heavily weighted in favour of benefits to retailers (significantly reduced production, delivery, product promotion and infrastructure costs, enhanced competitiveness and profitability) rather than their workforces. However, as Schwab and Samans (2016) have suggested, most retail occupations are undergoing a fundamental transformation, 'but the reality is highly specific to the industry, the region and occupations in question as well as the ability of various stakeholders to manage change' (p. v). Thus, at the lower end of the occupational spectrum in retail distribution centres and shops, jobs such as inventory management, forklift drivers, packers and stackers, cleaners, shelf-stackers, checkout operators and sales assistants will be the most susceptible to displacement by the new technologies; whilst at the high end, jobs such as marketing analysts, senior sales staff ('expert brand advocates' – Dwyer/SDA 2018: 4), data analysts, software engineers and social media experts (Dwyer/SDA 2018: 5) are positioned to increase significantly.

However, the COVID-19 virus has demonstrated the fragility of most (if not all) retail supply chains, notably concerning subsectors such as domestic and international travel, threatening the livelihood of travel agents and their associated networks; and has highlighted the difficulties of maintaining product supply in bookshops, newsagents and office supply stores, to identify a few examples.

The overall shift in emphasis away from semi-skilled or skilled jobs to highly-skilled professional roles is likely to specifically disadvantage women, transitional workers (school and university students) and retail employees in rural and remote areas of Australia. This is due to their generally lower education levels and lack of digital or technological skills and is expected to lead to increasing wage inequalities. It may, however, fit well with the growing generational preference for zig-zag careers 'whereby workers accumulate experience across multiple employers' (Dwyer/SDA 2018: 12) or the gig economy (individual contractors on time-bound contracts), rather than more traditional career ladders or structured pathways. This shift, however, also raises the issue of precarious employment, with its associated spectre of job insecurity, minimal employment conditions and a lack of protection from relevant unions. As Dwyer/SDA (2018) pointed out, 'expansion of the new technologies is a major driver of the growing inequalities' (p. 8) across the retail sector. Additional contributing factors in Australia are the variable internet access capacities in rural and remote locations and the scarcity of specialist staff there to deal with customer enquiries and service complaints.

With respect to the strategies that employers in the sector might adopt to maximise opportunities provided by the implementation of these new 4IR technologies and to minimise their adverse impact on existing and future employees, many authors have suggested that they should be predicated on the principle of 'a fair distribution of the benefits' (Dwyer/SDA 2018: 7), balancing financial and business needs with those of all stakeholders (AISC 2020; Ge et al. 2019); Khadem 2019; Powell 2020; Scarpetta 2017; Yip and Jones 2019). In pursuit of these aims, a plethora of integrated approaches by employers is recommended, including prioritising job creation and reskilling, the provision of decent wages and conditions, some degree of assured job security, employee consultation concerning planned technological changes, and attention to ways of mitigating the gender impact on women in the retail workforce (WEF 2016: 40).

Penprase (2019) further suggested that education of the workforce is a crucial element of retail employers' responsibilities in the implementation of these new technologies, especially 'ethical thinking, inter-cultural awareness and critical thinking, to enable thoughtful and informed applications of the exponentially developing technologies' (p. 220). Schwab and Samans (2016) emphasised the importance of a tripartite approach – 'businesses should take a proactive role in supporting their current workforce through retraining; individual (employees) should take a proactive approach to their own learning; and governments should create the enabling environment, rapidly and creatively, to assist these efforts' (p. v). On the latter point, other authors suggested that employment legislation needs to enshrine corporate accountability with respect to employer responsibilities in the implementation of new technologies which might lead to job displacement (Dwyer/SDA

2018: 7). Additionally Dwyer/SDA (2018) argued for a review of the Australian industrial relations system to allow for binding arbitration processes and 'portable entitlements' for employees which allow them to seamlessly take their entitlements (annual leave, sick leave, parental leave and superannuation) to their post-displacement employers (Dwyer/SDA 2018: 8).

Conclusion

Transformation of the retail sector is progressing towards digitally-enhanced automation, including the use of 4IR technologies such as robotics and machine learning. Investment in such technologies by the large players, both national and international, are already generating efficiencies that challenge SMEs to keep up. With employment costs only second to inventory costs, it will come as no surprise to stakeholders to see a shift in the traditional landscape of retail sector employment from low skilled, front-facing staff toward data specialisation positions. This shift will not be equal in terms of employment numbers, with the automation of the sector most likely to have consequences for many of the current traditional jobs, and especially for part-time and casual employees in low-skilled positions. It will likely decimate job opportunities for high school and university or TAFE students to gain work experience or support themselves through their studies.

These transformations are, without a doubt, most favourable to both the larger retail organisations and customers, leaving SMEs and many already vulnerable employees as potential victims of these new technologies. Of course, optimists view such transformations as opportunities for growth, re-skilling and related opportunities in new jobs yet to be defined. It may, however, be prudent for retailers to move cautiously, as those vulnerable to unemployment today will be unable to provide tomorrow's customer base. All of these factors have inevitably been complicated in the advent of COVID-19, with its specific impacts yet to be experienced or fully appreciated.

References

ABS. (2019). 8501.0 – Retail Trade, Australia, July 2019, Explanatory Notes, Australian Bureau of Statistics, ONLINE. https://abs.gov.au/AUSSTATS/abs@nsf/Lookup/8501.0.

ABS. (2020). 8501.0.55.008 – Retail Trade, Australia, Preliminary, Australian Bureau of Statistics, ONLINE. https://www.abs.gov.au/ausstats/abs@.nsf/mf/8501.0.55.008.

ACS. (2020). *Technology impacts on the Australian workforce*. Sydney: Faethm. ONLINE. www.acs.org.au/content/dam/acs/acs-publications. Accessed 31 Oct 2020.

Aguirre, E., Mahr, D., Grewal, D., de Ruyter, K., & Wetzels, M. (2015). Unravelling the personalization paradox: The effect of information collection and trust-building strategies on online advertisement effectiveness. *Journal of Retailing, 91*(1), 34–49.

Australian Small Business & Family Enterprise Ombudsman (ASBFEO). (2019). *Small business counts*. www.asbfeo.gov.au/sites/default/files/documents/ASBFEO-small-business-counts.pdf

Australian Industry & Skills Committee (AISC). (2020). *Industry insights: Retail & wholesale*. https://nationalindustryinsights.aisc.net.au/industries/retail-and-wholesale. Accessed 4 Apr 2020.

Balakrishnan, A., Sundaresan, S., & Zhang, B. (2014). Browse-and-switch: Retail-online competition under value uncertainty. *Production and Operations Management, 23*(7), 1129–1145.

Bennett, T., & Brookes, J. (2019). *The business of retail is changing as robots run warehouses and stores*, ONLINE https://which-50.com/cover-story-the-business-of-retail-is-changing-as-robots-run-warehouses-and-stores/.

Bernstein, F., Song, J. S., & Zheng, X. (2008). "Bricks-and-mortar" vs. "clicks-and-mortar": An equilibrium analysis. *European Journal of Operational Research, 187*(3), 671–690.

Bradlow, E. T., Gangwar, M., Kopalle, P., & Voleti, S. (2017). The role of big data and predictive analytics in retailing. *Journal of Retailing, 93*(1), 79–95.

Brynjolfsson, E., Hu, Y. J., & Rahman, M. S. (2013). Competing in the age of omnichannel retailing. *MIT Sloan Management Review, 54*(4), 23–29.

Chaturvedi, N., Martich, M., Ruwadi, B., & Ulker, N. (2018). *The future of supply chains*. https://www.mckinsey.com/~/media/mckinsey/dotcom/client_service/retail/articles/future_of_retail_supply_chains.ashx. Accessed 14 Mar 2020.

Dwyer, G/SDA. (2018). *Submission to the inquiry into the future of work and workers*. Melbourne: Shop Distributive & Allied Employees' Association (SDA).

Feller, D. (2020). *Industry report X0004 online shopping in Australian* IBIS World Melbourne.

Ge, D., Pan, Y., Shen, Z.-J., Wu, D., Yuan, R., & Zheng, C. (2019). Retail supply chain management: A review of theories and practices. *Journal of Data, Information & Management, 1*, 45–64.

Grace, K., Salvatier, J., Dafoe, A., Zheng, A., & Evans, O. (2018). Viewpoint: When will AI exceed human performance? Evidence from AI experts. *Journal of AI Research, 62*, 729–754.

Grewal, D., Levy, M., & Kumar, V. (2009). Customer experience management in retailing: An organizing framework. *Journal of Retailing, 85*(1), 1–14.

Grewal, D., Roggeveen, A. L., & Nordfält, J. (2017a). The future of retailing. *Journal of Retailing*, Elsevier, *93*(1), 1–6.

Grewal, D., Roggeveen, A. L., Sisodia, R., & Nordfalt, J. (2017b). Enhancing customer engagement through consciousness. *Journal of Retailing, 93*(1), 55–64. https://my-ibisworld-com.ezproxy.lib.rmit.edu.au/au/en/industry/home. Accessed 3 July 2020.

Inman, J. J., & Nikolova, H. (2017). Shopper-facing retail technology: A retailer adoption decision framework incorporating shopper attitudes and privacy concerns. *Journal of Retailing, 93*(1), 7–28.

Janda, M. (2020). Woolworths to eliminate 700 jobs in Sydney and Melbourne, *ABC News*, https://www.abc.net.au/news/2020-06-23/woolworths-automation-will-eliminate-700-jobs/12385292.

Khadem, N. (2019). *Australian has a high rate of casual work, and many jobs face automation threats: OECD*. https://www.abc.net.au/news/2019-04-25/australia-sees-increase-in-casual-workers-ai-job-threats/11043772. Accessed 9 Mar 2020.

Penprase, B. E. (2019). The fourth industrial revolution and higher education. In N. W. Glease (Ed.), *Higher education in the era of the fourth industrial revolution* (pp. 216–228). Singapore: Palgrave Macmillan.

Pentina, I., Pelton, L. E., & Hasty, R. W. (2009). Performance implications of online entry timing by store-based retailers: A longitudinal investigation. *Journal of Retailing, 85*(2), 177–193.

Powell, D. (2020). *Customers will just walk out: Coles exec flags 'checkout-free' stores within 10 years*. https://www.aacs.org.au/customers-will-just-walk-out-coles-exec-flags-checkout-free-stores-within-10-years/.

Scarpetta, S. (2017). *What future for work?* Retrieved from http://oecdobserver.org/news/fullstory.php/aid/5433/What_future_for_work_.html. Accessed 4 Apr 2020.

Schwab, K., & Samans, R. (2016). *Preface: The future of jobs: Employment, skills and workforce strategy for the fourth industrial revolution* (pp. v–vi). Geneva: World Economic Forum. ONLINE. Accessed 2 Oct 2019. Available at http://www3.weforum.org/docs/WEF_Future_of_Jobs.pdf.

Szana-Hopgood, A. (2018). The rise of automation: Should retailers be worried? *Retail Gazette*, October 11. https://www.retailgazette.co.uk/blog/2018/10/the-rise-of-automation-in-retail-should-retailers-be-worried/.

Taylor, J. (2019a, August). *Supermarkets are among the key businesses forging ahead with new technology, and observers warn that cutting jobs is a prime motive*. https://www.theguardian.com/australia-news/2019/aug/03/buy-now-pay-later-ai-and-the-red-light-risk-for-millions-of-australian-jobs.3.

Taylor, J. (2019b). Buy now pay later. AI and the red-light risk for millions of Australian jobs. *The Guardian*. ONLINE. www.thheguardian.cm/australia-news/2019/aug/03/buy-now-pay-later-ai-and-the-red-light-risk-for-millions-of-australian-jobs.

Verhoef, P. C., Lemon, K. N., Parasuraman, A., Roggeveen, A., Tsiros, M., & Schlesinger, L. A. (2009). Customer experience creation: Determinants, dynamics and management strategies. *Journal of Retailing, 85*(1), 31–41.

Verhoef, P. C., Kannan, P. K., & Inman, J. J. (2015). From multi-channel retailing to omni-channel retailing. Introduction to the special issue on multi-channel retailing. *Journal of Retailing, 91*(2), 174–181.

von Briel, F. (2018). The future of omnichannel retail: A four-stage Delphi study. *Technological Forecasting and Social Change, 132*, 217–229.

World Economic Forum (WEF). (2016). *The future of jobs: Employment, skills and workforce strategy for the fourth industrial revolution*. Geneva: World Economic Forum. ONLINE. Accessed 2 Oct 2019. Available at http://www3.weforum.org/docs/WEF_Future_of_Jobs.pdf.

Yip, R., & Jones, E. (2019). *Inside Australian online shopping: eCommerce industry report*. Australia Post. ONLINE. Accessed 2 Oct 2019. Available at https://auspost.com.au/content/dam/auspost_corp/media/documents/inside-australian-online-shopping-ecommerce-report.pdf.

Zhang, J., Farris, P. W., Irvin, J. W., & Kushawa, T. (2010). Crafting integrated multichannel retailing strategies. *Journal of Interactive Marketing, 24*(2), 168–180.

Chapter 5
Accommodation & Food Services

Subas P. Dhakal

Abstract Tourism industries, inclusive of the accommodation and food services [AFS] sector, are considered one of the main drivers of economic growth in Australia. Tourism industries collectively contributed over $100 billion to Australia's GDP and employed nearly one million people in 2019. One of the emergent issues associated with tourism industries is the Fourth Industrial Revolution (4IR) and the impacts of transformative digital technologies. Globally, it has been rightfully pointed out that digital technologies have advanced rapidly in recent years and are now considered as game-changers for tourism industries. However, although the business-centric view of digital opportunities associated with the 4IR has received significant attention, the policy-centric examination of the 4IR and tourism industries nexus remain under the radar in Australia. This chapter responds to this gap and draws on the three pillars of the Automation Readiness Index (EIU 2018a, b) – innovation, education and employment policies landscapes – in order to explore the challenges and the potential way forward for the AFS sector within tourism industries.

Keywords 4IR readiness · Accommodation and food services sector · Automation · COVID-19

Introduction

Tourism industries, inclusive of accommodation and food services [AFS] sector, are considered one of the main drivers of economic growth in Australia and are engaged in a variety of activities including but not limited to: travel agent service provision; tour operation; accommodation provision; domestic air service provision;

S. P. Dhakal (✉)
UNE Business School, University of New England (UNE), Armidale, Australia
e-mail: Subas.dhakal@une.edu.au

A. Nankervis et al. (eds.), *The Fourth Industrial Revolution*,
https://doi.org/10.1007/978-981-16-1614-3_5

international air service provision; cafe and restaurant operation, and hiring out motor vehicles (see IBISWorld 2020). Tourism industries collectively contributed over $100 billion to Australia's GDP and directly or indirectly employed nearly one million people in 2019 (AISC 2020). However, while the advent and proliferation of the digital economy is likely to accelerate the growth of tourism opportunities, bring the supply and the demand sides closer, streamline travel booking, transform marketing operations and reinvent the business models of different types of tourism enterprises (Guerriero 2019), tourism related occupations such as tourism & travel advisers are highly automatable and are likely to face potentially significant job losses in the future (FAETHM 2020). As discussed earlier in this book, the World Economic Forum [WEF] (2018) has argued that the world has entered the era of the Fourth Industrial Revolution [4IR] – the era characterised by 'a fusion of technologies that blurs the lines between the physical, digital and biological spheres' (Schwab 2017: 1). The extant literature on the 4IR and tourism industries nexus has primarily focused on to what extent technologies can help jobs to become more efficient and cost effective (Peceny et al. 2019; Pinzone et al. 2017). Although the techno-centric view has put a spotlight on the tourism opportunities associated with the 4IR, there is a limited understanding of its implications for Australia. This chapter responds to this gap and draws on the three pillars of the Automation Readiness Index (EIU 2018a, b) – innovation, education and employment policies landscapes – in order to explore the challenges and the potential way forward for the AFS sector within tourism industries.

The AFS sector is selected because it is (a) one of the fastest growing components of tourism industries in the past 5 years in Australia (Australian Jobs 2020) and (b) has a high automation potential (Muro et al. 2019). The chapter is structured in four parts, with the next section providing a brief overview of the tourism labour market, followed by a review of the 4IR and tourism industry-nexus. The subsequent section of the chapter describes the research study design and findings. Finally, the chapter will discuss the implications, including the context of an ongoing COVID-19 pandemic, before presenting concluding remarks.

Industry Overview

The United Nations World Tourism Organisation's [UNWTO] website characterises tourism as: a social, cultural and economic phenomenon which entails the movement of people to countries or places outside their usual environment for personal or business/professional purposes. These people are called visitors (which may be either tourists or excursionists; residents or non-residents) and tourism has to do with their activities, some of which involve tourism expenditure (UNWTO n.d.: paragraph 1). This description indicates that tourism activities are complex and wide ranging in nature and involves multiple components. For example, as Table 5.1 depicts, tourism includes multiple components including but not limited to promotion, attraction, services, transport, accommodation, food, and retail. Nonetheless, the Australian and New Zealand Standard Industrial Classification (ANZSIC) does not recognise tourism as one industry. According to the Australian Bureau of Statistics [ABS] (2012), industries are defined on the basis of the primary goods and services that they produce, whilst tourism instead is defined according to the status of the consumer, that is, the characteristics of the consumer determine whether the production is included within the scope of tourism (paragraph 1). In line with the argument made by Leiper (2008) that tourism industries is a more appropriate term and the singular expression is misleading, the likely rationale for the ABS is the fact that tourism activities bring together diverse components that directly or indirectly cater to the needs of the tourists or consumers and their actual tourism related experiences (Table 5.1).

Employment Trends

According to Tourism Research Australia [TRA], there were 302,520 tourism-related enterprises in Australia accounting for about 13% of a total of 2.3 million enterprises in the country (TRA 2019: 2). Micro enterprises with up to four employees, and small enterprises with 5–19 employees made up about 95% of total tourism-related businesses and accounted for 38% of the workforce in 2018. Whereas medium enterprises with between 20 and 199 employees and large enterprises with more than 200 employees made up 5% of the total businesses and accounted for 62% of the workforce (TRA 2020: 3). The latest World Travel & Tourism Council's [WTTC] country report on Australia indicates that tourism industries collectively

Table 5.1 Main components of tourism industries

Components	Examples
Attraction	Natural capital i.e. national parks
	Built capital i.e. monuments
Promotion	Marketing
	Communications
Services	Travel agents
	Event managers
Transport	Airlines
	Train
	Ship/cruise
	Taxi services
	Car rentals
Accommodation	Formal i.e. hotels, motels
	Informal i.e. Airbnb
Food	Restaurants/cafes
	Takeaway

Source: Author

contributed to nearly 11% of the total economy and supported over 1.6 million direct and indirect employment jobs (WTTC 2020:1).

The ABS collects and reports labour market data under the umbrella of Tourism Characteristics Industries and Connected Industries. The employment figures for the financial year 2018–2019 indicated that 666,000 people were directly employed in tourism industries, with most jobs (52.5%) being full-time and slightly more female (54%) compared to male (ABS 2019). Tourism-related jobs have specifically increased by more than one-third in the last 10 years and it was close to overtaking the manufacturing sector jobs in the country (Ludlow and Housego 2020) before the COVID-19 pandemic. Furthermore, a granulated scrutiny of the employment data on AFS (Table 5.2) reveals two interesting trends. The first is that most of the frontline hospitality related employment (for example, café, restaurants and takeaway food services) are part-time (or casual) in nature, with a greater female proportion. Secondly, women make up almost two-thirds of the workforce in the accommodation sector.

Labour Market Challenges

The Australian Tourism Labour Force Report: 2015–2020 (Deloitte Access Economics [DEA] 2015) highlighted that while the easing of the mining boom and general softening in the national labour market was assisting tourism enterprises to find workers, the country was facing a shortage of skilled and unskilled labour. The report stated that: 'in the absence of any change in policy or industry initiatives it is expected 123,000 new workers will need to be sourced by 2020. The skilled labour shortage is expected to be 30,000 workers, while an additional 63,000 unskilled workers are also required to be sourced' (p. i). Pre COVID-19 analysis suggested that cafés and restaurants as well as accommodation services providers were particularly facing greater labour market difficulties. For example, over 50,000 additional workers (inclusive of waiters, kitchenhands and chefs) in the food services sector and nearly 1000 additional managers were expected to be needed in the accommodation sector (SKILLSIQ 2019).

It has been posited that the productivity growth within tourism industries is crucial to Australia's transition from a resources-based economy to a services-based

Table 5.2 Employment in the AFS sector in Australia (in '000)

Sectors	Total	Part-time (%)	Full-time (%)	Male (%)	Female (%)
Cafes, restaurants & takeaway food services	181	117.70 (65.03%)	63.30 (34.97%)	86.20 (47.62%)	94.80 (52.38%)
Accommodation	86.1	41.50 (48.2%)	44.60 (51.80%)	30.80 (35.77%)	55.30 (64.23%)

Source: Australian Bureau of Statistics [ABS 2019)
https://www.abs.gov.au/AUSSTATS/abs@.nsf/DetailsPage/5249.02018-19?OpenDocument

economy, and that the growing shortage of skilled and semi-skilled labour is a threat to Australia's tourism strategy (TAA 2017: 5). Although there is documented evidence of discrepancies between governmental and recruiter evaluation of tourism industry related skilled migrant expertise (Treuren et al. 2019), Australia has a long history of demand-based skilled migration program in order to overcome specific shortages. As depicted in Table 5.3, the current skilled migration program addresses shortages in four of the main components of tourism industries namely: transport, accommodation, food, and promotion. These shortages have implications in the 4IR and tourism industry nexus, in particular the AFS sector and will be discussed later in the chapter.

Key Technologies

Various stakeholders of tourism industries are currently consumed with the ongoing disruptions associated with the COVID-19 pandemic (Cockburn 2020) as well as a diplomatic row with China (ABC 2020), the focus in this chapter is on the implications of the application of 4IR technologies for the AFS sector within tourism industries. As discussed throughout this book, the 4IR (also known as Industry 4.0) is disrupting almost all industries and sectors around the world with the use of transformative technologies to connect the physical world with the digital world. For example, OECD (2018a, b) has identified enabling technologies as one of the four megatrends that are likely to have significant impacts for the viability of various components within tourism industries (p. 61). According to the Australian Department of Industry, Science, Energy and Resources [DISER] 2019), these technologies include but are not limited to industrial and social robots, self-service kiosks, artificial intelligence [AI], chatbots, face recognition technology, voice controlled technologies, wearable and implanted technologies, 3D printing, the internet of things [IOT], and other automation technologies that are used for the production and delivery of goods and services instead of human employees. It is not surprising

Table 5.3 The AFS sector-related skilled migration occupation list

Component	Occupation
Accommodation	Accommodation and Hospitality Managers
	Hotel or Motel Manager
Food	Baker
	Cafe or Restaurant Manager
	Chef
	Cook
	Pastry-cook

Source: Department of Home Affairs 2020 https://immi.homeaffairs.gov.au/visas/working-in-australia/skill-occupation-list

that in recent years tourism enterprises have increasingly recognised that emerging technologies have the potential to foster their competitiveness by changing the way customers are targeted, disrupting existing service offerings, and forcing a re-imagining of the actual tourism experiences (TRA 2019: 2).

Tourism industries, however, are not only the enabler of, but are also shaped by, advances in technological innovations. Several key drivers such as, (a) increasing data volumes, computational power and connectivity, (b) emerging analytics and business-intelligence capabilities, (c) augmented and virtual reality systems are shaping new business models within tourism industries of the future (OECD 2016; OECD 2020). In addition, various components of tourism industries are increasingly embracing the 4IR and labelling themselves with expressions such as Tourism 4.0 or Smart Tourism (Lee et al. 2020; Pencarelli 2019). For example, as a part of the Smart Tourism initiative, the state of Queensland installed 150 *iBeacons* in 13 destinations including airports, information centres, national parks and other popular attractions which use location-based technology to automatically deliver users of the "This is Queensland" app with information about the top things to see and do in the vicinity (Tourism and Events Queensland 2015). The nature of the 4IR is such that it has accelerated the growth of tourism opportunities, transformed booking marketing operations, reinvented the business models of tourism enterprises, and enhanced immersive experiences in the AFS sectors around the world. For example, the Hen-na Hotel in Japan is Guinness-certified as the world's first robot-staffed hotel. Robots, equipped with the artificial intelligence and facial recognition technologies are used on the front desk, as customer information points and for storage purposes (Hen-na Hotel 2020). Fast-food outlets around the world have enthusiastically adopted the AI robots in recent years. For example, Oracle Food and Beverage (2017) reported that: a) KFC in China has showcased AI robots capable of complex customer service related tasks such as order changes and substitutions, and b) Dominos Pizza's delivery service in New Zealand has tested AI robots i.e. three-foot-tall carrier with storage space for up to 10 pizzas – that drives autonomously within a 20 kilometers range (p 3).

Although these examples indicate that the adoption of technologies have evolved at a rapid pace, the challenges as well as the opportunities for national governments, tourism-related enterprises and those employed within the sector remain poorly understood even amongst the world's most advanced economies (OECD 2016) including Australia. The 4IR and associated proliferation of transformative technologies identified earlier have not only excited cautious optimism about the future, but also fuelled an apprehension that large numbers of semi-skilled and unskilled jobs carried out by humans will be potentially replaced by machines (APEC 2017). For instance, the FAETHM (2020) report predicts that nearly half of all travel advisory jobs are automatable and almost 12,000 jobs are at risk in Australia (p. 20). It is in this context, this chapter contends that it is imperative to explore the operating environment of tourism industries in Australia at the macro level, if the potential associated with the 4IR is to be harnessed and its pitfalls minimised.

Given that the 4IR readiness of tourism industries is dependent upon sound employment, education, and innovation policy infrastructure, this chapter examines the question: "what insights can be generated from the current state of tourism industries related 4IR initiatives in Australia?" As indicated earlier, the AFS sector is the main focus of the chapter. The Economist Intelligence Unit's (EIU's) (2018b) Automation Readiness Index [ARI], which compared twenty- five countries in terms of their preparedness for the era of automation, provides a useful framework to explore policy developments, discussions and directions that directly contribute to the country's preparedness and ability to harness 4IR. The ARI focuses on the three key areas: innovation policies that directly or indirectly support research into and business adoption of advanced technologies; education policies that aim to develop the human capital needed to take advantage of these technologies; and on labour market policies needed to manage the workforce's transition to a highly automated economy (EIU 2018b; 8). For the purposes of this chapter, drawing on Dhakal et al. (2020) and Dhakal and Tjokro (2020), 4IR readiness is understood as the degree to which policy infrastructure (macro level) is responsive to the changing external environment – global and regional trends in order to build tourism enterprises' (meso level) – and individual workers' (micro level) abilities to harness emerging transformative technologies within tourism industries in order to gain desired outputs. This chapter primarily concerns a macro level 4IR readiness in the context of AFS sector within tourism industries and adopts an exploratory approach making use of documentary analysis (Bowen 2009; Johnston 2017) of selected key reports in order to answer the research question.

While the primary merit of exploratory research is that it allows researchers to uncover meaning, develop understanding, and discover meaningful insights of the emerging issue or phenomenon, the main limitation of the approach is that the analysis is primarily qualitative and may suffer from researcher's bias (Brown et al. 2019). Moreover, as Tussyadiah (2020) observed, there are limited in-depth studies of the nexus between 4IR and components of tourism industries not only from the readiness perspectives but also from the standpoints of stakeholders involved in the production and consumption of tourism products and services. Future studies in the post COVID-19 research environment might use a multi-method approach to comprehensively examine the implications of 4IR beyond the AFS sector in Australia from multiple stakeholder's perspective. This chapter is also cognisant of the fact that while both the 2019 Bushfires and COVID-19 pandemic have affected the Australian tourism industries (Cockburn 2020), the analysis presented here does not take into account the full extent of adverse impacts associated with these disruptions on all tourism industries.

Employment Impacts

As Nankervis et al. (2019) observed, AI, automation, digital disruption and robotics are some of the elements associated with the phenomenon of the 4IR that have gained policy momentum across the Asia Pacific region. For instance, the Asia–Pacific Economic Cooperation [APEC] acknowledges that the magnitude and scale of the rapid transformations in digital trends should not be underestimated, and states that 'digital technology, innovation and entrepreneurship are key to securing quality economic growth and employment in the 4IR revolution which is upon us' (APEC 2017: 1). This is particularly noteworthy in terms of harnessing the potential associated with the 4IR, as Australia ranks tenth out of 25 nations (Singapore is the leader in the region ranked 3rd) on the Automation Readiness Index (EIU 2018a, b). Although discourse on the 4IR is still nascent in the region, high income countries like Singapore and even middle-income countries such as Malaysia have already developed national frameworks and begun to implement programs by exploiting digital opportunities (MITI 2018; SEDB 2017). For example, the Tourism Board of Singapore recently launched a digital platform with an aim to not only help tourism businesses build capabilities and succeed in the digital age but also to put them in a better position to recover from COVID-19. A component of the platform is the Tourism Transformation Index, a self-diagnostic tool that provides a holistic snapshot of the tourism enterprises' current status across six domains: leadership and organisation, process and operations, customer, innovation, technology and data (Sagar 2020). While Singapore is at the forefront of exploiting digital capabilities, Australia is yet to formulate a national policy or roadmap, and a recent KPMG (2020) report highlights the fact that compared to countries like China and USA that have been making strategic investment in 4IR related technologies, without an overarching national policy initiative, Australia is at risk of being left behind (p. 3).

Innovation Landscape

Cloutman (2020) indicates that the rate of technological change in tourism industries in Australia is moderate, and technological advancements have largely focused on increasing efficiency and improving traveller comfort. Although some components such as frontline services in the AFS sector are still associated with long working hours and low wages, the adoption of transformative technologies and automation has begun to permeate them. For example, Copper City Motel in the regional Queensland town of Mt. Isa has introduced a state- of-the-art keyless entry self-check-in system via automated kiosk that operates 24 h (Copper City Motel 2020). In addition, the Case 5.1 highlights holiday rentals providers in the state of Queensland that have embraced a fully automated online business model without any face-to-face contact with customers.

Case 5.1: Holiday Rentals Surfers Paradise

Increasing financial burden associated with labour as well as cut-throat sectoral competition means that a new genre of accommodation services providers – a fully online holiday rentals – have emerged in Australia. The Holiday Rentals Surfers Paradise [HRSP], formerly known as the Gold Coast Holiday Rentals [GCHR], was one of the pioneering specialist/boutique providers of holiday apartments that aims to cater to a high-end target market who seek to choose the precise holiday accommodation in which they will be staying. This small business operates under a fully automated online business model without any face-to-face contact with customers at the time of bookings, making payments for the services and during the stay i.e. checking and checking out. The HRSP was established in 2008 and employs three full time staff and had an annual turnover $3.3 million in 2013. It offers nearly 60 accommodation choices across 10 different locations in Southeast Queensland and focuses on providing customised and personalised service for travellers. Each of the accommodation options e.g. holiday homes and resort apartments are featured in an interactive website with a full set of details and photographs for better appreciation of amenities, floor plans and a virtual tour of the apartments. A fully online business model means that the HRSP has been able to maintain competitive advantage over offline competitors because of lower operating costs. The business has received multiple awards and recognitions from Airbnb, Booking.com, TripAdvisor.com, and Hotels.com. However, a trend of diminishing bookings and growing competition means that the HRSP is keen on identifying opportunities for growth and survival by focusing on repeat visitors. The study carried out by Dhakal et al. (2014) indicated that customers who were more likely to be repeat visitors were those who felt positively about the business after visiting its website, and whose expectations at the time of booking matched with the actual experiences without any face-to-face contacts whatsoever.

Sources: Dhakal et al. (2014), Holiday Rentals Surfers Paradise (2020).

The lack of availability of skilled baristas (as mentioned earlier) as well as their rising wages, at least partially have meant that innovation around automation and virtual reality (VR) are now considered a good business proposition. Fist, an Australian engineering firm Aabak has created a wholly automated robotic coffee maker. The robot barista named "Rocky" is equipped with a state-of-the-art fusion of hardware and software functions generally in the coffee making by observing every single step needed – from grinding the beans to tamping the coffee and putting the lid on the cup. Designed to function as a replacement of human baristas, Rocky can make a cup of coffee within 60–90 s (Aabak 2020). The Rocky has been installed by Melbourne's "Once alike", a coffee-automation start-up business that aims to specialise in autonomous preparation and seamless service of delivering coffee through an app (Once Alike 2020). The main aim of the company is to reduce labour inputs but with greater output and better quality (Aabak 2020; Once Alike 2020). A business case for the synergy between Aabak and Once Alike is strong due the fact that one automated barista reduced wages to as much as $70,000 per annum per human Barista (Carey 2018) coupled with decreased costs of coffee sold per cup have enabled the café to reduce waste and offer competitive prices and speedy automated services (via app) to its customers. Second, a popular Melbourne restaurant Lûmé has adopted VR in order to augment the way the guests experience their meal. The innovative technology has allowed the restaurant to create a digital dining narrative showcasing the key ingredients, food preparation process and the restaurant into a VR experience with perceptible smell, sound and sensations (Catalyst VR 2020).

The IBISWorld report (2020) anticipates that various actors within AFS sector will enhance their digital presence and boost their technology capabilities over the next 5 years as technology transforms the way tourism services are provided and experienced. For example, accommodation services providers are likely to build up their social media presence and allow social media algorithms to influence marketing and promotional campaigns in order to target and engage with consumers (Appel et al. 2020). In addition, IBISworld (2020) also projects that AFS enterprises in regional Australia will increasingly adopt smart payment options for international tourists by offering contactless payment options, such as Visa payWave and Alipay. For example, one of the leading mobile payment and lifestyle platforms in the world – Alipay – recently partnered with Tourism Australia and piloted interactive mobile map services (operated through the Alipay app) in Sydney in order to promote tourist accommodations and food outlets to Chinese visitors (Tourism Australia 2019).

Education and Skills Landscapes

Trends associated with the 4IR combined with growth in international competition, workforce mobility, and growing customer demand and expectations for lived experiences have shifted educational and skills needs of the workforce. Tourism industries in Australia have collectively gone through a significant shift in terms of jobs growth and skills related challenges in the past two decades. For instance, two of the main challenges and opportunities associated with the AFS sector in the first decade of the new millennium revolved around the critical shortage of qualified and skilled labour, and the need for a comprehensive policy initiative to overcome the skills gap (Service Skills Australia 2013).

In recent years, challenges and opportunities have been framed around the implications of innovations in information and communication technologies (ICT) and associated digital disruptions, as well as digital transformative abilities on top of skills shortages. For instance, the Australian Government (2018a, b) report indicated that: '… advances in technology will provide opportunities for tourism businesses to improve productivity and efficiency … the tourism industry must be equipped with appropriately skilled ICT and social media marketing prodigies … the development of artificial intelligence and virtual/augmented reality, data personalisation and privacy are necessities today …' (p. 4). This shift is not unexpected in the global and regional context of evolving 4IR – as it has been rightfully pointed out that transformative digital technologies have advanced at a fast pace and have been viewed as game-changers for a variety of sectors within tourism industries (OECD 2020). However, what is unexpected is the lack of national strategic workforce related policy discussions and preparedness specific to the tourism industries and 4IR nexus in Australia when compared to other OECD countries. For instance, the policy focus in destinations such as Switzerland that is significantly more costly than its competitors has been on ensuring the digital skills of the workforce as well as high quality network infrastructures in order to ensure differentiation and competitive advantage (OECD 2018b: 67).

It is worth noting that the non-governmental actors in Australia have been calling for and leading the upskilling the semi-skilled workforce with emphasis on digital competency and skills for the future. For example, an online community of tourism operators, industry and digital experts called the Tourism Tribe (2020) believes in allowing tourism enterprises to exploit cloud-based solutions to improve and speed up services. It has captured this need succinctly as: "… we need to innovate, learn from other industries, take the best and give it a crack in tourism. In order to find the workforce of the future, we need an upskilling model that works with the digital generation's lifestyle, needs and expectations. They move around, they are the social generation – driven to connect, contribute and create – and the training needs to reflect that" (Tourism Tribe 2020: paragraph 7). A recent significant development on the governmental side is the review and renewal of tourism related training courses albeit beyond the AFS sector. For example, SkillsIQ (n.d.) has undertaken a number of projects with an objective to update tourism, travel and hospitality training packages with an emphasis on digital competency. The case for updating certificate III, Diploma and Advanced Diploma courses on Event Management stated that: '… the adoption of technology in the Events industry is vital and presents opportunities to improve business processes and enhance customer experiences. The workforce needs to be equipped with the confidence and skills to embrace technology and to continue supporting employers to innovate in this space …' (p. 6).

These initiatives are particularly relevant in relation to the increasing adoption of technologies involving online engagement and automation. That means, as SkillsIQ (2019) rightfully noted, that workforce skills requirements for tourism industries will continue to evolve, and demand digital competency of the workforce in the AFS sector, as employees are already having to adapt to new devices to take orders and payments as well as deliver meals. For example, UberEATS is already utilising machine learning to help recommend 30 min delivery options, and popular choices near the location of customers based on order history including time of day and delivery location (Lee and Lin 2020). Businesses like UberEATS and their employees will be relying on more in-depth customer data to recognise consumer behaviour to refine their products and services.

Employment Landscape

In one of the landmark reports of this decade, Edmonds and Bradley (2015) indicated that the retail trade, transport, and the hospitality sectors have the highest level of automation susceptibility in Australia (p. 2). In this regard, the CSIRO-led 'Tomorrow's Digitally Enabled Workforce' Report (Hajkowicz et al. 2016) provides a significant basis for informing policy developments around the 4IR related digital disruptions and the future of jobs within tourism industries. Mainly because as IBISworld (2020) observed, while tourism industries have been affected by technological innovation, diverse disrupting elements have impacted different components and sectors differently. For example, traditional accommodation services providers have struggled due to the arrival of accommodation-sharing app such as Airbnb. On the one hand, Tourism Australia (2019) reported that while the number of businesses in the food services sector has skyrocketed in the past 5 years, the accommodation sector had the largest number of business closures in recent years. Figure 5.1 depicts the change in numbers of enterprises, and small businesses were the hardest hit with over 84% of total business closures. On the other, the overall contribution of Airbnb to the Australian GDP was estimated to be AU$ 1.6 billion with more than 14,000 jobs supported (see Deloitte Access Economics 2018a, b). In Western Australia's [WA], however, the stifling competition with potential business closures and job losses associated with Airbnb, as it accounted for a quarter of total room capacity, meant that the traditional accommodation sector ended up mounting a campaign against Airbnb (Bankwest 2018). A recent survey carried out by the Restaurant & Catering Australia (2019) revealed that more than 70% of businesses respondents believed that digital disruption linked to online food delivery had negative impacts in terms of profitability and viability. Hospitality industry. The other aspect of employment associated with rapid digital transformations that has been on

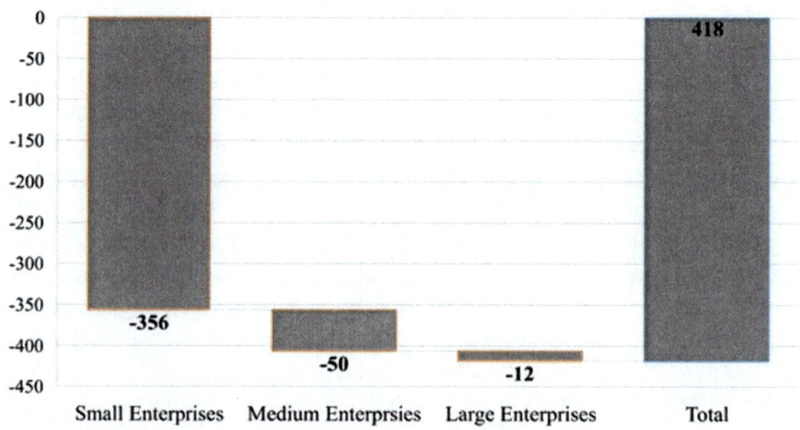

Fig. 5.1 Changes in number of businesses in the accommodation sector between June 2013 and June 2018. (Source: Graph created by the author based on the TRA (2019:1) data)

the spotlight in recent years is the precarious nature of the employment itself. For example, app delivery riders associated with UberEATS, Deliveroo, and Foodora in Australia are considered independent contractors and not employees (see Chau 2019) and it has been reported that these independent contractors get paid about $6 per hour (Zhou 2018) in a country where the current minimum wage is nearly $20.

Challenges & Opportunities

Although the outcomes of education, employment, and innovation related policy initiatives in the context of 4IR and tourism industries nexus cannot be expected instantaneously, policy discussions do need to capture their preparedness and implement an adaptive framework as a matter of urgency if the full potential of transformative technologies are to be realised. From the analysis above it is clear that tourism industries collectively are a significant driver of innovation and economic opportunities in Australia. However, the COVID-19 pandemic coupled with lacklustre 4IR readiness at the national level means that there is an urgent need to strategically address both issues simultaneously. It is in this context, COVID-19 and beyond as well as the 4IR as a way forward are briefly discussed below.

COVID-19 and Beyond

Australia remains one of the top ten popular destinations in the world (WEF 2019) and has been ranked one of the most advanced in the world in terms of competitiveness. For example, the TRA (2020) reported that over nine million international tourists visited the country in 2018–2019 and spent over AU$44 billion dollars. While visitors from China and New Zealand collectively made up almost one-third (30%) of the total tourists arriving in the country, it was the spending of Chinese tourists that accounted for over a quarter (27%) of overall expenditure (p. 5). The COVID-19 pandemic, coupled with the deteriorating diplomatic relations with China, (Tan 2020) means that the number of Chinese tourists visiting Australia is likely to take a nose dive in short and medium terms. For example, citing the Chinese Ministry of Culture and Tourism, the ABC (2020) reported: 'Due to the impact of the COVID-19 pandemic, racial discrimination and violence against Chinese and Asian people in Australia have seen a significant increase … the Ministry of Culture and Tourism reminds Chinese tourists to enhance their safety awareness and do not travel to Australia.'

Cloutman (2020) indicated that the revenue of tourism industries is expected to decline by at least 10% in 2019–20 due to a) the COVID-19 outbreak, and the associated strict travel restrictions which are significantly limiting tourism prospect, and b) severe bushfires earlier in 2019–20 discouraged both inbound and domestic tourism. Based on government modelling it was recently reported that tourism industries will incur losses of up to $55 billion loss this year alone (Macmillan 2020). ABS (2020) reported that one third of AFS sector related jobs were lost due to disruptions caused by the COVID-19. For example, in the early days of the pandemic, Santonerous (2020) reported that Chinese restaurant owners in Sydney and Melbourne saw a 60% drop in sales on weekends and an 80% hit on weekdays as a result of the coronavirus. In addition, up to 20% of the total tourism workforce could vanish with the estimated reduction of nearly 130,000 jobs – mostly part-time, casual and contract/seasonal jobs/positions, resulting in lost salaries and wages into broader economy worth over AU$ 5 billion (TTF 2020). It can be expected that the future tourism industry- related strategies will focus on diversifying the market (Cranston 2020) on the other side of the pandemic. For example, a recent study indicates that the lack of overseas travel means that post COVID-19 domestic tourism is likely to get a boost as Australians are keen to travel regional destinations (see UQ News 2020).

4IR as a Way Forward

Although the level of AI and automation growth within tourism industries is inevitable, the impacts will vary according to the geographies and specific sectors. For example, Muro et al. (2019) reported that since the AFS sector in the United States has the highest potential for automation (p. 36). The analysis presented in this chapter revealed that the emphasis on digital approaches to transform tourism industries in Australia has so far been an ad hoc in nature rather than being a strategic imperative. It can be expected that the upcoming Tourism 2030 Strategy will have concrete and targeted emphasis on transformative technologies. For instance, the report on the Tourism 2030 consultation workshop (KJA 2019) stated: '…discussion on infrastructure honed in not only on transportation and connectivity of geographic areas, but also on technology. Digital connectivity was raised numerous times as a lever to drive more tourists to specific areas and to identify unique experiences…' (p. 35). However, the primary motivation of 4IR related macro level policy initiatives should be much more than just doing analogue tourism in digital ways. It should be guided by the desire to improve the quality of actual tourism practices and ensuring better socio-economic outcomes of both guests and hosts (Pencarelli 2019).

The Travel & Tourism Competitiveness Index, compiled by the WTTC, that measures enabling factors and policies of the travel and tourism sector contributing to the development and competitiveness (WEF 2019: xiii), ranked the country seventh out of 140 countries in the world. While it can be expected that domestic side of tourism industries is likely to bounce back immediately after COVID-19 due to international border closures, improved connectivity and technological innovations are likely to drastically transform tourism industries in the long run (OECD 2018a, b). In line with the WEF's (n.d.) Closing the Skills Gap Project which puts emphasis on the fact that higher education and vocational education systems need to be adaptive in order to meet the evolving demands of labour markets, the rational way forward for ensuring 4IR readiness of Australian tourism industries would be to urgently develop national policies that focus on preparedness and ensures digitally competent employees and employers for the future.

Conclusion

This chapter focused on the AFS sector within tourism industries and examined the question: 'what insights can be generated from the current state of tourism industries related 4IR initiatives in Australia?' The chapter made broader analytical contributions towards evaluating the 4IR readiness of tourism industries in two fronts.

First, there are not only skills shortages but also gaps in the digital competencies of the tourism workforce in Australia. Unless efforts to invest in digital infrastructure in order to exploit the potential associated with the 4IR are tailored to meet the needs of tourism industries, rather than being made on the assumption that 'one size fits all', there is a risk that tourism businesses in Australia will not be able to maintain the competitive advantage. In addition, although it is likely the labour shortages within tourism industries is expected to be improved due to the decrease in demand caused by COVID-19, the reality has been that over two-thirds (69%) of employers within tourism industries have been reporting skills deficiencies in their workforce (SkillsIQ Limited 2019: 13). A strong case can therefore be made for the current occupation lists for migration program to be reassessed and calibrated in line with the skills and digital competencies of the future.

Second, although the impact of the current pandemic on the 4IR and tourism industries nexus is still evolving, one of the key findings is that while the awareness of the 4IR has certainly increased at the national level (KPMG 2020), a comprehensive and strategic readiness has been hindered by the lack of policy impetus when compared to other advanced economies in the region such as Singapore (SEDB 2017). An absence of national roadmap as well as regulations around the 4IR and tourism industries nexus highlight two specific issues. First, the fact that investments into 4IR are primarily driven by the private sector means that the policymakers are playing catch-up in relation to the development of associated transformative technologies such as automation and AI. Second, influential actors within tourism industries with expertise and influence on transformative technologies, in most cases are external to the country and connected to the global technological giants and multinational enterprises which are largely opposed to potential regulation.

It is clear that the AFS sector cannot remain competitive in the post COVID-19 era without significant investment in digital infrastructure and workforce competencies, and there is a danger that the lack of 4IR readiness will cost Australia's tourism industries.

References

Aabak. (2020). *Aabak*. Viewed 17 June 2020. https://aabak.com/

ABC. (2020). *China warns citizens not to travel to Australia amid 'increased' racism since coronavirus outbreak*. ABC News June 6th 2020. https://www.abc.net.au/news/2020-06-06/do-not-travel-to-australia-china-warns-citizens-of-racism/12328488

ABS. (2019). *Characteristics of employment, Australia, August 2019*. Canberra, Australian Bureau of Statistics [ABS]. Viewed August 1st 2020. https://www.abs.gov.au/ausstats/abs@.nsf/mf/6333.0

ABS. (2020). One third of Accommodation & food services jobs lost. Viewed 10 August 2020. https://www.abs.gov.au/ausstats/abs%40.nsf/mediareleasesbyCatalogue/C9E9F14708FC0AE7CA25855E0018F325?OpenDocument#:~:text=%3A30am%20(AEDT)-,One%20third%20of%20Accommodation%20%26%20food%20services%20jobs%20lost,Australian%20Bureau%20of%20Statistics%20today

AISC. (2020). *Tourism, travel and hospitality. Australian Industry and Skills Committee*, viewed 7 May 2019. https://nationalindustryinsights.aisc.net.au/industries/tourism-travel-and-hospitality

APEC. (2017). *Developing the tourism workforce of the future in the APEC region APEC tourism working group*. Singapore: APEC Secretariat.

Appel, G., Grewal, L., Hadi, R., & Stephen, A. T. (2020). The future of social media in marketing. *Journal of the Academy of Marketing Science, 48*(1), 79–95.

Australian Bureau of Statistics [ABS]. (2012). *Tourism industry*. Viewed 10 August 2020. https://www.abs.gov.au/ausstats/abs@.nsf/Lookup/by%20Subject/1301.0~2012~Main%20Features~Tourism%20Industry~135

Australian Government. (2018a). *Australia's Tech future: Delivering a strong, safe and inclusive digital economy*. Canberra. Viewed 5 September 2019. https://www.industry.gov.au/sites/default/files/2018-12/australias-tech-future.pdf

Australian Government. (2018b). *Beyond tourism 2020 Steering Committee*. Canberra. Viewed August 2 2020. https://www.tourisminvestment.com.au/content/dam/assets/document/1/7/4/7/s/2011672.pdf

Australian Jobs. (2020). *Accommodation and food services*. Canberra, Australian Government. https://australianjobs.employment.gov.au/jobs-industry/accommodation-and-food-services#:~:text=Accommodation%20and%20Food%20Services%20is,entry%20level%20opportunities%20for%20workers

Bankwest. (2018). *Focus on hospitality 2018*. Perth: Bankwest Future of Business.

Bhattacherjee, A. (2012). *Social science research: Principles, methods, and practices* (2nd ed.). University of South Florida. Open Access Textbooks Collection, Book 3. http://scholarcommons.usf.edu/oa_textbooks/3.

Bowen, G. A. (2009). Document analysis as a qualitative research method. *Qualitative Research Journal, 9*(2), 27–40.

Brown, K., Dhakal, S. P., Wiedemann, M., & Daniel, L. (2019). *Enhancing niche tourism: Prospects for South West Western Australia to integrate tourism and Agri-food systems* (Research report no. 21/19). Perth: Bankwest Curtin Economics Centre.

Carey, A. (2018). *Parliament of NSW advertising two barista jobs that come with a seriously generous wage*. https://www.news.com.au/finance/work/careers/parliament-of-nsw-advertising-two-barista-jobs-that-come-with-a-seriously-generous-wage/news-story/7b053d57b654ed91d01df6308810ff43

Catalyst VR. (2020). *Taste of Melbourne and Lûmé partner on a Festival First, a multi-sensory virtual dining experience like no other*. https://catalystvr.com.au/works/lume-through-the-looking-glass/

Chau, D. (2019). *Uber drivers are not employees, Fair Work Ombudsman finds. Sydney, ABC News*. Accessed 17 January 2020. Available at: https://www.abc.net.au/news/2019-06-07/uber-fair-work-ombudsman-investigation-contractor-employee/11189828

Cloutman, N. (2020). *Tourism in Australia no holiday: Revenue is expected to fall in the current year due to the COVID-19 outbreak*. Melbourne: IBISWORLD.

Cockburn, G. (2020). *Tourism jobs hard hit by bushfires and COVID-19 with further job losses expected later in the year*. The Australian August 6th 2020. https://www.theaustralian.com.au/breaking-news/tourism-jobs-hard-hit-by-bushfires-and-covid19-with-further-job-losses-expected-later-in-the-year/news-story/2807b2453707379c38742f7bc955306f

Copper City Motel. (2020). About us. http://www.coppercitymotel.net.au/content/about-us

Cranston, M. (2020). Australia has trade avenues beyond China, CBA says. *Australian Financial Review*, July 10th 2020. https://www.afr.com/policy/economy/australia-s-alternative-to-china-s-threat-on-trade-20200710-p55avd

Deloitte Access Economics. (2018a). *Tourism 2030 supply side requirements to support the development of the 2030 tourism strategy Austrade 2018*. Canberra: Deloitte Access Economics.

Deloitte Access Economics. (2018b). *Economic effects of Airbnb in Australia*. Viewed 3 August 2020. https://www2.deloitte.com/au/en/pages/economics/articles/economic-effects-airbnb-in-australia.html

Deloitte Economics Access. (2015). *Australian tourism labour force report: 2015–2020*. Canberra: Australian Trade Commission.

Department of Home Affairs. (2020). *Skilled occupation list*. Viewed August 15 2020. https://immi.homeaffairs.gov.au/visas/working-in-australia/skill-occupation-list

Dhakal, S. P., & Tjorko, S. P. (2020). Chapter 13: Travel and tourism workforce planning and development for sustainable development in Indonesia. In K. Dayaram, L. Lambey, J. Burgess, & T. W. Afrianty (Eds.), *Developing the workforce in an emerging economy: The case of Indonesia* (pp. 165–176). London: Routledge.

Dhakal, S. P., Mahmood, M. N., & Brown, K. (2014). *Segment analysis for specialist/boutique holiday accommodation provider in Southeast Queensland* (Project completion report). Gold Coast: Collaborative Research Network. Enterprise Connect, Canberra ACT.

Dhakal, S. P., Mahmood, M. N., & Bogati, R. (2018). Bridging the energy access divide for sustainable development: Policies and prospects in Nepal. *International Journal of Public Policy, 14*(1/2), 104–118.

Dhakal, S. P., Dahal, D., & Dahal, S. (2020). Chapter 11: Nepal. In Nankervis et al. (Eds.), *The future of work in Asia and beyond: A technological revolution or evolution?* (pp. 167–183). London: Routledge.

DISER. (2019). *Industry 4.0*. Canberra, Department of Industry, Science, Energy and Resources [DISER] Viewed August 15 2020. https://www.industry.gov.au/funding-and-incentives/industry-40

Dwyer, L., Edwards, D. C., Mistilis, N., Roman, C., Scott, N., & Cooper, C. (2008). *Megatrends underpinning tourism to 2020: Analysis of key drivers for change*. Gold Coast: Sustainable Tourism Cooperative Research Centre.

Edmonds, D., and Bradley, T. (2015). Mechanical boon: will automation advance Australia? Canberra, Australian Government or the Department of Industry, Innovation and Science. Accessed 7 May 2019. Available at: https://www.industry.gov.au/sites/default/files/June%202018/document/pdf/mechanical-boon_-_will_automation_advance_australia.pdf?acsf_files_redirect

EIU. (2018a). *The automation readiness index: Who is ready for the coming wave of automation?* London: Economist Intelligence Unit (EIU) Limited. Viewed 19 July 2019. www.automationreadiness.eiu.com/static/download/PDF.pdf.

EIU. (2018b). *The automation readiness index: Who is ready for the coming wave of automation?* London: Economist Intelligence Unit (EIU) Limited, viewed 7 May 2019, https://www.automationreadiness.eiu.com/static/download/PDF.pdf.

Faethm. (2020). *Technology impacts on the Australian workforce*. Sydney, ACS. Viewed 6 July 2020. https://www.acs.org.au/insightsandpublications/redirect-20200626.html?report=technologyImpactsOnTheAustralianWorkforce

Guerreiro, S, (2019). *A roadmap for destination management in the digital economy*. World Economic Forum, Viewed 6 February 2020. https://www.weforum.org/agenda/2019/09/a-roadmap-for-destination-management-in-the-digital-economy/

Hajkowicz, S. A., Reeson, A., Rudd, L., Bratanova, A., Hodgers, L., Mason, C., & Boughen, N. (2016). *Tomorrow's digitally enabled workforce: Megatrends and scenarios for jobs and employment in Australia over the coming twenty years*. Brisbane: CSIRO.

Hen-na Hotel. (2020). About us. Hen-na Hotel, 2020. Viewed August 15 2020. https://www.henn-nahotelmaihamatokyobay.com/en-gb/about-us

Holiday Rentals Surfers Paradise [HRSP]. (2020). *Surfers paradise accommodation specialists*. https://hrsp.com.au/

IBISworld. (2020). *Tourism in Australia – Market research report*. Melbourne, IBISWORLD Viewed 1 August 2020. https://www.ibisworld.com/au/industry/tourism/1903/

Johnston, M. P. (2017). Secondary data analysis: A method of which the time has come. *Qualitative and Quantitative Methods in Libraries, 3*(3), 619–626.

KJA. (2019). *Tourism 2030 strategy consultation workshop report – Summary report*. Canberra: Austrade. Viewed August 15 2020. https://www.austrade.gov.au/ArticleDocuments/10476/2019-austrade-tourism-2030-workshop-webinar-summary.pdf.aspx.

KPMG. (2020). *The 2020 fourth industrial revolution benchmark*. Melbourne: KPMG.

Lee, C., & Lin, R. (2020). *UberEATS: Using technology to build a reliable food delivery experience*. UberEATS Viewed July 15 2020. https://www.uber.com/en-AU/newsroom/ubereats-tech-update-2/

Lee, P., Hunter, W. C., & Chung, N. (2020). Smart tourism city: Developments and transformations. *Sustainability, 12*(10), 3958.

Leiper, N. (2008). Why 'the tourism industry' is misleading as a generic expression: The case for the plural variation, 'tourism industries'. *Tourism Management, 29*(2), 237–251.

Ludlow, M., & Housego, L. (2020). Tourism now employs one in 13 Australians. August 15th 2019 *Australian Financial Review*. https://www.afr.com/companies/tourism/tourism-now-employs-one-in-13-australians-20190815-p52hbv

Macmillan, J. (2020). *Warning to states on coronavirus border closures as tourism industry takes $55 billion hit*. ABC News, 3 September 2020. https://www.abc.net.au/news/2020-09-03/government-state-borders-coronavirus-tens-billions-tourism-loss/12622982

MITI (2018). *Industry 4WRD: National Policy on Industry 4.0*. Kuala Lumpur, Ministry of International Trade and Industry (MITI). Viewed 5 September 2019. https://www.miti.gov.my/miti/resources/National%20Policy%20on%20Industry%204.0/Industry4WRD_Final.pdf

Muro, M., Maxim, R., & Whiton, J. (2019). *Automation and artificial intelligence: How machines are affecting people and places*. Massachusetts: Metropolitan Policy Program at Brookings. https://www.brookings.edu/wp-content/uploads/2019/01/2019.01_BrookingsMetro_Automation-AI_Report_Muro-Maxim-Whiton-FINAL-version.pdf.

Nankervis, A., Connell, J., Cameron, R., Montague, A., & Prikshat, V. (2019). 'Are we there yet?' Australian HR professionals and the fourth industrial revolution. *Asia Pacific Journal of Human Resources*. https://doi.org/10.1111/1744-7941.12245.

OECD. (2016). Tourism trends and policy priorities. In OECD (Ed.), *OECD tourism trends and policies*. Paris: OECD.

OECD. (2018a). *OECD tourism trends and policies 2018*. Paris: OECD Publishing.

OECD. (2018b). *Effective policy approaches for quality Investment in Tourism* (OECD tourism papers, no. 2018/02). Paris: OECD Publishing. https://doi.org/10.1787/88ea780c-en.

OECD. (2020). *OECD tourism trends and policies 2020*. Paris: OECD Publishing.

Once Alike. (2020). About us. https://oncealike.com/about

Oracle Food and Beverage. (2017). *Restaurant 2025 emerging technologies destined to reshape our business*. California, Oracle. Viewed 19 August 2020. https://www.oracle.com/a/ocom/docs/dc/restaurant2025-report-latest.pdf?elq_mid=73491&sh=&cmid=BUMK170313P00052

Peceny, U. S., Urbančič, J., Mokorel, S., Kuralt, V., & Ilijaš, T. (2019). Tourism 4.0: Challenges in marketing a paradigm shift. In *Consumer behavior and marketing*. IntechOpen.

Pencarelli, T. (2019). The digital revolution in the travel and tourism industry. *Information technology & tourism*. Viewed August 15 2020. https://link.springer.com/content/pdf/10.1007/s40558-019-00160-3.pdf

Pinzone, M., Fantini, P., Perini, S., Garavaglia, S., Taisch, M., & Miragliotta, G. (2017, September). Jobs and skills in industry 4.0: An exploratory research. In *IFIP international conference on advances in production management systems* (pp. 282–288). Cham: Springer.

Restaurants and Café Australia. (2019). *Online delivery gobbles up profits as restaurants find themselves forced into partnering with them*. Media Release. http://rca.asn.au/rca/wp-content/uploads/2019/12/RAC-Disrupter.pdf

Sagar, M. (2020). *Singapore's Tourism Board uses technology and digitisation to support sector during pandemic*. Viewed August 15 2020. https://opengovasia.com/singapores-tourism-board-uses-technology-and-digitisation-to-support-sector-during-pandemic/

Santonerous, A. (2020). *'A dead town': Restaurants take whopping 80% hit from coronavirus*. February 19 2020. Viewed July 2 2020. https://au.finance.yahoo.com/news/chinese-restaurants-take-whopping-80-hit-from-coronavirus-231826224.html

Schwab, K. (2017). *The fourth industrial revolution*. Geneva: World Economic Forum.

SEDB. (2017). *The Singapore smart industry readiness index*. Singapore: Singapore Economic Development Board (SEDB).

Service Skills Australia. (2013). *Tourism, travel & hospitality workforce development strategy 2014–2019*. Canberra: Commonwealth Government.

SkillsIQ Limited. (2019). *Tourism, travel, and hospitality 2019 industry reference committee industry skills forecast*. Sydney: SkillsIQ Limited. Accessed 17 January 2020. Available at: https://www.skillsiq.com.au/ResourcesResearchandSubmissions/2019IndustrySkillsForecasts

SkillsIQ Limited. (n.d.). *Events qualifications – A case for change*. Sydney, SkillsIQ Limited. Accessed August 1st 2020. https://www.skillsiq.com.au/site/DefaultSite/filesystem/documents/Cases%20for%20Change/FINAL%20Events%20Case%20for%20Change.pdf

Tan, S. L. (2020). Why has the China-Australia relationship deteriorated into what some are calling 'trade war 2.0'? *South China Morning Post* July 1st 2020. Accessed August 1st 2020. https://www.scmp.com/economy/china-economy/article/3091182/why-has-china-australia-relationship-deteriorated-what-some

Tourism & Events Queensland. (2015). *Beacons signal new way for visitors to explore Queensland 29 March 2015*. https://teq.queensland.com/news-and-media/past-media-releases/beacons-signal-new-way-for-visitors-to-explore-queensland

Tourism Accommodation Australia. (2017). *Submission to the Department of Immigration & Border Protection Changes to the Temporary Skilled Migration Programme*. Accessed August 1st 2020. https://www.tourismaccommodation.com.au/wp-content/uploads/2017/06/010617Temporary-Skilled-Migration-Submission-FINAL.pdf

Tourism Australia. (2019). *Sydney to host Alipay Global Pilot Program*. Viewed August 15 2020. https://www.tourism.australia.com/en/news-and-media/news-stories/Sydney-to-host-Alipay-global-pilot-program.html#:~:text=Alipay%2C%20the%20world's%20leading%20mobile,Chinese%20New%20Year%20festive%20period

Tourism Tribe. (2020). *Tourism industry benefits from new technology to meet 2020 capacity requirements*. Viewed 2 July 2020. https://www.tourismtribe.com/tourism-industry-benefits-from-new-technology-to-meet-2020-capacity-requirements/

TRA. (2019). *Technology disruptors in tourism*. Canberra: Tourism Research Australia [TRA]. Viewed August 1 2020. https://www.tra.gov.au/ArticleDocuments/185/Disruptor%20report%202019.pdf.aspx.

TRA. (2020). *Tourism Businesses in Australia June 2018*. Canberra, Tourism Research Australia, Viewed 1 July 2020. https://www.tra.gov.au/Economic-analysis/tourism-businesses

Treuren, G. J., Manoharan, A., & Vishnu, V. (2019). The hospitality sector as an employer of skill discounted migrants. Evidence from Australia. *Journal of Policy Research in Tourism, Leisure and Events*, Viewed 1 July 2020. https://doi.org/10.1080/19407963.2019.1655859.

TTF. (2020). *Estimated impact of coronavirus on the Australian visitor economy*. Sydney: Tourism and Travel Forum [TTF]. https://www.ttf.org.au/wp-content/uploads/2020/03/Economic-Impact-of-Coronavirus-TTF.pdf.

Tussyadiah, I. (2020). A review of research into automation in tourism: Launching the annals of tourism research curated collection on artificial intelligence and robotics in tourism. *Annals of Tourism Research, 81*, 102883.

UNWTO. (n.d.). *Glossary of tourism terms*. Madrid: UNWTO. Viewed 10 August 2020. https://www.unwto.org/glossary-tourism-terms#:~:text=Tourism%20is%20a%20social%2C%20cultural,personal%20or%20business%2Fprofessional%20purposes.

UQ News. (2020). *Sunny outlook for domestic tourism post COVID-19 restrictions*. Brisbane: University of Queensland. Accessed 1 December 2020. Available at: https://www.uq.edu.au/news/article/2020/04/sunny-outlook-domestic-tourism-post-covid-19-restrictions.

WEF. (2018). *The global competitiveness report*. Geneva: World Economic Forum (WEF).

WEF. (2019). *The travel & tourism competitiveness Report 2019 travel and tourism at a tipping point*. Geneva: The World Economic Forum [WEF]. Viewed June 10 2020, http://www3.weforum.org/docs/WEF_TTCR_2019.pdf.

WEF. (n.d.). *Closing the skills gap*. Geneva: World Economic Forum (WEF). Viewed June 10 2020, http://www3.weforum.org/docs/WEF_System_Initiative_Future_Education_Gender_Work_Closing_Skills_Gap_pagers....pdf.

WTTC. (2020). *Australia 2020 annual research: Key highlights*. Geneva: The World Travel & Tourism Council [WTTC]. Viewed August 1st 2020. https://wttc.org/Research/Economic-Impact.

Chapter 6
Transport and Logistics

Richard Tay, Victor Gekara, and Aida Ghalebeigi

Abstract The fourth industrial revolution (i4.0) is transforming the workplace in every sector of the economy, including transport and logistics, with many jobs expected to decline over time while creating new jobs and spurring growth in some existing jobs. With changing employment comes the need for new skills. This chapter provides an overview of the impact of i4.0 on the transport and logistics sector worldwide and in Australia. Several case studies from Australia are presented to provide insights on how Australia is coping and expected to manage in the future to meet this technological challenge.

Keywords Connected and automated vehicles · Logistics · Supply chains · Transport

Introduction

Labour markets around the world are undergoing significant changes due to several major disruptions like the fourth industrial revolution, unexpected pandemics, shifts in globalisation and climate change. Any significant disruptions to the economy will create both opportunities and challenges. Although these changes are expected to create millions of new jobs and opportunities, they will also lead to job displacement and a redistribution of income and wealth. It has also changed the nature of work and the skills needed for the new jobs, resulting in significant changes in the skills demanded by the labour market. To prepare for these changes, governments, industry, education institutions, and workers need to have an understanding of how these disruptions will impact the various sectors of the economy.

According to the WEF (2017), the speed at which jobs are changing and the ability of workers to reskill varies across countries. Australia is rated as a country with slower labour market disruption and higher adult skills, implying that Australia should be able to manage the transition more smoothly than other developed

R. Tay (✉) · V. Gekara · A. Ghalebeigi
School of Accounting, Information Systems and Supply Chain,
RMIT University, Melbourne, VIC, Australia

A. Nankervis et al. (eds.), *The Fourth Industrial Revolution*,
https://doi.org/10.1007/978-981-16-1614-3_6

countries. Nevertheless, 44% of Australian jobs are at high risks due to automation alone (Hajkowicz et al. 2016). Moreover, the disruption and transition are also not uniform across different sectors, with the transport and logistics sector expected to experience more significant challenges.

There are two routes of change in the transport and logistics sector due to i4.0. One route is the indirect impact through changes in the demand for transportation and logistic services. Since much of transport demand is a derived demand, it is highly dependent on the need to travel and move freight, which will be significantly affected by i4.0. For example, there may be an increase in telework in all sectors of the economy, resulting in a reduction in commute trips and demand for passenger or people transport. One the other hand, there may be an increase in trip chaining with greater access to digital mobility services (trip planning, ticketing, payment systems, etc.). On the freight transport side, eCommerce and mCommerce have significantly change the retail shopping sector, resulting in a reduction in in-store shopping and distribution but an increase in automated supply chain and home delivery services. Also, i4.0 will disrupt the supply chain of companies in most sectors of the economy, which will have an impact on the demand for transport and logistic services.

The second route is the direct impact of i4.0 on the transport and logistic sector itself and how businesses in this sector will need to adapt their operations due to advances in technologies, wireless and cloud computing, mobile network and devices, analytics and big data. This chapter will focus mainly on the direct impacts of i4.0 and adjustments needed by the transport and logistics sector, particularly on its impact on the workforce in the transport and logistic sector.

The i4.0 related trends driving industry growth include (WEF 2018):

- Increasing computing power
- Increasing adoption of new technology
- Progress in artificial intelligence
- Expansion of big data
- Progress in mobile internet
- Improvement in cloud technology
- Advances in human-machine interfaces

The above changes are expected to have significant impacts on the composition of the workforce in the transport and logistics sector. As shown in Table 6.1, some of the declining jobs that have a 41% share in 2018 are expected to be reduced to 26% by 2022 while some emerging jobs are expected to increase from 8% to 21% in the same period.

However, identifying the needs of some subdivisions of the transport sector may be more difficult. According to a survey conducted by the WEF (2018), 20% of companies surveyed expect to expand their workforce due to automation, whereas 40% expect to reduce their workforce due to automation. Therefore, the expected impacts are not evenly distributed across the sector.

One of the reasons for the uneven distribution of expectations is the differences in technology readiness. As shown in Fig. 6.1, different firms face different

Table 6.1 Changing workforce in transport and logistics

Jobs with decreasing demand	Jobs with increasing demand
Accountants and auditors	AI and machine learning specialists
Accounting, bookkeeping & payroll clerks	Data analysts and scientists
Administrative and executive secretaries	Innovation professionals
Assembly and factory workers	Process automation specialists
Business services & admin managers	Product managers
Client info and customer service workers	Industrial and production engineers
Data entry clerks	Sales and marketing professionals
General and operations managers	Service and solutions designers
Material-recording and stock-keeping clerks	Software and applications developers and analysts
Transportation attendants and conductors	Supply chain and logistics specialists

Source: WEF (2018)

Fig. 6.1 Technology adoption barriers. (Source: WEF 2018)

perceived barriers to adopt new technology (WEF 2018). 50% of the firms surveyed do not understand the opportunities afforded by modern technology, 26% perceived a lack in investment capital, and 28% lack flexibility in hiring and firing employees. Interestingly, the skills gap in the local market is identified by 59% of the firms surveyed.

Revel et al. (2017) argued that "ensuring that the skills of the graduates match the industry needs is a real challenge for the future: industry needs are difficult to assess, and they are evolving more rapidly than the contents of academic programs. This challenge has been recognized by PEGASUS, and an innovative project, PERSEUS, was launched in 2015–2016 with the support from EU funding, in order to address it."

Industry Overview

The transport and logistic sector is one of the main economic engines of many countries, including Australia. According to the Australian Bureau of Statistics, the transport, postal and warehousing sector comprises 7.2% of the Australian economy and employs about 5.2% of the workforce in 2018 (ABS 2018). The transport industry alone accounts for about 4.6% of the Gross Domestic Product (GDP), with a further 2.7% coming from transport activities in other sectors. Moreover, according to the Australian Logistic Council (2020), the Australian freight logistics industry accounts for 8.6% of GDP, adding $131.6 billion to the Australian economy in 2013, and employs about 1.2 million people. An increase in logistics total factor productivity of 1% is estimated to increase GDP by $2 billion.

Figure 6.2 below represents the complex layout of the sector, which diversely comprises many different but closely related subsectors, including road, rail, air and water transport. They are further sub-sectored into passenger, freight and parcel services.

The sector workforce is equally diverse, although some key occupational groups are specific to the subsectors. For example, drivers, in the road and rail transport, seafarers in the water transport, straddle drivers and crane operators, in port operations, pilots and flight attendants in air transport and pickers in warehouse operations. Behind the scenes, however, are many different occupations which are essential to the sectors' operations, including planners and schedulers, airport

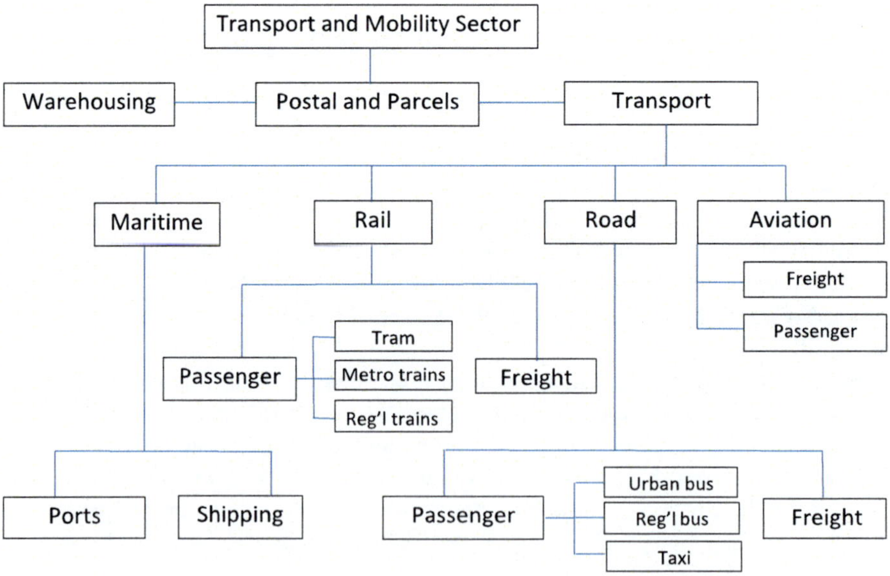

Fig. 6.2 The transport and logistics sector layout

ground crew, train station crews, maintenance personnel as well as many different functional management staff.

The disruptive impact of i4.0 cuts across the majority of the above sub-sectors and occupations. While automation has displaced some jobs in modern advanced warehouses and automated container terminals, associated digitalisation of operations has significantly altered the nature and texture of work in the remaining occupations. Significantly, new occupations have emerged as a result of these disruptive technologies (Gekara and Fairbrother 2013). The conventional work of drivers, for example, has been replaced by the need to possess digital knowledge and competencies to be able to understand and operate highly complex digital dashboards and remote-control systems, as well as digital mobile device enabled data management operations. The challenge for the sector's workforce is that not only is it a sector characterised by an ageing workforce, it also struggles to attract younger workers (Gekara et al. 2015). Furthermore, the technological changes have happened swiftly, in the last 20 years, leaving little room for an effective response from employers and the training establishment.

Without an effective and sustainable response to the skills question in the sector, the entire Australian economy faces significant challenges since efficient transport services are critical to Australia's access to domestic and international markets. Australia's national land freight task is expected to grow by around 75% between 2011 and 2031, with over three-quarters of the non-bulk freight carried on roads (DIRD 2016). Nevertheless, Australia's rail networks carried 1.3 billion tonnes of freight and contributed about $5.1 billion to the Australian economy in 2013–2014. More importantly, automation, such as driverless trains and trucks, is expected to drive future growth in the land freight sector. With regards to maritime transport, automation of stevedoring operations has improved the operational efficiency of major transport and logistic hubs in Australia, such as the Port of Brisbane and Port Botany (DIRD 2016).

Key Technologies and Skills Impact

Technological advances, such as Connected and Automated Vehicles (CAVs), are having a significant impact on the design and operation of Australia's transport systems. Reducing new infrastructure cost, improving road safety, and improving the efficiency of freight transport can be counted as such impacts (DIRD 2016). CAVs are expected to have a significant impact not only on cars and trucks but also on other transport options like freight trains, light rail, taxis and bus services, which will have a drastic effect on the supply chain, especially in first-and-last mile deliveries.

According to the 2019 Transport and Logistics Skills Forecast, advanced computer systems and big data to create 'smart' processes and products are changing the skills requirement of the workforce in the sector (AIS 2019). The impending introduction of CAVs will replace most of the existing drivers with employees with new skills in cybersecurity and automated systems. The adoption of collaborative electronic platforms will replace many administrative staff with employees with skills in digital literacy, data management, and cybersecurity. This rise of the gig economy will also create a labour market characterised by the prevalence of short-term contracts or freelance work as opposed to permanent jobs (AIS 2019). The internet-of-things and big data will generate a vast flow of information that requires new skills in data management, business analytics, and business systems.

Australian Industry Standards (AIS 2019) lists the top five generic skills required by the transport and logistics sector in order of importance as:

- Design mindset/Thinking critically/ System thinking /Solving problems
- Learning agility / Information literacy/Intellectual autonomy and self-management (adaptability)
- Technology
- Managerial/Leadership
- Communication /Virtual collaboration/Social intelligence

The above list indicates the impacts of big data and technology on the required skills. Competencies in digital technologies, analytical skills, critical thinking, problem-solving or the ability to interpret information to make data-driven decisions are considered as essential skills.

In summary, automation and digital transformation have revamped many facets of the transport and logistics industry. Expertise in robotics, systems and electronics engineering, as well as digital literacy, digital business, business analytics and computer science, are required in the future workforce to meet the requirements of new and emerging jobs.

Australian Case Studies

The Victorian Public Transport Rolling Stock Sector

Young et al. (2020) conducted an industry-funded study to understand the current and future workforce needs in the public transport rolling stock sector in Victoria. The project focused on the strengths, opportunities and challenges facing the sector in overcoming the projected skills and capability crisis in organisations that design, manufacture, maintain and operate rolling stock in trains, trams and buses. The authors concluded that with the emergence of digital and cyber technologies (Industry 4.0), the sector needed to look beyond its current technological focus to the people needed to enable and sustain these changes.

More importantly, the authors conclude that "there is limited literature that offers the insights needed to guide organisations in understanding who their potential future workforce may be, and how they can be recruited most effectively. It is also unclear as to what level of innovation or inclusion exists within the current supply chain, or the broader social and environmental benefits generated through procurement. As a result, it is not possible to ascertain the current composition of the workforce, where strengths and capabilities exist, or what the most effective economic and social levers are. Since 2006, specific recommendations concerning workforce issues have been periodically raised and repeated, which suggests that deeper systemic issues are yet to be fully understood or addressed" (Young et al. 2020, p. 7).

The study also suggests that "the rolling stock sector exists within an inward and change-resistant culture, which can create barriers to workforce development and retention of younger employees, women, people from different cultural backgrounds, and those with non-standard skills and abilities" (Young et al. 2020, p. 7), "a lack of clarity of the specific training needs related to rolling stock, particularly in relation to delivery of training (p. 8), and "quantified estimates of the economics of skills shortage and training in the rolling stock industry are hard to find in the economic literature" (p. 9).

One of the challenges facing the rolling stock sector is that the major employers of many workers are operators on fixed-term contracts and may not have a strong incentive to reskill workers for future jobs (Shah 2017). Workers in the sector tend to focus on the requirements of current jobs (Shah 2017). In an analysis of the National Workforce Development Fund training in the transport and logistics industry, Shah (2017) found that about two-thirds of all the qualifications were for jobs as machinery operators and drivers (38.3%) or labourers (26.8%), while 10.2% was for clerical and administrative training. Also, the most common reasons given by workers for undertaking training were 'job requirement' and 'to develop extra skills for the current job.' However, the demand for many of these jobs has been forecasted to be decreasing due to the advent of i4.0. Therefore, there appears to be a mismatch between current skills training and the skills required to meet the changing job market. Therefore, industry and/or government leadership to address this market failure is critical to managing a smooth transition.

Australian Container Terminals

The Australian ports industry comprises over 60 ports of all sizes and varying significance. According to Ports Australia trade statistics, 48 of these are considered significant gateways and while all of them handle ranging combinations of bulk commodities, including iron ore, LNG, oil, grains, coal, forestry products, fertiliser, manganese and sugar, only eight include containerised cargo and account for an annual throughput of 8 million TEU. The four key container ports, which account for 90% the total throughput include Port of Melbourne (37.5%), Port Botany (31.3%), Brisbane (16.3%) and Port Adelaide (5%). Technological changes in the industry, particularly container terminal operations can be traced back to the late 1990s when the dominant operator, Patrick Terminals, sought to transform its operations to enhance efficiency and productivity while reducing operating costs. An additional but crucial driving factor was also the need to reduce the power of the

Maritime Union of Australia workers union (MUA). These led to the historical waterfront dispute of 1998/9; the outcome of which reaffirmed the right of the terminal operator(s) to implement a wide range of cost-saving strategies targeting labour reduction (Griffin and Svensen 1998; Dabscheck 2000; McConville 2000). The following 20 years were characterised with rapid technology and digital transformation, which have placed Australia at the top of the advanced container terminal technology league (Gekara and Nguyen 2018).

Gekara and Nguyen (2018) have examined the technological developments at Australian ports and the implications for work, workforce skills and employment. This study builds on earlier research by Gekara and Fairbrother (2013), which focused more on the employment and union organising capacity. These studies conclude that the digital and automation changes taking place have significantly altered both the nature and texture of work.

> Apart from the increasing displacement of the last few remaining jobs by the robotic equipment, digitalisation of the entire process also means that those that remain have undergone significant change, particularly with regard to the tasks performed and the skills required (Gekara and Nguyen 2018).

The adoption and implementation of new technologies in the container terminal industry is mainly driven by the dominant global container terminal operators. The capability and specific interests of each operator ultimately shape the types of technologies adopted and the extent of implementation. Thus, around the world, the extent of technology adoption ranges on a scale of manual, through partial, to full automation.

In Australia these developments are driven by four competing operators – Patrick Terminals, Dubai Ports World (DP-World) and Victoria International Container Terminal (VICT) and Hutchinson, which handle the entire national container throughput. Of the three, Patrick is the most dominant (43.5%), followed by DP-World (39%), then Hutchinson (6.6%) and VICT (5.3%) (ACCC 2019). VICT, is also the youngest of all the operators, having been launched in 2017. Patrick has also been the most influential concerning the development and implementation of automation and digital technologies. There are three discernible models and levels of technology adopts, which we loosely label as the Patrick model, the DPW model and the VICT model.

The Patrick Model

Patrick Container Terminals is the largest operator in Australia. It is also unique in that, unlike the other two global operators, it is an Australian domestic company both in operations and location. Out of the nine major container terminals, Patrick operates four of them in Melbourne, Brisbane, Sydney and Fremantle and handles

43.5% of the total container throughput (ACCC 2019[1]). Not only is Patrick the largest, but it has also been leading in the advancement of terminal operating technologies. It has developed one of the most advanced systems called AutoStrad, based on automated straddles (see Gekara and Nguyen 2018 for more details). However, Patrick has only rolled out the AutoStrad system in its Sydney and Brisbane terminals, surprisingly maintaining manual operations at the Melbourne terminal, which handles the largest proportion of its containers.

Furthermore, while 90% of the AutoStrad terminals are automated, the quay cranes remain manual. This is, however, not likely to stay for long since the automated quay crane technology is readily available. Overall, including the digitalisation of processes, Patrick is one of the few highly automated terminals in the world, with roughly 80% of all operations automated. Across all its terminals, Patrick employs a staff of about 1000 workers.

As observed in Gekara and Nguyen (2018), the implication on work and workforce skills is significant. Not only has it resulted in a considerable reduction in the number of workers physically on-site, it has also transformed the nature of work and job roles. The large majority of the workers at the Autostrad terminals in Brisbane and Sydney occupy desk-top based monitoring and data analysis roles as opposed to previously where the bulk of the work was container yard-based. The few surviving yard-based positions are found in repair and maintenance as well as a new role created to assist in the first and last-point container truck grid operations where lifting off and loading onto the truck bed requires manual assistance. These are called tele-ops (Gekara and Nguyen 2018).

Consequently, the skills composition of the remaining jobs has also changed. While container yard workers' core skills included equipment operation, e.g. straddle, crane and truck driving, the tele-ops supposedly assisting in 'manual' first and final truck grid operations require digital skills as they use miniature yard control consoles. The work of a "Terminal Technical Engineer" for example is no longer hands-on as the designation suggests but instead involves remote desktop monitoring of the operations of the automated straddles and intervening where needed, e.g., in cases of malfunction, breakdown and emergency. The "Terminal Production Manager", on the other hand, monitors productivity statistics and adjust speed and rates of equipment operations as necessary. Consequently, Gekara and Nguyen (2018) observe that

> for most of the remaining workers, it is no longer about pushing buttons and shifting levers; it requires understanding and use of complex computer systems through both mobile and fixed digital devises and touch-pads.

[1]ACCC (2019) Container Stevedoring Monitoring Report, https://www.accc.gov.au/system/files/Container%20Stevedoring%20Monitoring%20Report%20-%202018-19.pdf

The DP-World Australia Model

Unlike Patrick, DP World Australia is a global terminal operator and is part of the DP World global group of companies and a leading provider of container terminal services internationally. In Australia, it is the second-largest operator, and like Patrick, it operates four terminals located at the Brisbane, Fremantle, Melbourne and Sydney ports. It handles about 39% of the total throughput in Australia (ACCC 2019) and employs about 1800 workers.

Interestingly, however, DP World Australia has taken a different approach towards its technology adoption. On a scale of minimal to full automation, DP World Australia may be located in the semi-automated category. Although they have implemented highly advanced Information and Communication Technologies and automated management processes (Gekara and Fairbrother 2013), yard operations still remain predominantly manual.

A number of explanations may be presented for the deliberate decision not to advance the technology to the level of their key competition – Patrick. First, there is no significant value add in terms of operational efficiency and productivity, labour savings and overall profitability. The narrow difference in annual throughput between Patrick and DP World terminals implies that any additional productivity gains might not sufficiently justify the huge extra investment in full automation. The second explanation relates to the second move advantage. A delay in adopting the technologies would allow for first movers, in this case Patrick, to advance and test the technology so that by the time DP World decides to automate, it will be highly advanced, adequately tried and tested and possibly cheaper. Should this be the case, it is highly likely that DP World will begin automating its yard operations very soon.

The implications for the workforce, especially concerning skills and job roles, is not very different from the Patrick case. Although they continue to employ a comparatively large workforce, the nature and functions of jobs and work have changed significantly as a result of the extensive digitalisation of operations. Like in Patrick, digital skills have become an essential part of workforce competency across all job roles, including those that have been traditionally viewed as physical and manual.

The VICT Model

The Victoria International Container Terminal was formally opened in 2017 as a subsidiary of the International Container Terminal Services Incorporated (ICTSI). It currently operates only at Melbourne port and has a capacity of 1 million TEU although, as per the 2018/19 throughput, it now handles approximately 423,000 TEU, which represents 5.3% of the country's total throughput. On the scale of minimal to full automation, VICT is at the fully automated end with more than 90% of its operations automated. Consequently, with a total workforce size of about 54 employees, it has the least number of workers when considering workforce size per terminal (see Dagge 2016; VCIT 2020; ACCC 2019). Gekara and Nguyen (2018) observe that

> …[it] stands out as one of the very few fully automated terminals in the world—from the terminal gate to the ships rail… the entire terminal cargo process is both paperless as well as with minimal and peripheral ground human intervention.

Like the Patrick AutoStrad terminals at Brisbane and Sydney, VICT's workforce is both lean and highly digitalised in terms of the skills they require to perform their roles.

Discussion

The fourth industrial revolution (i4.0) has changed the way firms operate in every sector of the economy. The uptake of technologies has changed the production and delivery methods and processes. These disruptions have a significant impact on the labour force. The transition in the transport and logistics sector in Australia has been disparate, with some industries better prepared to adapt than others. The impact of industry 4.0 workforce in the transport and logistics sector, is not merely new technologies and job replacements. It is instead a more complex scenario of workforce displacement, job reconfiguration and the emergence of new job roles. Automation and digital transformation have revamped many facets of the transport and logistics industry. Expertise in robotics, systems and electronics engineering, as well as digital literacy, digital business, business analytics and computer science, are required in the future workforce to meet the requirements of new and emerging jobs. Skills such as critical thinking, problem-solving, data-driven decisions, leadership, and information literacy have become the generic skills required in this sector. These changes are continuous and transformative. The presence of competitive pressures, as well as industry and/or government leadership, is critical to managing a smooth transition.

The need for government leadership is evident is the Victorian rolling stock sector. Specific recommendations in relation to workforce issues have been periodically raised and repeated in the industry forums. This suggests the presence of deeper systemic issues. One possible reason is the change-resistant culture of both the firms and their employees in the sector, and a lack of clarity on training needs and the delivery of training. Also, due to the nature of fixed-term contracts in sector for operators, firms may not have a strong incentive to reskill workers for future jobs, and workers in the sector tend to focus on the requirements of current jobs, many of which are expected to decrease over time due to advent of 1.40. Therefore, the market has not functioned efficiently, and more government leadership and incentives are needed to ensure a smoother transition.

The cases of the three major port operators, for example, Patrick Terminals, Dubai Ports World and the newly introduced Victoria International Container Terminal (VICT), lead to the conclusion that the use of technology in various processes and operations has significantly impacted the workforce. There has been a significant reduction in workforce sizes across different terminals which occurred as a result of increasing automation in the past two decades induced by high operating costs and the need for operations efficiency and consistent productivity. The increased use of automated mobile-yard equipment such as straddles and cranes, where the largest proportion of the workforce was, hitherto, located explains the large reduction in the overall terminal workforce.

The impacts are not limited to number reduction. It has changed the required skills and expertise needed in port operations. Traditionally, the port operations required a largely unskilled workforce with little requirement for qualifications or any specific skills. Now, however, terminal operations require a workforce with highly defined skills, including digital literacy and competence. Most of the work has shifted from the yard to the office and involves remote equipment monitoring, control, intervention and data analysis, all of which need highly specialised computer and digital skills. Even employees engaged in the operations of the few remaining non- or semi-automated mobile yard equipment are required to be equipped with the skills to understand and operate the sophisticated systems that integrate their work, which often involves digital control and input, to the overall production process.

To develop these skills, terminal operators have adopted various strategies for training and workforce development, which complement any specific formal training and qualifications that workers may have acquired. These include mostly on-the-job training programs and strategies, with some terminals operators also running formally accredited training under the national vocational education and training system, as enterprise training organisations, to ensure that they equip their workers with the necessary skills but also effectively respond to continuous skills upgrade needs as technologies and systems change (Gekara and Fairbrother 2013).

Conclusion

The case studies in this chapter provide snapshots of the impacts of the fourth industrial revolution (i4.0) on the Australian transport and logistics sector. It can be concluded that the sector has undergone a complex transformation in its workforce skills requirement. The sector requires new job configurations, new skills and workforce development and training to be able to address the requirements of i4.0. However, as recent research indicates, employer response to the changing skills needs is varied, with the majority of organisations making little effort and investment in training (Gekara et al. 2019). Because of the rapid changes in skills requirement and considering that it is employers driving the technology change for enhanced productivity, the more significant burden for training rests with employers. While a comprehensive government policy on workforce digital transformation in Australia is lacking (Gekara et al. 2020), employers must not only implement extensive in-house re-and up-skilling for their workers but also actively participate in developing a sustainable pool of workers for the emerging i4.0.

References

ACCC. (2019). *Container stevedoring monitoring report*. Australian Consumer and Competition Commission.

AIS. (2019). *Skills forecast 2019*. Canberra: Australia Industry Standards.

Australian Bureau of Statistics. (2018). *Delivering the goods: Transport activity contributed $122.3 billion to GDP*. Canberra: Australian Bureau of Statistics.

Australian Logistic Council. (2020). *Key facts about the Freight Logistics Industry*. Available online, access 11/9/2020, https://www.austlogistics.com.au/about-us/key-facts-about-the-industry/

Dabscheck, B. (2000). The Australian waterfront dispute and theories of the state. *Journal of Industrial Relations, 42*(4), 497–516.

Dagge, J. (2016). *Port of Melbourne's Robo-dock*. Herald Sun, 7 October 2016.

DIRD. (2016). *Transport and Australia's development to 2040 and beyond*. Canberra: Department of Infrastructure and Regional Development.

Gekara, V. O., & Fairbrother, P. (2013). Managerial technologies and power relations: A study of the Australian waterfront. *New Technologies Work and Employment, 18*(1), 51–65.

Gekara, V. O., & Thanh Nguyen, V. X. (2018). New technologies and the transformation of work and skills: A study of computerisation and automation of Australian container terminals. *Journal of New Technology, Work and Employment, 33*(3), 219–233.

Gekara, V. O., Snell, D., & Chhetri, P. (2015). Are older workers 'crowding out' the young? A study of the Australian transport and logistics labour market. *Labour and Industry, 25*(4), 321–336.

Gekara, V., Molla, A., Snell, D., Karanasios, S., & Thomas, A. (2019). *'Skilling the Australian workforce for the digital economy', National Centre for Vocational Education Research (NCVER)*. Adelaide: NCVER.

Gekara, V., Snell, D., & Molla, A. (2020). *Australia's local and national approaches to supporting the existing workforce meet the challenges of digital transformation*. Melbourne: Australian Industry Standards.

Griffin, G., & Svensen, S. (1998). Industrial relations implications of the Australian Waterside Dispute. *Australian Bulletin of Labour, 24*, 194– 206.

Hajkowicz, R., Rudd, B., Hodgers, M., & Boughen. (2016). *Tomorrow's digitally enabled workforce: Megatrends and scenarios for jobs and employment in Australia over the coming 20 years (Megatrends)*. Canberra: CSIRO.

McConville, C. (2000). The Australian waterfront dispute 1998. *Politics & Society, 28*(3), 393–412.

Revel, P., Bauer, P., & Cotillon, A. (2017). Future workforce for aerospace: Risks and opportunities. *Journal of Aerospace Science, Technology and Systems, 96*(2), 81–85.

Shah, C. (2017). *Analysis of NWDF training in the transport and logistics industry*. Adelaide: National Centre for Vocational Education Research.

VCIT. (2020). *About Us, Victorian International Container Terminal*. Accessed 2/9/2020, https://www.vict.com.au/

World Economic Forum. (2017). Accelerating workforce reskilling for the fourth industrial revolution. *World Economic Forum., 2017*.

World Economic Forum. (2018). *The future of jobs*. Geneva: World Economic Forum.

Young, C., Jones, R. N., Heenetigala, K., Ooi, D., Lung, S., & Parry, N. (2020). *Reimagining the workforce: The Victorian rolling stock context. Literature review*. Melbourne: Rail Manufacturing Cooperative Research Centre.

Chapter 7
Arts and Communications

Lisa Dethridge

Abstract This chapter provides examples of how Fourth Industrial Revolution (4IR) technologies, including artificial intelligence (AI) are used in the Australian Media and Communications sector, including advertising, journalism, publishing, film, and TV production. One focus is the use of data analytics in advertising and journalism; another is the automation of roles previously performed by people in screen, literary and arts production. AI is now used as a production tool which has led stakeholders to suggest that in the future media production companies may work in collaboration with software and interface designers to ensure a sustainable, human-centred approach (Van der Bijli-Brouwer et al, 53:1–23, 2017). This means that the term "job sharing" takes on a new dimension as people share their jobs at increasing levels with AI technologies, as in other sectors covered in this book.

Keywords AI and libraries · Artificial intelligence · Australian media and communications automated advertising · Automated news & screen production · Data analytics · Authorship · Music and literary rights management

Introduction

This chapter explores the nature and characteristics of applications using artificial intelligence across the field of media and communications. As in other Australian industry sectors, media producers are reliant on information technology (computers and software) to drive content for the screen, the laptop or mobile phone. AI-driven information technology, web and network telecommunications are mainly used to deliver and enable the massive flows of information within what Seyfert and Roberge call an "algorithmic culture" (Seyfert and Jonathan Roberge 2016: 6).

L. Dethridge (✉)
School of Media and Communication, RMIT University, Melbourne, Australia
e-mail: lisa.dethridge@rmit.edu.au

A. Nankervis et al. (eds.), *The Fourth Industrial Revolution*,
https://doi.org/10.1007/978-981-16-1614-3_7

Industry Overview

The Australian Information Media and Telecommunications industry includes businesses engaged in newspaper and internet publishing, film production, television and radio broadcasting, telecommunications infrastructure and networks. Employment is concentrated in Sydney and Melbourne and growth has been relatively strong over the past 5 years.

Regional radio and TV take their material from city centres. Regional newspapers, often owned by family businesses, were hard hit by the COVID-19 virus (Howden 2020) The top employing occupations include journalists; film, television, radio and stage writers and directors; advertising and public relations managers; artistic directors, media producers and presenters (see Table 7.1). Employment figures for both city and regional operators can be found at the Australian Government Labour Information Portal (Australian Government 2019a).

The top three Internet Service Providers (ISPs) are Telstra, TPG and Singtel Optus (Ibis World 2019). Data Processing and web-hosting services include IBM Australia/New Zealand Holdings; Macquarie Telecom Group and the Arq Group (Ibis World 2020a). A 2020 analysis of these subdivisions suggests that they are all likely to face mixed effects from COVID-19. Growing demand for remote working and the ability to work on the cloud is anticipated to benefit Australian internet service providers and data processing services. However, the data storage services sector may face challenges from COVID-19 if demand begins to rapidly increase, as the technical resources used to construct and operate data centres are primarily sourced from overseas (Ibis World 2019, 2020a, b). It is worth noting that the COVID-19 pandemic has caused a high degree of volatility in the Australian media labour market (Australian Government 2019b).

Automation and the use of analytics to manage and optimise data are changing the configuration of workflows across media industries, especially in advertising, news journalism, libraries, publishing and the production of screen material for music, film and TV. Table 7.2 provides data on the job outlook of many occupations within the Australian media and communications industry, including specific occupations in the media and communications industry, together with the growth and impact of artificial intelligence on these occupations.

Jobs in the media and communications industry have been significantly affected by the technology available to mega-corporations that disrupt both revenue and occupations (ACCC 2019; Kohler 2020). The escalating power of the digital platforms Facebook and Google has resulted in substantially reduced advertising revenue, particularly within "traditional print (now print/online) media businesses" (ACCC 2019: 1). "Many print/online news media businesses have struggled to survive and have reduced their provision of news and journalism" (ACCC 2019:1).

In the last decade, the print media experienced a decline in revenue of 45% to AU$3 billion (Kohler 2020). Television revenue also fell considerably, whereas for newspapers it collapsed (Kohler 2020). In the last 15 years online advertising grew

Table 7.1 Employment in Australian Information, Media and Telecommunications

Top employing occupations	This industry	All industries
Telecommunications Trades Workers	18,900	27,700
Journalists And Other Writers	11,800	22,200
Film, Television, Radio and Stage Directors	11,300	14,800
Telecommunications Engineering Professionals	9100	13,200
Ict Managers	8000	51,600
Advertising, Public Relations and Sales Managers	7100	141,200
Librarians	6800	13,900
Artistic Directors, Media Producers and Presenters	6700	13,100
Graphic and Web Designers and Illustrators	5900	62,800
ICT Sales Assistants	5900	17,000
Sales Representatives	5700	84,300
Computer Network Professionals	5300	37,700
Ticket Salespersons	4800	16,700
Performing Arts Technicians	4800	14,600
Software and Applications Programmers	3800	123,200
Library Assistants	3800	8400
Contract, Program and Project Administrators	3700	131,100
Information Officers	3700	86,900
Advertising and Marketing Professionals	3700	74,000
General Clerks	3500	281,800

Sources: Australian Government: Australian Bureau of Statistics, Labour Force (trend and annual averages of original data); ABS, Education and Work; Department of Jobs and Small Business, Employment Projections – added information is available on Labour Market Information Portal lmip.gov.au

from zero dollars to AU$8 billion, and more than half of this amount is accounted for as revenue by Google and Facebook (Kohler 2020).

The Australian Competition and Consumer Commission (ACCC) is an independent Commonwealth statutory authority with the role of ensuring fair trade. The ACCC's (2019) *Digital Platform Inquiry* investigated Facebook and Google's use of news material from Australian media companies without contributing revenue for it. Kohler (2020) and Zappone (2020) stated that the ACCC may enforce the Fair-Trade Act to induce the "global tech giants" Facebook and Google to pay for news content "harvested" from Australian media enterprises. In response, Facebook, for example, has threatened to 'block access within Australia to the news on its platform' (Kohler 2020; Zappone 2020).

> '… the ACCC, and by extension the Australian government, has decided to take on two of the world's richest and most powerful corporations, Google and Facebook, to take back some of the revenue they are sucking out of news media' (Kohler 2020)

Table 7.2 Impact of AI on jobs in Media Communication Industries

Occupations	Susceptibility to Automation %	Growth
Sales and marketing managers	14	Strong
Advertising managers	14	
Public relations managers	14	
Artistic directors	20	Moderate
Media producers	20	
Radio presenters	20	
Television presenters	20	
Authors	20	Moderate
Book and script editors	20	
Call centre team leaders and operators	20	Moderate
Computer network and systems engineers	25	Very strong
Network administrators	25	
Network of analysts	25	
Electronic engineering draughts persons and technicians	13	Moderate
Art directors, and directors (film, television or stage)	20	Moderate
Cinematographers	20	
Film and video editors	20	
Program directors (television or radio	20	
Stage managers	20	
Technical directors	20	
Video producers	20	
Gallery, library and Museum technicians	56	Decline
Graphic designers	17	Strong
Illustrators (including animators)	17	
Multimedia designers	17	
Web designers	17	
Graphic prepress trade workers	66	Stable
Chief information officers	12	Stable
ICT project managers	12	
Journalists and other writers	20	Stable
Broadcast transmitter operators	56	Decline
Camera operators	56	
Light technicians	56	
Makeup artists	56	
Sound technicians performing arts technicians	56	

Source: Created by the author using occupations listed in the information media and telecommunications industry by Job Outlook (2020), and job susceptibility due to automation forecasts by Byrd et al. (2017)

Google and Facebook depend on advertising revenue (Statista 2020). The ACCC (2019) and Kohler (2020) claim that these two digital platforms have impacted on many jobs in the Australian media sector due to the power of the digital platform corporations and the AI embedded in their operations.

AI Technologies & their Employment Impact

The following sections of this chapter summarise the main employment impacts of the 4IR technologies which are changing most components of the media and communications sector across Australia.

Automated Advertising

AI allows for concise record-keeping and helps enhance the predictive utility of data, which makes it the perfect management tool for both advertising and news journalism. Advertising, public relations and sales managers constitute the people who direct, control and coordinate advertising and marketing.

Australian researcher, Julian Thomas (2018), identifies two technologies which embody different visions of automation and the future of advertising. One is programmatic advertising 'defined broadly as the automation of the sale and delivery of digital advertising where the appearance of ads on a website is determined by software which can process user data and behaviour with high accuracy', making advertising sales "controllable, predictable and manageable at scale" (Thomas 2018: 36). Thomas (2018: 36) also describes the players in Australia's digital advertising field: the publishers who own inventory management systems and data management platforms which accumulate user data; the ad-servers which provide advertising content and measure delivery; the inventory management systems controlled by publishers and on the demand-side, inventory platforms controlled by ad buyers and finally the advertisement traders who match-make those who are buying and those who are selling, often through auctions .

Within this industry configuration, data analysts have the opportunity to design and manage a range of content-filtering and anti-tracking tools. Some AI tools can limit the reach of automated advertising, including "tactical tools which create worthless data trails, control browsers and provide some security against malvertising" – advertisements that contain malware or viruses (Thomas 2018: 37). Some software developers even play both sides of the market. They do this by forming a two-sided business model offering adblockers to consumers, while also luring advertisers for inclusion on a "white list" which guarantees that their advertisements will not be blocked. (Thomas 2018: 37). The Australian Government Job Outlook suggests that employment in these sectors shows strong future growth while jobs for journalists and other technical writers will remain stable (Job Outlook 2020), as discussed in the next section.

AI Automated News Journalism

Reuters Digital News Report examined data from 2016–2020, finding that Australian news media remains strong and steady as the primary news source although newspaper readership continues to drop. During the COVID-19 and the Australian bushfire crises, television news services and online sources experienced a surge in demand, with more people identifying television as their primary source of news. That said, increasing numbers of Australians are using mobile phones to access news, widening the use gap between mobiles and computers. Reportedly only 6% of Australian audiences use Commercial FM radio to source news. (Reuters 2020).

Since 2017 cuts have decimated mainstream Australian newspaper operations. News institutions such as Fairfax Media have lost staff, while the national news agency Australian Associated Press (AAP) shut down incurring 500 job losses in March 2020. Such cutbacks, closures and reduction in news coverage reflects a global reduction in the customers who will pay for news content when they can access free news from Google or Facebook (Reuters 2020). This leads to the question - what are the job implications for those journalists who remain employed in the field?

In 2019, *Journalism and Mass Communication Quarterly* reported on a special forum on the use of AI in journalism. Several challenges were identified by participants in relation to the use of artificial intelligence as a news-gathering tool (Broussard et al. 2019). Journalists stated that while they perceived AI as a tool that can enhance and augment professional reporting processes it was not perceived as a suitable replacement for journalism. Often journalists are confronted by huge volumes of text in the form of reports and government or civil documents such as court or media archives and records. Journalists may use AI to analyse and process data within such a massive range of documents to find story leads and relevant data. The Australian software company Nuix provides software and data analytics for the analysis of unstructured data in email, phone calls and other daily traffic. The AI can pinpoint data with forensic accuracy (Nuix 2020).

The Nuix software company has grown from a one-person company to a global operation with 2000 customers in 75 countries, and will earn around $200 million in 2020 (Boyd 2020: 40). Nuix provides a program which is used globally "to uncover fraud, protect personal data, meet regulatory compliance obligations, win complex legal cases and to catch criminals" (Boyd 2020: 40). It was used by the International Consortium of Investigative Journalists to review documents from the Panamanian law firm Mossack Fonseca. The documents were leaked to the German newspaper *Suddeutsche Zeitung* and then shared with journalists around the world who used them to uncover a massive tax evasion racket (Boyd 2020).

According to Thurman et al. (2017), the availability of sophisticated data feeds, and the increased demand for more news, is leading to an increase in the prevalence of automated news systems. The authors interviewed journalists from the BBC, CNN and Reuters which used robot-news writing software to construct stories (Thurman et al. 2017: 1245). The journalists interviewed in this study stated that automated journalism would increase "the depth, breadth, specificity, and immediacy of information available" (Thurman et al. 2017: 1245). However, the journalists also raised ethical and societal issues emphasising "the need for skills—news judgement, curiosity, and scepticism—that human journalists embody" (Thurman et al. 2017:1252).

Meanwhile, Reuters published a 2020 global survey of publishers whose responses suggest that they are planning to invest more to harness the potential of Artificial Intelligence and Machine Learning – but not at the expense of editors and journalists. The publishing respondents considered that both investment in AI (78%) and more journalists (85%) are needed to help meet future challenges – but with their most robust preferences heavily stacked in favour of humans (Reuters 2020: Section 2.3).

The Reuters 2020 report also set out the different ways that AI is being used in (1) newsgathering, (2) production (including various kinds of newsroom automation), and (3) distribution/recommendation. In western newsrooms, AI is used to create more effective recommendations; to target potential subscribers and optimise paywalls to drive greater efficiency in the newsroom. AI can be used to assist with sub-editing or improve the consistency of tagging, which allows information to be located and stored with accuracy. (Reuters 2020: section 1.6). Some jobs which involve investigation, content production, robo-writing, and distribution are now automated by systems which have been in place since the 1990s within the fields of sport, medicine and financial reporting. These automated systems are an extension of automatic text summaries that were first used in weather forecasts in the 1960s. (Lemelshtrich Latar 2019: 42).

However, AI is about much more than glorified word processing or text recognition. The proliferation of 'fake news' online increasingly affects our ability to make informed choices; threatens the public's trust in the media; and interferes with the functioning of democratic processes. Upon the closure of the Australian Associated Press, the former chairman Campbell Reid warned that "professional information… is being substituted with the unresearched and often inaccurate information that masquerades as real news on the digital platforms" (Khadem and Pupazzoni 2020: 2).

The use of AI to organise and access human records raises many complex problems around intellectual property, the privacy of information, and the protection of journalistic sources. Ethical guidelines, special filtering or further research may be required in future to detect and disclose biases that may be inherent in the processes of machine learning that are the foundation of many AI procedures (Broussard et al. 2019: 678).

In his book, *Automating the News, how algorithms are rewriting the media,* Nicholas Diakopouos asserts that computer algorithms, machine learning and data mining are changing the fundamental structures of how news is created, disseminated and received. (Diakopoulos 2019:6). Diakopoulos gives the example of newsbots which communicate with social media audiences to distribute and comment on stories with online media, and suggests that journalists may be challenged by such new workflows and publication strategies to tell stories that may compromise their journalistic principles. He insists that AI will not replace journalists but should be seen as an augmentation of the human processes of journalism and advocates for more study of the process of "hybridisation: of people and computers" (Diakopoulos 2019:8). It seems clear that journalists need to be proactive in shaping the way AI is deployed in their industry (Broussard et al. 2019: 673).

Clearly AI will allow journalists to do more work that constitutes journalism and less data processing which can be more effectively undertaken through automation (Lewis et al. 2019). In the case of automated journalism, the software assumes a news-writing role that has, until now, been a human domain (Lewis et al. 2019: 409). Despite disruption by AI automation, the Australian Government Job Outlook (2020) report suggests that employment prospects show strong future growth for copywriters, technical writers, editors, journalists, bloggers and journalists for print, radio and television.

The next section outlines how AI is also augmenting and supplanting human craft activity in the screen industries, which are using increased automation to control production elements such as the scripting, shooting, post-production and distribution of media materials.

Artificial Intelligence and Screen Production

The companies holding the largest market share in the Motion Picture and Video Production in Australia industry include NEP-GTV Holdco Pty Limited, Endemol Shine Australia Holdings (producers of *Big Brother*) and Freemantle Media Australia. According to an industry market report, the Australian Film and TV industry has a market size of around AU$2 billion, with approximately 5800 businesses employing 11,000 people (Ibis World 2019: 1). This industry has displayed significant volatility over the past five years. The Federal Government's financial incentives include cost rebates for domestic and international film and TV producers. These government rebates have encouraged overseas producers to shoot several large projects in Australia during 2015–2020, including *Thor: Ragnarok* and *Aquaman*. However, the project-based nature of film production means that industry revenue can fluctuate from year to year. Overall, industry growth has declined by 3.1% from 2015–2020 (Ibis World 2019:1).

The Australian Government Job Outlook suggests that Film TV, Radio and Stage directors have moderate future growth prospects as do artistic directors, media producers and presenters (Job Outlook 2020). Technicians who work alongside producers and directors also show only moderate future growth prospects: camera operators; sound and lighting technicians; make-up artists, and transmitter operators

(Job Outlook 2020). The industry is expected to experience substantial revenue declines in 2019–20. Film and television production activity has largely been delayed or postponed due to public health measures implemented to curb the COVID-19 outbreak (Chapman 2020). Any drop in revenue may further compromise the industry, where wage costs are relatively high as a share of the revenue (Ibis World 2020b). Australian film producer Tim White remarks that despite industry contraction, the industry remains optimistic – "people who are talented and dedicated will ride through this" (Siebert 2020: 3). Nonetheless, some may experience lean times before recovery. Australian screen industry advocates like the *Make it Australian* Campaign espouse the need to reinstate Australian screen content quotas, to prevent Australian viewers being swamped by overseas content on large AI-driven streaming platforms like Netflix, Amazon Prime and Stan (Make it Australian 2020). Advocates from the Screen Producers Association of Australia, the Media, Entertainment and Arts Alliance; and the Australian Directors and Writers Guilds, suggest that up to 15,000 jobs are at risk and advocate government tax support for small screen production businesses, especially after COVID-19 (Make it Australian 2020).

AI and Libraries, Authorship, Music and Literary Rights Management

Australian librarians, who develop, organise and manage collections and services show stable job prospects; while those of the library assistants, who handle and maintain the shelves and records for books and items, are in decline (Job Outlook 2020). One reason for this decline is that sophisticated computer algorithms are dedicated to managing the public library E-lending landscape. A study by Giblin et al. (2019) investigated the availability of e-books in five countries and analysed the licence terms and prices for 100,000 titles and 388,000 e-lending licenses across Australia, New Zealand, Canada, the United States and the United Kingdom. The investigators created a dataset using the aggregator "Overdrive", which is a global distributor of E-books with a focus on libraries, schools and those with special needs. It provides an example of how AI can help manage intellectual property and licenses, thus making human librarians and assistants redundant (Overdrive 2020).

Screenwriting is another skilled occupation that is being disrupted by AI. The Australian government supports local and overseas screen productions through eight federal, state and local funding agencies: Film Victoria, Create New South Wales, Screen Queensland, ScreenWest, The South Australian Film Corporation, Screen Territory, Screen Canberra and Screen Tasmania. (Australian Government 2019c). One of these government agencies, Screen Queensland, is using AI to find script ideas that will resonate with audiences. Screen Queensland producers are collaborating with an artificial intelligence and machine learning platform called *Wattpad* to determine what audiences want from a story (Quinn 2020). The platform is driven by AI and boasts a readership of 80 million, distributed across the Asia-Pacific, USA, South America and Europe. Authors post material regularly on the platform; engaging an audience, inviting suggestions and responses about the writing (Wattpad 2020). The Wattpad company uses AI to collect around a billion points of data a day using "Story DNA" analytical software to calculate which story elements resonate with readers (Quinn 2020). Screen projects based on literary properties developed on the platform include Emmy-winning TV Series and hit Netflix releases (Quinn 2020). This joint Australian government-industry project means that the Screen Queensland production agency will use AI to find a pathway to their global audience, as a way of ensuring a return on production investment funds.

In this example of AI the author, publisher or distributor are involved in a more intimate relationship with an audience or reader. Audience responses are invited and then harvested as data which can further develop the property or the license, extending its reach across ever broader platforms. AI and interactive social media platforms can also be used to activate audiences who gather around specific online documentaries which may have a social activist objective related to climate change or democratic expression. AI can potentially focus the interaction of media producers with an audience in a way that fosters community-building, where audiences or readers can form groups around special interests such as sustainable development goals for people and the planet (Griggs et al. 2013).

In another example of literary experimentation, concerns the integration of automation and AI in the creation or generation of content across text and photographic imagery. Two Melbourne authors, Donnachie and Simionato (2018) used machine learning to train a "reading machine" which was on display at the Melbourne Art Book Fair in March of 2020. The *Library of Nonhuman Books Reading Machine* uses a combination of optical character recognition and computer vision to "read" books and then uses machine learning and natural language processing to recombine these words in the form of poetry. The machine also illustrates the text it generates by searching Google image files for an image to match the text, before packaging the entire production using an online printing service.

Donnachie and Simionato (2018) have used their "reading machine" to reinterpret twelve major works of literature. According to one reviewer, the results were occasionally puzzling, often engaging, at times hilarious and intensely poetic (Quin 2020). The programmer Donnachie, stated this is an "attempt to grapple with the future of the book, an object we've had around us for so long and…that's changing so fast" (Quin 2020: 4). The author/programmers remind us that chance and imperfection within literature and art have a definite role in a world mediated by algorithms as they are "what makes us human and what often delights us in art" (Quin 2020: 5). The author/programmers suggest that their work demonstrates how technology may need to embrace aspects of uncertainty as a creative choice. They received the Tokyo Type Directors Club award for the project (Quin 2020: 3).

Similar experiments related to music composition during 2020 were observed in relation to the inaugural Artificial Intelligence Eurovision Song Contest. In May 2020 the global competition was won by an Australian group "Uncanny Valley" who wrote their song *Beautiful the World.* Organised by the Dutch broadcaster

VPRO, this event invited global contestants to use algorithms to compose original music. The competition was judged by an expert panel and public votes. The Australian team won by using an AI system that was trained with audio samples derived from native Australian animals; koalas, kookaburras and Tasmanian devils.

These examples demonstrate that the use of AI in film, literature and music may be about to emerge from the experimental avant-garde to become mainstream (Fildes 2020: 34). The next section investigates the impact of AI on jobs in the TV production industry.

AI and TV Production

The Australian screen industry includes many small independent boutique production houses such as Jumpgate, Ignition Immersive, Liminal VR, Phoria, Opaque Media, StaplesVR and VRTOV. These virtual-reality (VR) and 360 video production studios combine traditional narrative with ground-breaking VR content that is produced using sophisticated data analytics (Film Victoria 2020). In mainstream TV production, AI-driven automation has already totally changed the workflows around camera operation and switching. For example, *Viz Mosart* software is typical of the AI systems used to control TV production equipment to mix vision, sound, effects, graphics, cameras, microphones, lighting and all screen functions. The system may receive news reports from international and local sources, via satellite, internet or local reporters. With the introduction of 24-hour news cycles, the automated control system allows studios to reduce personnel costs while maintaining quality and reducing human error (Vizrt 2020).

Previously in TV Studio workflows, the control room would include a camera control operator, a sound operator, director, vision mixer and computer graphics operator. Also, a studio manager, floor manager and assistant director, lighting, sound and camera people would share information about various camera angles, microphones, and the position of acting talent which need to be aligned for a particular shot or sequence. Nowadays, fully automated systems allow the running of a live-to-air program using only two staff; the director and one technical assistant. Before broadcasts occur, other news reporters and graphics staff shape the packages using the systems which are then loaded into the computerised system by the director before going to air. An automated studio control system picks up and saves the metadata about various shots which are then automatically executed by automated studio components, including robotic cameras: no humans required.

The traditional TV news studio evolved as a combination newsroom and film studio. The crew worked holistically to coordinate production processes which are now managed by an automated system. The action focused on the integrated teamwork of a crew who, while they collaborated, were each specialised in various crafts. The directors who spruik the Viz Mosart software on company YouTube promotions seem very happy with their now deserted studios. However, images of the director in a silent, fully automated studio depict an individual alone in a high-tech bunker; a lonely technocrat whose studio crew has been replaced by robotic cameras, lighting and sound instruments (Vizrt 2020). As a result, the film and television industry is in a state of flux, due to the disruptive advent of AI systems. Consequently, we need to envisage retraining and job redesign programs that use AI to augment rather than eliminate human input.

It is clear from this brief survey of the AI and media industries that those who previously worked within complex workflows have now been superseded by digital production processes. These may include commissioning media editors, journalists, creative writers, camera operators, library assistants or media producers. Such workers may benefit from further specialist training in aspects of digital production that can enhance their digital literacy. This is not to suggest that they have abandoned their vocations, but to point out that they need to boost their skills with some basic training in programming, data analytics, virtual or 360 production skills, web or software design. Any such upskilling would enhance a worker's digital literacy enabling them to talk to other teams and comprehend the new workflows. Further, this upskilling may allow media workers to be less dependent on information technocrats and technicians who may otherwise tend to over-determine the direction of evolution in the field.

Challenges & Opportunities

We have seen that in some aesthetic endeavours, such as in media related to poetry and music, AI programs already achieve a tolerable simulation or simulacrum of human agency. In other fields, such as news journalism and studio production, AI-driven processes can achieve a high level of technical precision and organisation which promises a positive future for AI processes as augmenting agents which assist the work of humans in the field. The examples of AI use in film, literature and music discussed here suggest that AI may be used increasingly as a tool to augment the work of creative humans in the composition of artistic and cultural products. For some, AI will be considered a friendly companion. For others in more regimented environments, it may represent an onerous system which requires more IT and administration skills than creativity. In the film industry example, AI may be used to gather data and identify global audience responses to a story or theme. That said, it is not clear that consulting a multitude of user opinions on the progress of a story will guarantee a better or more coherent story. It is perhaps just as likely to produce that well-known literary euphemism for messy confusion - an “elephant designed by committee”.

These examples of AI use in literary and music rights management illustrate the use of AI as a means of managing multiple sets of data about users, IP rights and literary or media properties from diverse locations, diverse authors, sources and audiences. In each case, AI helps to organise a coherent view not only of audience location but also audience engagement and preferences. However, not all agree that the AI future is rosy. The examples covered in this chapter demonstrate that, while media professionals such as TV producers and journalists, may not program the computers that govern their daily activities, they contend with increasingly complex interfaces where the input and output of data and the management of files and interfaces require unique skillsets.

Human operators will need the right employee skills to achieve the right effects with the machines in their studios. Aside from cost-cutting, what are the benefits for human craftspeople in handing over their hard-earned skills to an inanimate workmate? In many contexts, human operators become programmers and machine minders. As such will they retain their pride and passion in their work when programming tasks replace their ability to exercise methods and techniques of a profession or craft?

As the editors of this volume point out, employee-readiness in the current work environment relates to the ability of humans to develop and apply automated solutions. In the examples of automated journalism, it seems that the journalist's existing jobs of investigation would expand into the realms of data analysis. In screen production, the use of automated studio systems already reduces the number of specialists in the workflow process. The professional camera operator is simply eliminated and replaced outright by a fully automated camera and AI lighting. In other parts of the same studio, remaining workers will need to take on new skills to adapt to the processes of graphic arts, editing and sound engineering to automated, AI-driven systems.

In the film industry, we see AI being used to augment the process of deciding which films to commission. This example also signals the use of audience data in a more collaborative or participatory way. Audiences can contribute creatively to the outcome of stories, not just consume them passively. However, the Cambridge Analytica scandal illustrates that there is a human tendency to enter a bubble or bell-jar of reductionist thinking, where editors may choose to give us more of what we already like and know, rather than extend our intelligence through exposure to challenging or "foreign" ideas. Surely it is this process of expanding the known universe which helps the species evolve? Thus a question remains - how can serendipity and aspects of both the feared and the unknown be considered if the system is programmed within predictable or the same boundaries?

Putting AI at the centre of our media and communication industry recalls what Seyfert and Jonathan Roberge (2016:2) termed as algorithmic cultures which are "the product of a specific approach to the world (which) frames reality, while at the same time organizing how people think about society". It seems clear that creative media professionals such as authors, composers, journalists and other media professionals may benefit from their ability to collaborate with software and hardware designers, programmers and manufacturers, using human-centred design processes. This kind of collaborative design process may ensure that media workers can directly access the technology to assess how AI can best assist with the development of editorial processes and policy. Further, industry and user/audience groups may advocate that the already well-developed ethical codes of twentieth-century journalism are carried over into the new regime. Within a utopian vision, such collaborations could focus on the use of interaction design and user-profiling that encourages the sustainable development goals for people and planet (Griggs et al. 2013).

We have seen how the use of AI to organise and access human records raises many complex problems around intellectual property, the privacy of information and the protection of journalistic sources. Ethical guidelines will be needed to guide journalists in the ways that data can be used. Further, while jobs may be lost as a result of automation, new jobs will arise. For example, analysts and machine trainers may be needed to ensure that special filtering is used to detect and disclose biases that may be inherent in the processes of machine learning, the foundation of many AI procedures. Nicholas Diakopoulos insists that AI should be seen as augmenting the human processes of journalism, and advocates more study of the process of "hybridisation: of people and computers" (Broussard et al. 2019: 678). Michael Dupagne and Ching-Hua Chuan argue that journalists need to be proactive in shaping the way that AI is deployed inside their industry (Broussard et al. 2019: 673).

Maleki (2020) argues that the challenge in media industries is to design AI systems that are personal and humane, suggesting that researchers need to focus on what AI should do, not what AI can do. For example, when we discuss human-centred AI, we need to ask: which humans? Who is doing what? And who may be marginalised as part of this process? Thomas (2018) expresses concern that digitisation may cause increased inequality and exclusion, which he considers to be a complex and evolving issue of critical importance in Australia and beyond. Research shows that those Australian citizens who are either elderly, lowly-paid, in precarious employment, or lacking tertiary education, are less likely to be "digitally" included than their counterparts (Wilson et al. 2019).

So how can future iterations of AI design ensure that the end-user is placed at the centre of the design equation, and not be treated merely as a point of purchase within a larger industrial system? Concerns about the use of AI to promote "surveillance capitalism" is a prominent issue in this context (Zuboff 2019). Zuboff (2019) defined this late phase of capitalism as "instrumentarian power that challenges market democracy with a collective order that expropriates critical human rights… that claims human experience as free raw material for hidden commercial practices of extraction, prediction and sales" (p. 1). This raises a few important questions. How are we to prevent business managers from chasing fast results apparently offered by data platforms that convert behavioural data into sales? How are we to prevent the exploitation of workers and citizens who may be lulled into false comfort by the colourful and fast-moving allure of such platforms? The final section examines some ethical options for managing these future challenges.

Conclusion

This chapter suggests that AI technology may augment the creative, knowledge-based work undertaken by higher-skill workers in media industries, improving their productivity and increasing the demand for such workers. A 2018 discussion paper by the Australian Institute of Machine Learning states that increased AI and automation will lead to both job losses and job creation - those industry sectors which invest in 'skills development and technical competence in AI will benefit' (Australian Institute of Machine Learning 2018:1). The report concludes Australia urgently needs a 'formal, national strategy for Artificial Intelligence" to ensure they are "beneficiaries and not…powerless recipients' of AI technology (Australian Institute of Machine Learning 2018:1).

As with many debates around the future of technological development, the discussion of Artificial Intelligence implies a spectrum of utopian and dystopian potentials for industry. The dystopian vision has become more prevalent due to our sense of responsibility (and helplessness) around the threats of global warming and viral pandemics. A human-centred approach may encourage system designers to recalibrate their thinking, discarding old values of the first industrial revolution (competition, maximised profits). System designers may move toward values where human fulfilment and satisfaction are considered through a lens of inclusion, diversity and the equitable distribution of resources.

The Australian Government Department of Industry, Science, Energy and Resources (DISER) engaged with industry, academia and business in a 2019 public consultation. The goal was to formulate an ethical framework for Australia to realise the benefits of artificial intelligence (Australian Government 2019d). Its first principle is that the public needs the ability to trust that any AI application is safe, secure and reliable. The report further emphasises that AI systems need to benefit individuals, society and the environment; should respect data privacy; should be fair and inclusive (Australian Government 2019d).

These large scale industrial AI systems must provide transparency and disclosure to ensure that people know when they are engaging with an AI system. This means those responsible for 'different phases of the AI system lifecycle should be identifiable and accountable for the outcomes of the AI systems' (Australian Government 2019d:1). Finally, such systems should be overseen by humans. The Australian Consumer and Competition Commission emphasises this need for transparency in its 2020 inquiry into the impact of Google and Facebook and their use of AI to organise user data for commercial purposes (Karp 2020). Inquiries like this will shine welcome light on the use of AI and data analytics in the Australian and global media industries. Scrutiny of AI and automation in media industry workflows is particularly relevant to the supply of news and the implications for media content providers, advertisers and consumers.

References

Australian Government. (2019a). *Australian jobs, Information media and telecommunications*. https://australianjobs.employment.gov.au/jobs-industry/information-media-and-telecommunications. Accessed 20 Oct 2020.

Australian Government. (2019b). *Labour Market Information Portal*. https://lmip.gov.au/maps.aspx?layer=EmploymentRegions&region=EmploymentRegion. Accessed 17 Oct 2020.

Australian Government. (2019c). *Ausfilm: Why film in Australia* https://www.ausfilm.com.au/why-film-in-australia/work-with-the-best/federal-state-local-government-agencies/. Accessed 11 Nov 2020.

Australian Government. (2019d). *AI ethics framework*. Australian Government Department of Industry, Science, Energy and Resources. https://www.industry.gov.au/data-and-publications/building-australias-artificial-intelligence-capability/ai-ethics-framework. Accessed 20 Oct 2020.

Australian Institute of Machine Learning. (2018). *Submission to the Australian senate inquiry on the future of work and workers*. https://www.aph.gov.au/Parliamentary_Business/Committees/Senate/Future_of_Work_and_Workers/FutureofWork/Submissions. Accessed 20 Oct 2020.

Boyd, T. (2020). Australia's next tech unicorn, *Australian Financial Review*, 16 May. https://www.afr.com/chanticleer/australia-s-next-tech-unicorn-20200515-p54t9i. Accessed 21 Oct 2020.

Broussard, M., Diakopoulos, N., Guzman, A., Abebe, R., Dupagne, M., & Chuan, C. (2019). Artificial Intelligence and Journalism. *Journalism & Mass Communication Quarterly, 96*(3), 673–695.

Byrd, J., Spraggon, B., O'Neill, M., & Liddy, M. (2017). *Could a robot do your job?* Sydney: ABC News. Available at www.abc.net.au/news/2017-08-08/could-a-robot-do-your-job-artificial-intelligence/8782174. Accessed 26 Apr 2021.

Chapman, W. (2020). *Motion Picture and Video Production in Australia Industry* (ANZSIC) Report J5511.

Diakopoulos, N. (2019). *Automating the News, how algorithms are rewriting the media*. Cambridge, MA: Harvard University Press.

Donnachie, K., & Simionato, A. (2018). The trumpet of the swan. *MatLit (Centro de Literatura Portuguesa Da Universidade de Coimbra), 6*(1), 177–186.

Film Victoria. (2020). https://www.film.vic.gov.au/virtual-reality

Giblin, R., Kennedy, J., Pelletier, C., Thomas, J., Weatherall, K., & Petitjean, F. (2019). What can 100,000 books tell us about the international public library e-lending landscape? *Information Research, 24*(3).: Paper 838. https://osf.io/preprints/lawarxiv/6bcmg/. Accessed 30 Oct 2020.

Gildes, N. (2020). Robo Eurovision in *The Australian Financial Review*, 16 May 2020, 16.

Google Developers. (2019). *ARCore Overview*, Google Developers. https://developers.google.com/ar/discover. Accessed 15 May 2020.

Griggs, D., Stafford-Smith, M., Gaffney, O., et al. (2013). Sustainable development goals for people and planet. *Nature, 495*, 305–307, https://www.nature.com/articles/495305a. Accessed 30 Oct 2020.

Guardian Newspaper Online, Cambridge Analytica Files. (2018). https://www.theguardian.com/news/series/cambridge-analytica-files. Accessed 20 June 2020.

Howden, S. (2020). As the pandemic cuts a swathe through newsrooms, *communities will count the toll.* https://www.croakey.org/as-the-pandemic-cuts-a-swathe-through-newsrooms-communities-will-count-the-toll/. Accessed 20 Oct 2020.

Ibis World. (2019). Internet service providers in Australia, *2014–2019 Industry Trends*. https://www.ibisworld.com/au/industry/internet-service-providers/1832/. Accessed 11 Oct 2020.

Ibis World. (2020a). Data processing and web hosting Services in Australia, *2014–2019 Industry Trends*. https://www.ibisworld.com/au/industry/data-processing-web-hosting-services/2246/. Accessed 20 June 2020.

Ibis World. (2020b). Motion picture and video production in Australia industry trends 2015–2020, *Industry Trends*. https://www.ibisworld.com/au/industry/motion-picture-video-production/634/. Accessed 22 Nov 2020.

Job Outlook. (2020). *Information media and telecommunication industry.* National Skills Commission. Australian Government Canberra. https://joboutlook.gov.au/careers/explore-careers?keywords=&industry=10&skilllevel=0. Accessed 22 Sept 2020.

Karp, P. (2020). *Australian consumer watchdog to examine anti-competitive behaviour by Google and Facebook*. https://www.theguardian.com/australia-news/2020/feb/15/australian-consumer-watchdog-to-examine-anti-competitive-behaviour-by-google-and-facebook. Accessed 23 June 2020.

Khadem, N., & Pupazzoni, R. (2020). AAP newswire service closes after 85 years with 500 job losses, blames free online content. *ABC News* https://www.abc.net.au/news/2020-03-03/aap-newswire-closes-after-85-years/12020770. Accessed 30 Mar 2020.

Kohler, A. (2020). Global tech giants Facebook and Google are ramping up their attacks on Australia's proposal to make them pay for news content. *ABC News Victoria*. Sunday 13 September 2020 Australian Broadcasting Commission Sydney. https://iview.abc.net.au/show/abc-news-vic. Accessed 14 Sept 2020.

Lemelshtrich Latar, N. (2019). *Robot journalism; can human journalism survive?* Singapore: World Scientific.

Lewis, S., Guzman, A., & Schmidt, T. (2019). Automation, journalism, and human–machine communication: Rethinking roles and relationships of humans and machines. *News in Digital Journalism, 7*, 409–427.

Make it Australian. (2020). https://makeitaustralian.com/

Maleki, S. (2020). Rediet Abebe: The mechanism for social good. *Crossroads, Association for Computing Machinery, 27*(1), 42–43.

Overdrive Library Data Aggregator https://company.overdrive.com/company-profile/who-we-are/

Quin, M. (2020). *AI powered robot reads novels and writes poetry*. https://www.rmit.edu.au/news/all-news/2020/feb/ai-reading-machine. Accessed 4 May 2020.

Quinn, K. (2020). *Australian screen agency to develop film TV using artificial intelligence*. https://www.theage.com.au/culture/movies/australian-screen-agency-to-develop-film-tv-using-artificial-intelligence-20200620-p554io.html. Accessed 23 June 2020.

Reuters Institute. (2020). *Digital news report*, http://www.digitalnewsreport.org/. Accessed 20 June 2020.

Seyfert, R., & Jonathan Roberge, J. (2016). *Algorithmic cultures: Essays on meaning, performance and new technologies*. Oxfordshire: Routledge.

Siebert, B. (2020). Coronavirus pandemic spurs Australian movie producers to favour feel-good films. *ABC News online*. https://www.abc.net.au/news/2020-04-08/producers-pivot-to-feel-good-films-amid-covid-19/12120126. Accessed 20 June 2020.

Statista. (2020). *Leading internet billionaires as of March 2020, by net worth*. Statista New York City. https://www.statista.com/statistics/267581/net-worth-of-the-ten-richest-internet-billionaires/. Accessed 22 Sept 2020.

Thomas, J. (2018). Programming, filtering, adblocking: Advertising and media automation. *Media International Australia, 166*(1), 34–43.

Thurman, N., Doerr, K., & Kunert, J. (2017). When reporters get hands-on with Robo-writing: Professionals consider automated Journalism's capabilities and consequences. *Digital Journalism, 5*(10), 1240–1259.

Van der Bijli-Brouwer, M., & Dorst, K. (2017). Advancing the strategic impact of human-centred design. *Design Studies, 53*, 1–23.

Vizrt. (2019). The big AR Sports Show, *Youtube Video* https://www.youtube.com/channel/UCbm48EShieyuFzgXKwwjzBA. Accessed 17 Oct 2020.

Vizrt. (2020). https://www.vizrt.com/products/viz-mosart

Wattpad. (2020). https://www.wattpad.com/

Wilson, C., Thomas, J., & Barraket, J. (2019). Measuring digital inequality in Australia: The Australian digital inclusion index. *Journal of Telecommunications and the Digital Economy, 7*(2), 102–120.

Zappone, C. (2020). Making good on Facebook's threat to Australia. *Opinion. Sydney Morning Herald. Opinion.* https://www.smh.com.au/world/oceania/making-good-on-facebook-s-threat-to-australia-20200914-p55vb7.html. Accessed 16 Sept 2020.

Zuboff, S. (2019). *The age of surveillance capitalism*. London: Profile.

Chapter 8
Financial and Insurance Services

Alan Montague, Jan Svanberg, Francesco Maisano, and Venesser Fernandes

Abstract In this chapter, the authors focus on the impact of artificial intelligence (AI) and associated technological changes on work and jobs in Australia's Financial and Insurance Services industry sector. Extensive commentary on the cumulative effects of AI, a term that incorporates machine learning, big data, blockchain, chatbots and financial technology (fintech) and other technological advances, are distilled for consideration. The intention in this chapter is to attempt to predict vocational areas in this specific industry sector that may diminish, noting that it is a challenging task amidst wide-ranging views. The commentary primarily focuses on disruptive technology in a relatively broad context to complement knowledge contributed within other chapters that focus on different industry sectors.

Keywords Artificial intelligence · Disruption · Jobs · Financial and insurance services industry sector

Introduction

This chapter focuses on the impact of artificial intelligence (AI) and associated technological changes on work and jobs in Australia's Financial and Insurance Services sector. Scholarly commentary on AI, machine learning, big data, blockchain, chatbots and financial technology (fintech), has been increasing recently. The commentary and analysis has primarily focused on disruptive technology in a relatively broad context – an area where this chapter intends to contribute to current understanding.

A. Montague (✉)
School of Management, RMIT University, Melbourne, VIC, Australia
e-mail: alanjmontague@gmail.com

J. Svanberg · F. Maisano · V. Fernandes
RMIT University, Melbourne, Australia
e-mail: jan.svanberg@hig.se; frank.maisano@rmit.edu.au;
venesser.fernandez@monash.edu.au

A. Nankervis et al. (eds.), *The Fourth Industrial Revolution*,
https://doi.org/10.1007/978-981-16-1614-3_8

Climate change, globalisation, increasing urbanisation, an ageing population, and high-tech development are cumulatively transforming Australia and other countries across the globe faster than ever before. Such extensive transformation offers excellent opportunities for the advancement of Australia and its industry sectors, although there are considerable insecurity concerns about what may unfold in the future (Nankervis et al. 2019). To cope with this transformation, Australia needs policy measures that offer its citizens a sense of security and confidence in a better future. As outlined in this chapter, the finance and insurance industry sector is pivotal in this process, given its prominence and economic power in the Australian context.

This chapter begins with a brief definition of AI and machine learning. This is followed by defining the industry sector, the number of workers and capital generated, and basic demographics. Issues related to government policy will also be included with an emphasis on AI and emerging technologies. A review of literature outlining the potential impact of AI on the fintech sector is featured in the context of the possible effects on jobs. Machine learning products and other technological aids that may impact jobs partly or wholly are also explored.

The imperative for profits in the face of practices deemed to be unethical (Hayne 2019) is also covered briefly in the context of the potential impact on jobs in the sector. The Hayne (2019) Royal Commission into Misconduct in the Banking, Superannuation and Financial Services Industry reported an element of greed, and that bonuses were driven by allegedly illegal activities aimed at increasing profits and delivering higher share market results and dividends representing a significant problem in the sector. This is of particular relevance, as it follows that this sector, in particular, may have a culture that is conducive to its arguably hyperactive appetite for profits by using technology to further reduce costs through slashing its human resources (Boobier 2020). Increasing profit margins using AI and machine learning, as opposed to staff salaries and on-costs, is an issue that is also discussed in the chapter. The literature review will explore the new technologies that are being implemented and are expected to be deployed in the next decade to "disrupt" existing jobs in the sector for profit maximisation. Emphasis is placed on the anticipated impacts on the labour market in this sector concerning jobs, skills and workplaces, and projected training needs for both new recruits and existing staff. The effects of AI and technological change on productivity, competitiveness and future jobs in the sector will also be considered. Observations on the disruption that the COVID-19 pandemic has wrought are also briefly covered, concerning how this disruption is affecting the current workforce as well as future implications for AI. The chapter will conclude with a synthesis of the critical consequences of the issues discussed.

Industry Overview

The Financial and Insurance Services sector has many subdivisions (Australian Bureau of Statistics 2020a).

The 2006 Australian and New Zealand Standard Industrial Classification (ANZSIC) provides a structure for managing and organising data about enterprises – by facilitating the alignment of business units conducting similar activities in the context of productivity (ABS 2008). Division K, the Financial and Insurance Services Division, includes entities principally engaged in financial transactions involving the establishment, liquidation, or transformation in ownership of financial assets and facilitating financial transactions where required (ABS 2008).

The range of activities is extensive. They include 'raising funds by taking deposits and/or issuing securities and, in the process, incurring liabilities; units investing their own funds in a range of financial assets; pooling risk by underwriting insurance and annuities; separately constituted funds engaged in the provision of retirement incomes; and specialised services facilitating or supporting financial intermediation, insurance and employee benefit programs' (ABS 2008: webpage). Central banking, regulation and monetary control of financial activities are all embedded in this division. Table 8.1 below, adapted from the RBA (2020), provides an example of the magnitude of this multilayered Financial and Insurance Services Division in Australia.

The high performing financial sector is crucial to Australia's economy (Hayne 2019). It acts as an intermediary between savers and borrowers, and along with other financial services illustrates the importance of the sector for economic and social sustainability in Australian society (Burns et al. 2019).

Hayne's (2019:8–9) Final Royal Commission report stated:

At their most basic, the underlying principles reflect the six norms of conduct I identified in the Interim Report:

- obey the law;
- do not mislead or deceive;
- act fairly;
- provide services that are fit for purpose;
- deliver services with reasonable care and skill; and
- when acting for another, act in the best interests of that other.

- These norms of conduct are fundamental precepts. Each is well-established, widely accepted, and easily understood.

The report made it clear what the role of the banking and finance industry sector should be. However, the findings called each of the points listed above into question as compelling evidence that emerged from the Royal Commission showed that some banks had allegedly flouted their social and economic responsibilities being driven by greed and bonuses.

In the finance and insurance sector, the largest business comprises the banks in terms of income compared with insurance companies (RBA 2020). There are 147 authorised deposit-taking institutions in which fifty-five per cent of Australia's financial institutions' assets are held. In Australia, banking is dominated by four leading banks (referred to as the 'Big 4'): the Commonwealth Bank of Australia, the Westpac Banking Corporation, the Australia and New Zealand Banking Group and the National Australia Bank (Hayne 2019; Wu 2020). Several foreign banks based in Australia, but few have retail banking (Commonwealth of Australia 2018). Retail banking assists consumers in managing their money through credit and depositing

Table 8.1 Main characteristics of finance and insurance industry Australia

Type of intermediary	Main characteristics
Banks	Provide financial services to all sectors, including (through subsidiaries) funds management and insurance services. Foreign banks authorised to operate as branches in Australia need to confine their deposit-taking activities to wholesale markets.
Building societies	Raise funds primarily by accepting deposits from households, provide loans (mainly mortgage finance for owner-occupied housing) and payments services. Traditionally mutually owned institutions, building societies increasingly are issuing share capital.
Credit unions	Mutually owned institutions, provide deposit, personal/housing loans, and payments services to members.
Money market corporations	Operate primarily in wholesale markets, borrowing from, and lending to, large corporations and government agencies. Other services, including advisory, relate to corporate finance, capital markets, foreign exchange, and investment management.
Finance companies	Provide loans to households and small to medium-sized businesses. Finance companies raise funds from wholesale markets and, using debentures and unsecured notes, from retail investors.
Securitisation vehicles	Special purpose vehicles that issue securities backed by pools of assets (e.g. mortgage-based housing loans). The securities are usually credit enhanced (e.g. through use of guarantees from third parties).
Life insurance companies	Provide life, accident and disability insurance, annuities, investment and superannuation products. Assets are managed in statutory funds on a fiduciary basis, and are mostly invested in equities and debt securities.
Superannuation and approved deposit funds (ADFs)	Superannuation funds accept and manage contributions from employers (including self-employed) and/or employees to provide retirement income benefits. Funds are controlled by trustees and fund managers/advisers. ADFs are generally managed by professional funds managers. Like superannuation funds ADFs may accept superannuation lump sums and eligible redundancy payments.Both these structures invest equities, property, debt securities and deposits).
Public unit trusts	Unit trusts pool investors' funds, usually into specific types of assets (e.g. cash, equities, property, money market investments, mortgages and overseas securities). Most unit trusts are managed by subsidiaries of banks, insurance companies or money market corporations.
Cash management trusts	Cash management trusts are unit trusts which are governed by a trust deed and open to the public and generally confine their investments (as authorised by the trust deed) to financial securities available through the short-term money market.
Trustee companies (common funds)	Trustee companies pool into common funds money received from the general public or held on behalf of estates or under powers of attorney. Funds are usually invested in specific types of assets (e.g. money market investments, equities and mortgages).
Friendly societies	These bodies represent mutually owned co-operative financial institutions offering benefits to members through a trust-like structure. Benefits and services include investment products through insurance or education bonds, funeral, accident, sickness, or other allowances.

(continued)

Table 8.1 (continued)

Type of intermediary	Main characteristics
General insurance companies	Provide insurance, including for property, motor vehicles and employers' liability. Assets are invested mainly in deposits and loans, government securities and equities.

Source: Adapted by the authors based on RBA 2020

money securely. Services offered by retail banks consist of cheque and savings accounts, mortgages, personal loans, credit cards, and certificates of deposit. The finance industry covers businesses that offer banking, lending services and investment trusts in Australia (Wu 2020). The most prominent industry subsectors in the Finance subdivision include 'domestic banks, foreign banks, non-depository financiers and financial asset investors' (Wu 2020: 4). In December 2017, 'banks, credit unions, building societies, general insurance and reinsurance companies, life insurance, private health insurance, friendly societies and the superannuation industry held a combined $7.6 trillion in assets' (Productivity Commission 2018: 57).

Workforce Characteristics & Trends

In May 2020, the number of employees in this sector comprised 489,800 within a total workforce of 12,214,700 people or 4.0% of the Australian workforce (ABS 2020b). The 'Big 4' banks together account for approximately 40% of total sector employment (ABS 2020a) and have already made moves to reduce workforce numbers. It is estimated that job losses will be in the order of forty thousand over the next 5 years (Reuters 2018).

As only one example of this trend, in late 2017, the National Australia Bank (NAB) announced that it would cut about 6000 jobs while recruiting 2000 technically savvy staff (Ziffer 2018). In 2020 further disruption has been reported, as over 2600 staff at the bank will need to reapply for jobs to maintain their employment in three divisions, as this financial giant restructures and reacts to the fallout from the coronavirus pandemic, with a further retrenchment estimated to involve 350 more staff (Bonyhady and Yeates 2020).

Australia's insurance industry comprises general insurers and reinsurers. 'General insurers underwrite insurance policies to cover individuals and businesses' financial loss associated with property, casualty, liability and other risks. Underwriting involves assuming risks and assigning premiums. Reinsurers assume all or part of the risk associated with existing insurance policies underwritten by other insurers' (Thomson 2019: 3).

The following table provides a snapshot of forecasts for the Finance sector prior to the COVID-19 pandemic wreaked havoc (Table 8.2).

The curious aspect is that the wages share of revenue may have declined as the employment growth increased by 59,400 or 14.6 per cent between 2015–2020

Table 8.2 Pre COVID-19 forecasts

2020 Forecast to have a total revenue	$AUD204.6 billion
2020 forecast profit margin	$AUD 613.8 billion
Annual growth 2015–2020	Decline .05 per cent
Growth forecast for 2020–2025	Growth 3.8 per cent
Staff wages as a share of revenue in 2020	Decline by 15.7 per cent in 2020
Increased number of businesses in the sector	Growth 2.6 per cent between 2015–2020

Source: Adapted by the authors from Wu 2020

Table 8.3 Profile of the insurance industry subsector

Female/Male employment	Female 48.6% Male 49.4%
Fulltime employment	83.6%
Projected employment May 2019–May 2020	Anticipated growth 4.6%

Source: Adapted by the authors from Australian Government 2020

(Australian Government 2020). This chapter aims to determine why this occurred through reviewing relevant literature and scrutinising the insights from experts in the field.

From February 2016 to February 2020, employment in the Financial and Insurance Services industry increased by 14.6 per cent (Australian Government 2020). The Australian Government (2020) estimated that, in 2020, the median age for people employed in this industry sector was 38 years, with median annual earnings being around AUD78,000, compared with $AUD89,700 across all industry sectors (Salaryexplorer 2020).

A further profile of the insurance industry subsector is outlined in Table 8.3 below.

The impact of COVID-19 and its continued influence inhibits accurate forecasts of growth in the insurance and finance sector (Wu 2020).

Australian Government's Policies on AI in Finance and Insurance Services

> Domestic policy covers priorities that affect the lives of all Australians. Our work involves advising the Prime Minister, the Cabinet and Portfolio Ministers on issues such as jobs and economic growth, the budget, industry, infrastructure, agriculture, innovation, health, education and the environment. (Department of the Prime Minister and Cabinet 2020: webpage).

Having well-formulated government policies to strategically address both the positive and negative impacts that AI poses would seem logical, given the prominence of AI in the finance and insurance sectors. The effect of AI on the workforce and future ways of working within all the Australian industry sectors, as well as Australia's economic position in a global market, are key issues that confront

Australia (Hajkowicz et al. 2019). This is of concern as policies are needed to safeguard jobs, particularly in this sector (Deloitte 2020; Hajkowicz et al. 2019).

Government policy is a difficult concept to define (Bacchi 1999) and policy-making processes require insight through visionary constructs and discourse (Bacchi 1999). The development of policy into "constructive schemes" involves numerous dimensions of discourse to determine policy problems (Bacchi 1999), This process then progresses to the formulation of policy generated by useful research to implement funded processes, and procedures built into strategies that produce solutions for the population (Bessant et al. 2006). Government policy signifies the implementation of activity in a society that is well funded and researched and designed to benefit most of the population. Along similar lines, Bacchi (1999) viewed government policy as a principle, or on occasion, a law, that aims to guide decisions with strategic thinking culminating in positive outcomes that enhance society. Government policies contain the reasons things are to be done in a certain way and why. Policies are not laws, but they can lead to laws.

It is important to note that information on the Australian Government's AI policies within the Finance and Insurance Services sector yields very little in terms of academic or government commentary. Hence, it is not surprising that Australia is lagging well behind other developed countries in this regard (Deloitte 2020; Hajkowicz et al. 2019, Loucks et al. 2019, Smith 2019a, b).

It is quite revealing how limited policy development in Australia is compared with other developed countries. The Australian Information Computer Technology (ICT) industry in its missive to a broad membership signalled problems stating that 'currently {Australia} lacks access to relevant local skills, and is not supported by an effective Research and Development Taxation Incentive (R&DTI) program that fosters an environment of innovation, commercialisation and export of high-quality Australian AI products and services' (Anonymous 2019: webpage).

Loucks et al. (2019) reported that Australian industry, including the finance and insurance sector, was ranked highly among industry adopters among developed countries, but revealed the government policies were inadequate:

While there is not yet a dedicated national AI strategy, the government recently published "Australia's Tech Future." The plan touches upon the economic importance of AI, as well as skills shortages in AI and data science, as part of a broader discussion of opportunities presented by digital technologies. The 2018–19 national budget allocated AU$29.9 million over 4 years to boost the country's AI capabilities, including the development of a technology road map and frameworks for standards and AI ethics. However, AI experts are issuing warnings that greater levels of spending will be needed for Australia to keep up with other countries that are lavishing public funds on AI initiatives (Loucks et al. 2019: 10).

Deloitte (2020: webpage) highlighted the lack of government policy with clarity in these words: 'No national strategy or proper funding.' It claimed that Australia did not have a 'dedicated national AI strategy' despite several 'prominent Australian business and industry leaders … urgently pushing for {a} national debate on the policies needed to address AI risks (Deloitte 2020: webpage). The same report cited industry leader comments critical of the meagre '2018-19 federal budget' allocation of 'AU$29.9 million over four years to boost the country's AI capabilities, including the development of a technology roadmap to build standards and ethics' (Deloitte 2020: webpage).

The report further stated that AI experts have warned that significantly increased levels of spending are required for Australia to keep pace with other countries. 'China for example … has a comprehensive national AI strategy and plans to spend billions to become a world-leading AI innovator. Beijing announced a US$2.1 billion AI-centric technology park, and Tianjin plans to set up a US$16 billion AI fund (Deloitte 2020: webpage).

Smith (Smith 2019a, b) reflected the concerns expressed by Deloitte (2020) and Loucks et al. (2019) and revealed added detail on what can be described as a paltry AI policy commitment by government. He stated that 'Australia's funding for AI-related initiatives has been comparatively thin' when compared with other developed countries' (p.5). In policy announcements before the last federal election, the Coalition government did not raise the AI challenges. The Minister for Industry, Science and Technology at the time and also and still occupying this position as this chapter is penned, The Honourable Karen Andrews MP said that 'the government had invested $29.9 million in artificial intelligence development under the 2018-19 budget' (Smith 2019a, b, p. webpage). But this was not reported. Deloitte (2020), however, reported that this money was spread over 4 years, which further dilutes the impact of this meagre investment. The policy on AI in terms of expenditure is out of fiscal context. Hajkowicz et al. (2019) outlined a catalogue of statistics emanating from compelling research which showed that 'digital technologies, including AI, is potentially worth AU$315 billion to the Australian economy by 2028 and AI could be worth AU$22.17 trillion to the global economy by 2030' (p.v). To state the obvious, the $29.9 million in artificial intelligence development under the 2018–19 budget spread over 4 years represents such a small fiscal commitment that Australia may arguably be destined for an economic state of disadvantage.

Smith (2019a, b) provided further insights into government policy inactivity by stating that the Minister for Industry, Science and Technology" admitted that political leadership in the area has been limited, but said she recognised that AI had the potential to provide significant social, economic and environmental benefits.'

In the past, I think politicians have been hesitant to talk about artificial intelligence because of the genuine concern in the community around the future of work," she said. "I want to assure Australians that AI will be a job creator, particularly if we get ahead of the curve and maximise Australia's role. (Smith 2019a, b, p.5, citing Minister Karen Andrews).

To summarise this section, fears that Australia will be left behind due to minimal AI spending and policy commitment appear to have some merit.

France has committed €1.5 billion ($2.4 billion) over 5 years leading up to 2022. The South Korean government committed to 2.2 trillion won ($2.7 billion) over the same period. India and the European Union also published ambitious AI strategies. Canada pledged $C125 million ($131 million) over 5 years starting in 2017. Singapore committed $S150 million ($155 million) from 2017 to 2022. Despite Australia's $29.9 million being almost fully committed already, Ms. Andrews told

The Australian Financial Review she didn't believe Australia was under-investing in AI initiatives. (Seo 2019: webpage).

Key Technologies

Five areas are outlined below where AI is expected to be influential. The examples mostly refer to banks, but similar examples will also apply to insurance.

AI Aided Customers and Self-Service

First, in the customer interface, this decision-making technology and other IT software can be made accessible for customers to produce services themselves (De Keyser et al. 2019; Larivière et al. 2017; Wirtz et al. 2018) with the effect of reducing the number of branch offices to the bare minimum and leading to the replacement of humans with robots call centres. Robo-advisors, which involves using software that enables customers to interact via a web interface to receive investment advice, moves this back-office activity to the front-office. Robo-advisors reduce fees and provide around the clock access to financial advice (Park et al. 2016). Robo-advisors have been embraced mostly by early adopters to date (Jung et al. 2018; Ryu 2018).

AI and Lending Decisions

Second, lending decisions are a typical application of standard machine learning. Decision support with regard to lending would, first of all, use the information that the manual banker uses for lending decisions, although many other data sources may be utilised such as the: online behaviour of potential clients, online ratings for small business (Sigrist and Hirnschall 2019), account-level credit card data, credit bureau data (Butaru et al. 2016), internal due diligence reports (Zhang et al. 2015), social media data, utility bills and telecom data (Onay and Öztürk 2018). Credit scoring with machine learning is sold by AI developers, who make tailored applications according to the data the financial institutions have. Where credit scoring has been undertaken with statistics (for example, logistical regression), it can be improved with the integration of various technologies, or as demonstrated by a recent finding, with Grabit. Grabit uses a combination of methods (Sigrist and Hirnschall 2019). Grabit can extract mega data from multiple file types that are readable and convert data sets into matrices that significantly improve predictions on likely defaults with business loans methods (Sigrist and Hirnschall 2019). This is because these methods can make more efficient use of data as well as data that has been found to be unsuitable for statistical methods (Khandani et al. 2010; Li et al. 2016).

AI – Deposits and Payments

Third, deposits and payments are computerised but require surveillance due to customer security needs and loss reduction. However, financial regulation and surveillance are expensive. A large fraction of the staff in banks and insurance companies work directly or indirectly with internal controls to ensure compliance with the regulations. The advantage of using AI for monitoring compliance in financial institutions is that computers can monitor all transactions all of the time and react to non-compliance instantly (Shilts 2017). In contrast, human surveillance uses sampling, and there is a time lag of weeks or months between the occurrence of a breach and corrective action (Alles et al. 2006; Sahin et al. 2013). Another benefit is that AI is more efficient. Its application in fraud prevention and it can detect more complex, nuanced, fraudulent attempts, predominantly due to the increased capacity of calculating and even predicting possible fraud. Software such as RegTech for banks is available that ensures that processes are compliant with regulations. There are modules for specific parts of banking such as investment management which is an application dominated by a few software suppliers (Butler and O'Brien 2019). The potential for the technology to survey regulatory compliance, referred to as RegTech, is large and a majority of large firms have had plans to use machine learning in continuous internal control which shows that constant auditing and similar applications will be used when applications are available (Baker 2009). AI is used in two predominant ways when detecting fraud and reducing losses. This includes front-end and back-end implementations (Choi and Lee 2018), which incorporates two stages that compare incoming transaction history to check for anomalies, use machine learning algorithms and resolve false alarms that identify suspected irregularities that are further checked via fraud history databases. Choi and Lee (2018) showed evidence supporting the conclusions that machine learning shows more efficiency in predicting and detecting fraudulent transactions than statistical methods. Machine learning is the standard approach in commercial applications of fraud detection and loss reduction (Choi and Lee 2018; Soviany 2018).

AI and Credit Card Fraud

Fourth, credit card fraud is a vitally important aspect in finance firms' fight against fraud. The massive increase in E-Commerce, and the use of credit cards online for purchasing, has led to more resources being used by financial firms to increase security on their financial instruments, such as credit cards. The previous strategy of simple data matching techniques is deemed insufficient in this age of online transactions. Methods related to new ways to prevent fraud and loss include data mining, fuzzy logic, sequence alignment and genetic programming. Sequence alignment and genetic programming involve the development of algorithms to signal suspicious transactions and identify patterns of behaviour warranting further investigation at a level beyond human capability as it applies to massive data sets. (Raj and Portia 2011). Such AI methods apply to insurance fraud monitoring, and accomplished fraud detection using the same technique (Raj and Portia 2011; Pathak et al. 2005).

Business Planning

Fifth, AI can assist top management with business planning as per its use by researchers and for the development of credit scores. Cash flows in ATMs can be predicted with an Artificial Neural Network (ANN) (Serengil and Ozpinar 2019). The number of cash transports related to ATMs and branch offices will be estimated with higher accuracy with machine learning than manual calculations (López Lázaro et al. 2018). Finally, marketing managers will use data to make targeted offers to customers in similar ways to those used in internet-based firms (Martens et al. 2016).

In something akin to a game of 'follow the leader', we can expect the testing of the processes implemented to achieve the desired outcomes viewed voraciously by competitor organisations as they learn which practices will be accepted by major stakeholders, such as the government, unions and society in general and what will and what will not be accepted, before embarking on what may be 'job-slashing expeditions'.

Employment Impact

A summary of the jobs that will be affected by AI is outlined in this section as well as some predictions concerning the impact of AI on finance jobs in the future.

Commissioner Hayne's (2019) final report on the Australian Royal Commission into Misconduct in the Banking, Superannuation and Financial Services Industry was released to the public on 4 February 2019. The findings from Hayne's (2019) report provide an interesting perspective on the ethics, governance, leadership and management within this sector. Specifically of interest is how the increased integration of AI within the sector, due to its cost-effectiveness and efficiency, might provide a strong impetus for change to occur much sooner than adequate policies and frameworks are developed to address malpractice and greed around AI integration. The final Hayne report detailed seventy-six recommendations and twenty-four referrals to the judiciary for criminal conduct among three of the four biggest Australian banks (Hayne 2019). There were also prominent recommendations that the senior figures in one bank were worthy of serious review, which resulted in resignations (Hayne 2019).

So the question arises as to whether the implementation of AI, given the apparent zeal for increased profits in this sector, will result in many redundancies? Jobs under the most significant danger from automation include those that are described as routine, repetitive tasks conducted physically and cognitively (Frey and Osborne 2017; Manpower Group 2018; O'Neill 2017; Susskind 2020; WEF 2016). The finance insurance industry is not immune to this problem. Frey and Osborne (2017) examined 702 occupations and identified significant risks for office and administrative support workers, and labour in production occupations – many of which permeate the insurance and finance industry. Manyika et al. (2017) also pointed to numerous large-scale studies which asserted that many jobs were at risk. They contended that the fourth industrial revolution, propelled by emerging technologies would "obliterate" activities that involve work of a routine nature. Susskind (2020), however, concluded that over the next two to three decades, as long as the pace of change is not too fast, employees will move to other jobs using many skills they already possess with a need to adapt to new tasks due to technological disruption.

Huang and Rust (2018) described AI as a source of innovation that will gradually replace human jobs in the future. They estimated that technology would develop through phases with mechanical intelligence first, then analytical capacity (for example, robo-advisors) and, in the distant future, intuitive and even empathetic intelligence (Huang and Rust 2018). These researchers reflected Susskind's (2020) research which asserted that the jobs requiring creativity, innovation and empathy were destined to be marginally impacted upon for well beyond three decades. The mechanical intelligence positions that Huang and Rust (2018) referred to would be at risk significantly within the next two decades. In the finance and insurance sector, these jobs would include accounts and bank clerks, secretaries, receptionists, call centre staff, credit and loans officers, debt collectors, financial dealers, financial investment managers and advisers, general clerks, and information officers and insurance, money market and statistical clerks, keyboard operators, and personal assistants would either decline or experience limited growth (Job Outlook 2020), for further details see Figs. 8.1 and 8.2 below.

The Following Case Study Illustrates the Effects of AI on Employment in One Key Australian Bank

Case Study 8.1 – National Australia Bank (NAB)

A point-to-case within the banking sector is NAB, as outlined above. NAB retrenchments began in February 2018 and were comprised mainly from the head office in Melbourne, where artificially charged software is now focused on tasks that were once considered too complicated (Ziffer 2018).

Primarily, the job losses were linked to the digitalisation and robotics of banking services, the loss of retail staff due to online banking and ATMs, and the loss of administrative support staff due to technological change and the offshoring of services (Ziffer 2018). Despite NAB being very profitable, in February 2018 the National Australia Bank (NAB) commenced departing with 6000 people as jobs were slashed (Ziffer 2018) The staff cuts represented 20 per cent of NAB's labour force (Ziffer 2018). The massive number of redundancies that occurred mainly in February 2018 was announced in November 2017 on the same date the bank announced its annual net profit of A$5.3 billion for the fiscal 2016/2017 year (Ziffer 2018).

Circumstances indicate the pressure is on for banks to reduce costs, increase productivity and eliminate jobs (Reuters News 2018). The question is, where is this "pressure" coming from? Internationally the sector was planning transformation in its production and service processes, and significant job losses are occurring with further job cuts projected (Reuters News 2018). New banks were predicted to emerge based on mobile phone technology and automated services with minimal local staffing requirements, leading to predictions that half of all jobs in the sector would disappear (Fletcher and Kreps 2017). At the same time, it was projected that new jobs, mainly in IT management would be generated; in the case of NAB, the forecast is for an additional 2000 jobs in this area (Ziffer 2018). While NAB had indicated that it would have a consultative and supportive approach to the process of managing the redundancies, the main union representing employees in the sector, the Finance Sector Union, had criticised the approach of NAB over its program of managing the redundancy process (Han 2018). 'NAB has since hired more than 2000 staff, almost exclusively in roles dealing with new technology, like augmented reality, artificial intelligence and machine learning' (Ziffer 2019: webpage).

Further disruption to NAB jobs is occurring as over 2600 staff reapply for jobs in three divisions as this 'financial giant restructures itself as it deals with the fallout from the coronavirus pandemic' (Bonyhady and Yeates 2020: webpage). In 2020 350 more NAB staff are facing likely redundancy (Bonyhady and Yeates 2020).

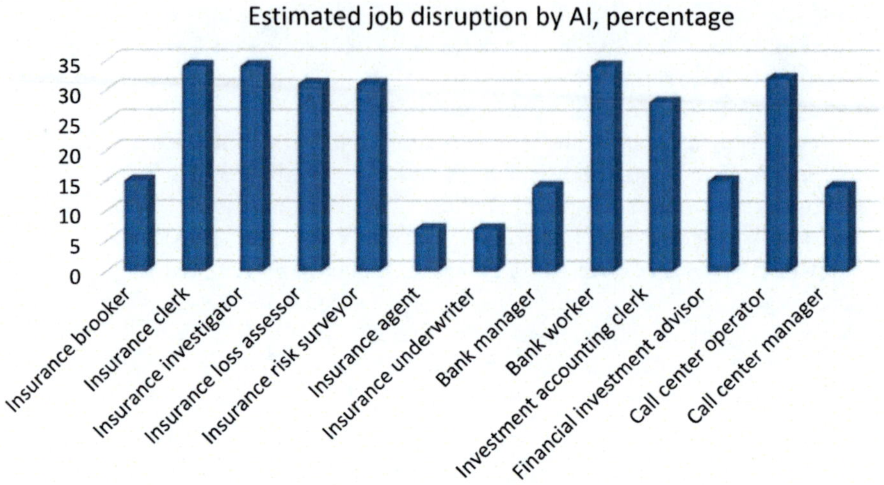

Fig. 8.1 AI disruption: Jobs in the finance/insurance sector "At Risk" (Byrd et al 2017)
Source: Developed by authors based on data from Bertomeu et al. (2020)

Challenges & Opportunities

We suggest that comparisons with previous technological changes may lead to false conclusions. The rationalisation of jobs that is now at our doorstep will create an effect on employment in a much more profound way than the automation of manufacturing because AI mechanises the minds, not the hands of skilled workers. The combination of two circumstances is why we anticipate that the broad entry of AI to the finance sector will be a discontinuity to the employment on a never-before-seen scale. The first circumstance is the general versatility of AI: AI is predominantly a set of techniques for making decisions automatically (Agrawal et al. 2019). As long as tasks can be described as decisions and as long as decision premises are made on data that can be made available in databases, there are is a good chance that some AI applications will be useful. The second circumstance is that most activities in banks and insurance companies are decision-making or can be rephrased as such. In addition, the data are, or soon will be, stored in databases.

The Economic modelling firm AlphaBeta have developed estimates for anticipated job disruption from AI adoption in Australian businesses (AlphaBeta 2017). Their estimates were derived from an analysis of the existing US government database ONET, which describes tasks in every occupation. The calculations were developed by converting the US data so that it would fit the Australian context. For example, a factory worker operates equipment and monitors facilities. The database contains more than 2000 such work-related activities covering a substantial number of jobs in the finance sector.

Tasks were placed into one of six groups depending on the type of work they represent. Tasks requiring interaction with other people were assigned to a group

Occupation	Susceptibility to Automation %
• Typist • Keyboard Operators • Data Entry Operators • Machine Shorthand Reporter	52%
• Receptionist (General)	35%
• Call Centre Supervisor • Call or Contact Centre Information Clerks • Information Officer	32%
• Debt Collector • Insurance Investigator • Insurance Loss Adjuster • Insurance Risk Surveyor • (Miscellaneous Clerical and Administrative Workers)	31%
• ICT Quality Assurance Engineer • ICT Test Analyst • (and ICT Network and Support Professionals)	25%
• General Clerk	21%
• Business Systems Analyst • Business and Systems Analysts • Programmers • Software Programmer • (Business and Systems Analysts, and Programmers)	17%
• Sales and Marketing Manager • Advertising, Public Relations and Sales Managers • Finance Manager	14%
• Insurance Agent • Insurance Agents and Sales Representatives	7%

Fig. 8.2 Can a robot perform jobs in finance and insurance?
Source: Created by the authors using occupations listed in the finance and insurance industry by Job Outlook (2020) and job susceptibility due to automation forecasts by Byrd et al. (2017)

named "interpersonal" and tasks such as reviewing documents or monitoring facilities were assigned to a group named "information analysis." Each of those groups of tasks was rated as "difficult to automate" or "automatable." Researchers could then calculate how much of any job was "difficult to automate" and how much was "automatable" (AlphaBeta 2017).

From Fig. 8.1 the estimate indicates that approximately twenty per cent of tasks for this sample of jobs can be automated. Because technological development is so rapid in the finance area, perceptions of what can be automated may change in just one or 2 years. Notably, insurance broker and financial investment advisor positions should probably be reassessed in the light of the recent deployment of robot advisors, despite these jobs involving empathy and interpersonal understanding. Moreover, several jobs are professional and require substantial education and would, therefore, traditionally not be the first to be replaced by machines.

Nevertheless, 14% of bank managers' jobs were labelled as automatable (AlphaBeta 2017). Several highly analytical jobs in insurance companies, e.g. insurance risk surveyor, which is an entirely analytical back-office job, and an insurance investigator involving the inspection and assessment of damage and loss to insured property and business may be hit by more than a 30 per cent decrease. The job of an insurance risk surveyor who assesses the potential financial risk posed by offering insurance cover, providing underwriters with information about how to reduce risk or whether insurance cover should be offered, may be even worse off because this job requires computerised data and ultimately comprises numerically supported decisions much like credit rating or fraud detection, which is exactly what a machine learning application can do better than most humans (Bertomeu et al. 2020). Call centre operator positions will also suffer more in the coming 10 years from the impact of chatbots. Figure 8.2 illustrates estimates of a selection of key roles in the finance and insurance industry.

If an occupational area is going to be disrupted by AI, by a certain percentage, this could signal redundancy. If computer technology, for example, can in time perform a third (33.3%) of a person's job this could mean that three people in the same job could be replaced by two people as one person may be surplus to needs and could face redundancy unless they can migrate to a new position with an organisation. Figure 8.2 provides an estimate of job disruption in the sector.

Impact on the Sector Due to COVID-19

The certainty of COVID-19 having a substantial negative impact on labour market activity in Australia in the next year or more is apparent (Australian Government 2020). There is considerable uncertainty around the economic implications of the virus and the magnitude of the changes to employment that will result (Australia Government 2020). While the overall finance industry subdivision is not directly affected in terms of trade and supply chain disruptions, it is projected that it can be indirectly impacted by movements in the financial markets and adjustments to the cash rate (Wu 2020). Furthermore, lender's profitability and net interest margins are likely to be squeezed with a significant impact on employment. However, the extent of this disruption is too complex to forecast, particularly given the volatility in financial markets both locally and abroad (Wu 2020).

Conclusion

This overview of the potential impact of AI on jobs and opportunities in the Australian finance sector suggests three conclusions.

First, we find that jobs will likely be substantially impacted in the foreseeable future, and most likely, 15–30 per cent of employment will be in the risk zone. Although some jobs may be even more in demand, the net effect will be that many tens of thousands of people will face the challenge of finding something else to do because their jobs will become redundant. It is anticipated that many of those employed in the finance and insurance sector will be professionals who never imagined that they would 1 day suffer the same fate as maybe their grandparents did who worked in factories or farming. Losses will occur repetitive jobs and in analytical and decision-making jobs that may currently be well-paid and highly regarded. If the Australian Government does not work to address the situation, we predict that many people are unlikely to manage a transition to the new finance sector.

Consequently, it is recommended that the Australian Government revise its policy when the COVID-19 pandemic subsides. It is essential for this nation's prosperous and productive finance sector to work to ensure that the positive aspects of the impending AI revolution are emphasised for the Australian people, their banks, insurance companies and the staff employed in the sector. The pandemic has shown that national and state leadership is essential for Australians, which means that tackling the AI revolution in finance should be approached with an effective and well-planned national policy which is currently conspicuous through absence.

Second, most of the potential for AI in banks and insurance companies is in places where it cannot be seen as it is invisible. The visible applications are in customer service, but while it is not impossible to make a chatbot that answers many questions, we are not the only customers who have felt frustration when dealing with a machine that will not comprehend the issue that requires resolution. Therefore, we assert that the myriad relegated tasks to the "back-office" are more at risk of being automated. Back-office automation may connect a human insurance salesperson with a sales support system that consists of purely AI-type software that every second computes optimum insurance terms for thousands of insurance policies. Based on the research in this brief chapter, the indications are that lending decisions, insurance policy agreements, deposits and payments, internal controls such as loss prevention and fraud detection are among an array of transactions that will be automated with machine learning applications within a foreseeable future.

Our third and final point is brief and concerns the Hayne (2019) Royal Commission into Misconduct in the Banking, Superannuation and Financial Services Industry. This report indicated that an element of greed and bonuses was driven by illegal activities to increase profits and deliver higher share market results and dividends in the sector. This industry sector allegedly indulged in a litany of misdemeanours leading to a crucial question. As banks and insurance companies have been exposed for their repeated practices of mistreating their customers, flouting regulations and the law and consequently have faced many financial penalties, will they now respect the work of their staff and strive to maintain people as employees? The track record of the four major banks in Australia suggests otherwise. The quest for profit and bonuses in such toxic cultures, as uncovered by the Royal Commission (Hayne 2019), means that it may be difficult for such a culture to change. Hence, as pointed out previously, embracing AI at the expense of people's jobs may be a problem needing government policy intervention, particularly in this sector.

Although the impact on jobs in the finance sector is difficult to predict, research suggests that many positions may be obliterated and disrupted in this industry sector to a level unimagined and unprecedented.

References

ABS. (2008). 1292.0 – Australian and New Zealand Standard Industrial Classification (ANZSIC), 2006 (Revision 1.0) https://www.abs.gov.au/ausstats/abs@.nsf/Previousproducts/AF04F89CEE4E54D6CA25711F00146D76?opendocument Accessed 19 Aug 2020.

ABS. (Australian Bureau of Statistics). (2020a). 1292.0 – Australian and New Zealand Standard Industrial Classification (ANZSIC), 2006 (Revision 2.0) Australian Bureau of Statistics Canberra. Retrieved from https://www.abs.gov.au/AUSSTATS/abs@.nsf/Latestproducts/1292.0Contents12006%20(Revision%202.0)?opendocument&tabname=Summary&prodno=1292.0&issue=2006%20(Revision%202.0)&num=&view= 10 May 2020.

ABS. (2020b). *Labour force, Australia, detailed.* Australian Bureau of Statistics Canberra https://beta.abs.gov.au/statistics/labour/employment-and-unemployment/labour-force-australia-detailed/may-2020 Accessed 19 August 2020.ABS.2018 Labour Force, Australia, Detailed, Quarterly – Table 04 Employed persons by Industry sub-division of main job (ANZSIC), 29 March, Cat. no. 6291.0.55.003.

Agrawal, A., Gans, J. S., & Goldfarb, A. (2019). Artificial intelligence: The ambiguous labor market impact of automating prediction. *Journal of Economic Perspectives, 33*, 31–50.

Alles, M., Brennan, G., Kogan, A., & Vasarhelyi, M. A. (2006). Continuous monitoring of business process controls: A pilot implementation of a continuous auditing system at Siemens. *International Journal of Accounting Information Systems, 7*, 137–161.

AlphaBeta. (2017). The automation advantage how Australia can seize a $2 trillion opportunity from automation and create millions of safer, more meaningful and more valuable jobs. https://www.alphabeta.com/wp-content/uploads/2017/08/The-Automation-Advantage.pdf Accessed 28 July 2020

Anonymous. (2019). *Digital skills shortages and R&D tax incentives remain obstacles to artificial intelligence development in Australia.* Targeted News Service: Says AIIA.

Australian Government. (2020). Employment portal. Australian Government Canberra. https://lmip.gov.au/default.aspx?LMIP/EmploymentProjections Accessed 30 July 2020.

Bacchi, C. (1999). *Women policy and politics; the construction of policy.* London: Sage.

Baker, N. (2009). Software trend spotting; recent IIA survey results show many auditors use software to Automate key tasks, though a surprising number have yet to adopt popular tools. *Internal Auditor, 66*(4), 30–34.

Bertomeu, J., Cheynel, E., Floyd, E., & Pan, W. (2020). Using machine learning to detect misstatements. *Review of Accounting Studies*, forthcoming.

Bessant, J., Watts, R., Dalton, T., & Smyth, P. (2006). *Talking policy: Making social policy in Australia.* Sydney: Allen and Unwin.

Bonyhady, N., & Yeates, C. (2020, August 12). C. NAB staff in firing line as bank pushes ahead with restructure amid pandemic. *The Age.* Nine Group Sydney. https://www.theage.

com.au/business/banking-and-finance/nab-staff-in-firing-line-as-bank-pushes-ahead-with-restructure-amid-pandemic-20200812-p55l13.html?btis Accessed 19 Aug 2020. August 12, 2020 – 6.12pm.

Boobier, T. (2020). *AI and the future of banking*. John Wiley & Sons Ltd..

Burns, C., Houghton, L., & Stewart, H. (2019). Sustainability – A key to Australian finance directors improving their organisation's CSR culture. *Corporate Social-Responsibility and Environmental Management, 27*(2), 1164–1176. https://doi.org/10.1002/csr.1870.

Butaru, F., Chen, Q., Clark, B., Das, S., Lo, A. W., & Siddique, A. (2016). Risk and risk management in the credit card industry. *Journal of Banking and Finance, 72*, 218–239.

Butler, T., & O'Brien, L. (2019). Understanding RegTech for Digital Regulatory Compliance, in: Disrupting Finance. (pp. 85–102).

Byrd, J., Spreaggon, B., O'Neill, M., & Liddy, M. (2017). Could a robot do your job? Australian Broadcasting Commission https://www.abc.net.au/news/2017-08-08/could-a-robot-do-your-job-artificial-intelligence/8782174?nw=0 Accessed 5 July 2021.

Choi, D., & Lee, K. (2018). An artificial intelligence approach to financial fraud detection under IoT environment: A survey and implementation. *Security and Communication Networks* 15.

Commonwealth of Australia. (2018). Royal Commission into Misconduct in the Banking, Superannuation and Financial Services Industry, Interim report, vol. 1, (pp. 1–347). Canberra, AU.

De Keyser, A., Köcher, S., Alkire (née Nasr), L., Verbeeck, C., & Kandampully, J. (2019). Frontline service technology infusion: Conceptual archetypes and future research directions. *Journal of Service Management*.

Deloitte. (2020). *Australia unprepared for AI risks. Australian businesses are the most concerned but least prepared for AI risks*. Deloitte Melbourne. https://www2.deloitte.com/au/en/pages/media-releases/articles/australia-unprepared-for-ai-risks-070519.html Accessed 28 July 2020.

Department of the Prime Minister and Cabinet. (2020). *Domestic policy*. Department of the Prime Minister and Cabinet Canberra https://www.pmc.gov.au/domestic-policy Accessed 27 July 2020.

Fletcher, G., & Kreps, D. (2017, September 12). Banking sector will be ground zero for job losses from AI and robotics. *The Conversation*.

Frey, C., & Osborne, M. (2017). The future of employment: How susceptible are jobs to computerisation? *Technological Forecasting and Social Change, 114*(C), 254–280.

Hajkowicz S., Karimi, S., Wark, T., Chen, C., Evans, M,, Rens, N., Dawson, D., Charlton, A., Brennan, T., Moffatt C., Srikumar S., & Tong K. (2019). *Artificial intelligence: Solving problems, growing the economy and improving our quality of life*. CSIRO Data61, Australia. https://data61.csiro.au/en/Our-Research/Our-Work/AI-Roadmap Accessed 4 Aug 2020.

Han, M. (2018). NAB's 6000 job cuts 'lazy option': Finance Sector Union. *Financial Review*. The Nine Group. Sydney. https://www.afr.com/companies/financial-services/nabs-6000-job-cuts-lazy-option-finance-sector-union-20180221-h0wedp. Accessed 10 Jan 2020.

Hayne, K. (2019). *Final report the royal commission into misconduct in the banking, superannuation and financial services industry*. Volume 1.Commonwealth of Australia, Canberra https://financialservices.royalcommission.gov.au/Pages/reports.aspx Accessed 12 July 2020.

Huang, M. H., & Rust, R. T. (2018). Artificial Intelligence in Service. *Journal of Service Research, 21*, 155–172.

Job Outlook. (2020). *Financial and insurance services*. National Skills Commission . Australian Government Canberra. https://joboutlook.gov.au/IndustrySpecific?search=Industry&Industry=K Accessed 20 July 2020.

Jung, D., Dorner, V., Weinhardt, C., & Pusmaz, H. (2018). Designing a robo-advisor for risk-averse, low-budget consumers. *Electronic Markets, 28*, 367–380.

Khandani, A. E., Kim, A. J., & Lo, A. W. (2010). Consumer credit-risk models via machine-learning algorithms. *Journal of Banking and Finance, 34*, 2767–2787.

Larivière, B., Bowen, D., Andreassen, T. W., Kunz, W., Sirianni, N. J., Voss, C., Wünderlich, N. V., & De Keyser, A. (2017). "Service encounter 2.0": An investigation into the roles of technology, employees and customers. *Journal of Business Research, 79*, 238–246.

Li, K., Niskanen, J., Kolehmainen, M., & Niskanen, M. (2016). Financial innovation: Credit default hybrid model for SME lending. *Expert Systems with Applications, 61*, 343–355.

López Lázaro, J., Barbero Jiménez, Á., & Takeda, A. (2018). Improving cash logistics in bank branches by coupling machine learning and robust optimization. *Expert Systems with Applications, 92*, 236–255.

Loucks, J., Hupfer, S., Jarvis, D., & Murphy, T. (2019). *Future in the balance? How countries are pursuing an AI advantage*. London: Deloitte Touche Tohmatsu Limited.

ManpowerGroup. (2018). Robots need not apply: human solutions for the skills revolution. *ManpowerGroup* https://www.voced.edu.au/content/ngv:79585 Accessed 16 Jan 2020.

Manyika, J., Chui, M., Miremadi, M., Bughin, J., George, K., Willmott, P., & Dewhurst, M.. (2017). *A future that works: Automation, employment, and productivity*. Summit: McKinsey Global Institute (MGI McKinsey & Company. Retrieved from https://www.mckinsey.com/global-themes/digital-disruption/harnessing-automation-for-a-future-that-works

Martens, D., Provost, F., Clark, J., & de Fortuny, E. J. (2016). *Mining massive fine-grained behavior data to improve predictive analytics*. MIS Quarterly: Management Information Systems.

Nankervis, A., Connell, J., Cameron, R., Montague, A., & Prikshat, V. (2019). 'Are we there yet?' Australian HR professionals and the Fourth Industrial Revolution. *Asia Pacific Journal of Human Resources*.

O'Neill, M. (2017). Explainer: What is artificial intelligence? Lateline 7 Aug 2017. *Australian Broadcasting Commission Sydney*. https://www.abc.net.au/news/2017-08-07/explainer-what-is-artificial-intelligence/8771632 Accessed 22 July 2020

Onay, C., & Öztürk, E. (2018). A review of credit scoring research in the age of big data. *Journal of Financial Regulation and Compliance, 26*, 382–405.

Park, J.Y., Ryu, J.P., & Shin, H.J., (2016). *Robo-advisors for portfolio management*. pp. 104–108.

Pathak, J., Vidyarthi, N., & Summers, S. L. (2005). A fuzzy-based algorithm for auditors to detect elements of fraud in settled insurance claims. *Managerial Auditing Journal, 20*(6), 632–644.

Productivity Commission. (2018). Competition in the Australian Financial System, Productivity Commission Inquiry Report, No. 89, 29 June 2018. https://www.pc.gov.au/inquiries/completed/financial-system/report/financial-system.pdf

Raj, S. B. E., & Portia, A. A. (2011). Analysis on credit card fraud detection methods. *International Conference on Computer, Communication and Electrical Technology (ICCCET)*, 152–156.

Reserve Bank of Australia. (2020). The structure of the Australian financial system. Reserve Bank of Australia https://www.rba.gov.au/publications/fsr/2020/apr/ Accessed 19 Aug 2020.

Reuters News. (2018, February 18). Australia's big banks focus on job cuts as inquiry looms.

Ryu, H. S. (2018). What makes users willing or hesitant to use Fintech?: The moderating effect of user type. *Industrial Management and Data Systems, 118*, 541–569.

Sahin, Y., Bulkan, S., & Duman, E. (2013). A cost-sensitive decision tree approach for fraud detection. *Expert Systems with Applications, 40*(15), 5916–5923.

SalaryExplorer. (2020). Average Salary in Australia 2020. http://www.salaryexplorer.com/salary-survey.php?loc=13&loctype=1 Accessed 15 July 2020)

Seo, B. (2019). Fears Australia will be left behind with minimal AI spending. *The Australian Financial Review*; Melbourne. https://www.afr.com/technology/fears-australia-will-be-left-behind-with-minimal-ai-spending-20190116-h1a4oo Accessed 28 July 2020.

Serengil, S.I., & Ozpinar, A. (2019). *ATM cash flow prediction and replenishment optimization with ANN*. Uluslararası Muhendislik Arastirma ve Gelistirme Dergisi (pp. 402–408).

Shilts, J. (2017). A framework for continuous auditing: Why companies don't need to spend big money. *Journal of Accountancy, 223*, 1–7.

Sigrist, F., & Hirnschall, C. (2019). Grabit: Gradient tree-boosted Tobit models for default prediction. *Journal of Banking and Finance, 102*, 177–192.

Smith, E. (2019a). Artificial intelligence could be worth $315b. *The Australian Financial Review*, p. 5. 15 November 2020. Fairfax Media Sydney.

Smith, E. (2019b). AI road map pitches $315b industry. *Financial Review*. The Nine Group. Sydney. https://www.afr.com/technology/ai-roadmap-forecasts-315b-industry-20191114-p53ali#:~:text=The%20report%20kicks%20off%20with,which%20found%20AI%20could%20be Accessed 28 July 2020.

Soviany, C. (2018). The benefits of using artificial intelligence in payment fraud detection: A case study. *Journal of Payments Strategy & Systems, 12*(2), 102–110.

Susskind, D. (2020). *A world without work*. London: Penguin Books Ltd.

Thomson, J. (2019). Industry Report K6322 General Insurance in Australia. IBISWorld Melbourne.

WEF. (2016). *The future of jobs: Employment, skills and workforce strategy for the fourth industrial revolution*. http://www3.weforum.org/docs/WEF_Future_of_Jobs.pdf Accessed 16 July 2020.

Wirtz, J., Patterson, P. G., Kunz, W. H., Gruber, T., Lu, V. N., Paluch, S., & Martins, A. (2018). Brave new world: Service robots in the frontline. *Journal of Service Management, 29*, 907–931.

Wu, T. (2020). Industry Report K6200 Finance in Australia. IBISWorld Melbourne.

Zhang, D., Xu, W., Zhu, Y., & Zhang, X. (2015). Can sentiment analysis help mimic decision-making process of loan granting? A novel credit risk evaluation approach using GMKL model. In: *Proceedings of the Annual Hawaii International Conference on System Sciences*. (pp. 949–958).

Ziffer, D. (2018, February 18). NAB workers latest to fall as automation transforms the economy. *ABC News, The Business*. http://www.abc.net.au/news/2018-02-21/nab-robots-taking-over-white-collar-jobs/9465524 Accessed 30 July 2020

Ziffer, D. (2019, June 27). Bank jobs shed as big four slim down amid tech spending and automation. *New Daily. Finance News*. New Daily Melbourne https://thenewdaily.com.au/finance/finance-news/2019/06/27/banks-big-four-smaller/ Accessed 3 Sept 2020.

Chapter 9
Local Government

Wajeeha Shaikh and John Burgess

Abstract The Australian public sector incorporates federal, state, and local government agencies. It is one of the largest employment sectors in the economy incorporating a range of occupations. Technology is key to the development of many sections of the public sector, for example the defence sector is driven by technological developments in hardware and systems. Given the range and coverage of the public sector, this chapter will examine AI and technological developments only in local government. The public sector is too large and diverse to capture in a single chapter, and while local government is immediate and spread across the country, it is under researched when compared to state and federal government. As with all areas of the public sector, local government has been subject to the reforms and pressures of new public sector management to improve service delivery and achieve cost reductions and efficiencies. These changes have also been associated with a range of organisational developments such as privatisation, public-private partnerships, and shared services. Information technology (IT) and automation have the potential to support both the quality and efficiency objectives of local government. However, there are challenges around the impact of the structural and technological change on employment, especially in regions; issues include the COVID impact on finances and the demand for services as well as skills development in the sector.

Keywords COVID19 · Local government · Managerialism · New public sector management · Outsourcing · Public goods · Shared services · Structural reforms

W. Shaikh
RMIT University, Melbourne, Australia
e-mail: wajeeha.shaik@rmit.edu.au

J. Burgess (✉)
Torrens University, Adelaide, SA, Australia
e-mail: john.burgess@torrens.edu.au

A. Nankervis et al. (eds.), *The Fourth Industrial Revolution*,
https://doi.org/10.1007/978-981-16-1614-3_9

Introduction

Local government in Australia represents the third tier of government after Federal and State government. It is responsible for local services and provides community and business services. There are over five hundred local councils across Australia that vary in terms of their budgets, size, responsibilities, and functions. In Western Australia, the size of local councils ranges from less than 2 square kilometres in Peppermint Grove, Perth, to over a hundred thousand square kilometres in the North West of the state around the Pilbara region. The long-term trend has been towards fewer and larger councils. In 1910 there were over a thousand local councils in Australia but now the number is around half that (Australian Services Union (ASU) 2016). According to the Australian Local Government Association (ALGA 2017), total employment in the sector is around 190,000 and it manages non-financial assets valued at over $400 billion. There are around 6600 elected councillors who are responsible for the funding, planning, organising, and assessment of services (ASU 2016). The labelling and classification of local governments varies across the states – varying from shires; boroughs; cities; councils and municipalities; and include indigenous local governments in Queensland, the Northern Territory, and South Australia. There is no local government in the Australian Capital Territory, and across the states there are areas that are without local government representation, either because they are too large and sparsely populated, such as Western NSW; or too small and remote, such as Lord Howe Island off the coast of NSW. These special areas, including ski resorts in Victoria, are directly administered by state governments.

Industry Overview

Local government is not recognised in the Australian Constitution and it has a perennial funding problem in that it has only one principal income source (property rates) and it is dependent on these together with grants from Federal and State governments (Dollery et al. 2006). There are also fees, charges, and fines that contribute a small share of local government revenue. Figs. 9.1 and 9.2 below show a sample breakdown of income and expenditure sources for local councils, in this case derived from Hornsby Council. a northern suburbs council in Sydney.

The Australian Local Government Association (ALGA 2018b: 6) identified the services offered by local government which include:

- infrastructure and property services, including local roads, bridges, footpaths, drainage, waste
- collection and management
- provision of recreation facilities, such as parks, sports fields and stadiums, golf courses, swimming
- pools, sport centres, halls, camping grounds and caravan parks

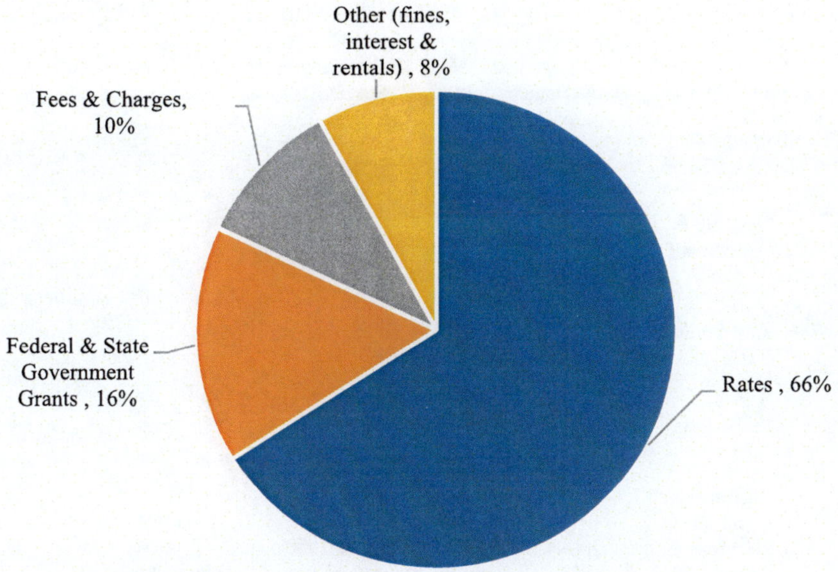

Fig. 9.1 Sample Council Income Sources

- health services such as water and food inspection, immunisation services, toilet facilities, noise
- control and meat inspection and animal control
- community services, such as childcare, aged care and accommodation, community care and welfare services
- building services, including inspections, licensing, certification, and enforcement
- planning and development approval
- administration of facilities, such as airports and aerodromes, ports and marinas, cemeteries, parking facilities and street parking
- cultural facilities and services, such as libraries, art galleries and museums
- water and sewerage services in some states
- other services, such as abattoirs, sale-yards and group purchasing schemes

There is no "typical" local council as the conditions governing operations vary across States and across regions. The ALGA (2018b) in a submission on regional inequality noted the gaps in financial capacity and infrastructure access between capital cities, and rural and regional cities. Given the dependence on local rate income, in capital cities with urban consolidation (high-rise and apartments) and increases in land values, the financial capacity of those councils improved. This was not the case in areas outside of the capital cities, especially in rural and remote regions. In its 2018/19 Federal budget submission the ALGA (2017) noted the increase in responsibilities and funding associated with disaster mitigation, recreational activities, health and well-being, environmental risk management, and climate change.

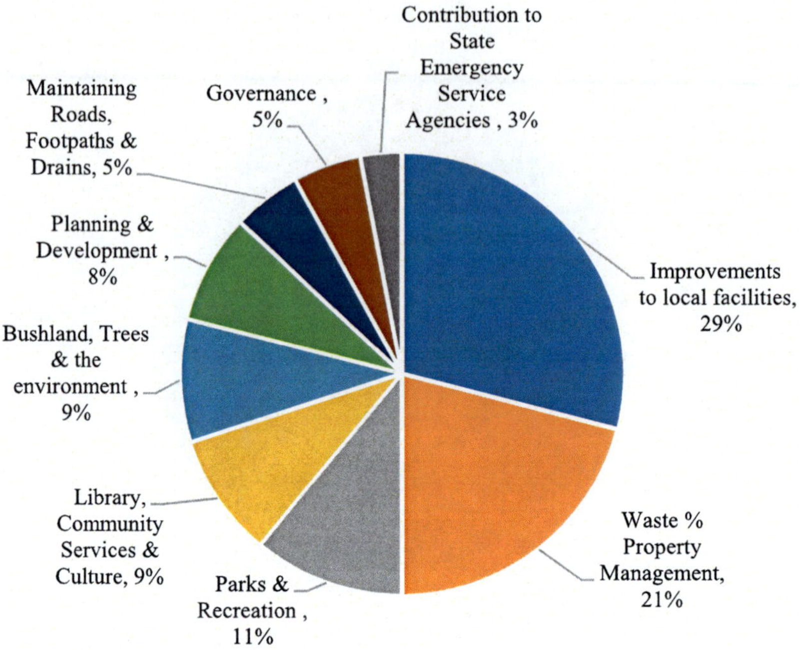

Fig. 9.2 Sample Expenditures
(Source: Hornsby Council 2019)
(Note that Hornsby is not considered to be representative, given the diversity across local government)

Local governments are controlled by State legislation and are required to comply with legislation regarding their operations. The size and boundaries of local government are determined by state governments, and council representatives are locally elected for a fixed term, but they can be dismissed by State governments and replaced by administrators. Local government provides services that are essential, and collective in nature, and many services are not priced by the market. Over the past century, the range of services provided by local government have changed from local infrastructure, property services, and utilities (roads, parks, footpaths, lighting, electricity, gas, water, and sewerage), towards community and business services. Utilities have been privatised by state governments and local governments have taken on services such as childcare, parking, environmental regulation, water safety, building and planning codes, and community centres (Dollery et al. 2006). There is a trend towards shared services to improve effectiveness and reduce costs (Dollery et al. 2016), and towards the delivery of services previously delivered by state governments (ASU 2016). Services associated with state and Federal governments are shared with, or delivered by, local government such as roads maintenance, disaster management, and environmental regulation.

The ALGA (2017, 8) stated that:

'Local governments are responsible for the streetscape, the operating environment for the cafes, restaurants and local business across municipalities. They provide individuals and families with access to public libraries, internet cafes, art galleries, museums, men's sheds, community halls, sports grounds, parks and gardens, showgrounds, individual properties, and local businesses. Councils manage municipal waste, provide local roads, run local airports and aerodromes in rural communities and sustain transport links for passengers and freight. They manage stormwater services, and in some states, councils provide and manage access to clean drinking water and waste water services. In short, they manage the cities and towns in which people live and work and the well-being of local communities'.

The services provided are intangible, and often do not enter the market, but are essential for the functioning of the community and organisations from schools and places of worship through to sporting organisations and businesses. While there is a natural monopoly with regard to many of the provided services, they are provided on a mixture of payment for service (planning permissions) incorporated into rates (such as garbage collection), or are available to all users without payment (such as gardens, parks, libraries). Other services, such as road maintenance and water management, indirectly support businesses and the community. Providing a combination of marketable and non-marketable services, and inputs that are essential to local businesses and communities.

Over the past hundred years the reduction in councils has, in part, been driven by consolidation forced by state governments, especially in Victoria. This has largely occurred based on economies of scale arguments that suggest that larger councils have lower unit costs of service delivery than smaller councils (Worthington and Dollery 2002).

However, the evidence on scale economies in local government is mixed, with Dollery et al. (2016) suggesting that service sharing without the amalgamation of councils is a more effective model for cost reductions. The other obstacle to amalgamations has been local opposition by the community on the grounds that imposed amalgamations compromise local democracy and the quality of services, and in some cases there is evidence of diseconomies of scale as the amalgamated councils become too large to effectively deliver services and reduce unit costs (Drew and Kortt 2015).

Public sector management principles have been influential in driving the legislative and structural reforms in local government since the 1970s (Parker and Guthrie 1993). These changes have encompassed contracting out; shared services; privatisation; public private partnerships; forced amalgamations; extensive governance and reporting requirements linked to performance indicators; and workplace/IR changes (Worthington and Dollery 2002). Local governments are regulated by state government legislation and are forced to operate within a legislative framework set by state governments. The state governments have control over the main income source, local rates, with (for example, in NSW and South Australia) the increase in rates pegged by the state government. Likewise, control over State and Federal grants to local government means that this source of funding is often dependent on the electoral cycle, government budget priorities, and whether the council is in a marginal electoral seat. Each local government submits an annual report to the state government that addresses key performance criteria in keeping with the new public sector and managerialist agenda. Occasionally, state governments dismiss local assemblies and replace them with administrators for a defined period. In 2020 the NSW state government dismissed the Balranald Shire Council on the grounds that it had "failed to act as a reasonable employer with valuable staff having to quit because of the work environment" (ABC News 2020).

To examine the impact of technological change on local government it is important to be cognisant of the differences across local governments in terms of financial, skills, and technological capacity; their limited financial base, the range of services offered, the public goods component of these operations, the controls and reporting requirements imposed by State governments, and the large number of different occupations that contribute to the delivery of local government services. Next, the discussion will examine employment, occupations, and skill sets for the sector, followed by an analysis of the impact of developments in ICT and robotics for the sector; a brief outline of several case studies that address technological developments in the sector; and emerging challenges for the sector are identified.

Jobs, Occupations, and Skills in Local Government

The ALGA (2018b) estimates that there are around 190 thousand employees across the sector. There are also private sector jobs that are linked to the provision of local government services from road maintenance and parks maintenance, to the use of call centres and consultants. As a result, the local government employment headcount by direct employees excludes those who are employed by the public sector in contracting skilled, semi-skilled, and unskilled services. The important employment feature of local government is that it is a major employer and a key source of professional employment (direct and indirect) in regions that have limited direct public sector representation (state and federal) and limited large corporate presence. Federal and State governments, and large corporations, all tend to concentrate employment, especially professional and highly skilled employment, in capital cities.

The main source of data on LG employment can be found in the annual reports by the relevant State government departments. In Queensland, the state government/local government annual report provides a workforce division by outdoor and indoor staff. The outdoor staff work on roads, footpaths, traffic conditions, gardens, parks, bushland, the environment, and public order. The indoor staff include administration, clerical, library services, customer services, legal and governance, community services and planning. Within the broad division there is a range of occupations and skills from labourers through to engineers, IT support, architecture, town planning and legal services. The distribution of indoor and outdoor staff is not standard, nor is the distribution of skills and occupations. From the Queensland annual report on local government, the emerging staff distribution indicates that the smaller the council (in terms of staff numbers) and the more remote it is in terms of distance from capital cities, the greater the share of outdoor staff (Queensland Government 2019). For example, Goondawindi, McKinlay Shire and Lockhart River Aboriginal Shire Council have relatively large outdoor staff numbers compared to indoor staff. For large urban councils, such as Brisbane City and the Gold Coast, the share of indoor staff exceeds that of outdoor staff, and the range of services provided is more extensive with both these councils responsible for managing large public sector transport networks.

The ALGA (2018b) report on skills for the sector reported that, within local government, there were over 390 occupations. Those occupations with over 5000 staff nationally included: specialist managers; engineering, ICT, and science technologist; childcare workers; community service workers; clerical and administrative workers; road and rail drivers; design, engineering, and transport professionals; animal and horticultural workers; office and administration managers; business, HRM, and marketing professionals. Over the period 2006–2016 the largest increase in percentage terms in occupational employment included specialist managers; education professionals; electrotechnology and telecommunication trades; and machine operators and drivers. The occupations with declining employment numbers included cleaners and laundry workers; construction, mining, and other labourers; mobile plant operators; and farm, forestry, and garden workers. Some of these changes may reflect contracting out, shared services, and privatisation, rather than technological displacement. The report identified the key drivers of the shifting occupational composition in local government which included: changes to Legislation/Acts; increasing levels of governance, compliance and integrated reporting requirements; increased devolution of services from state to local government; changes in the scope and level of services delivered; population growth; population demographics – ageing population; and changes in technology (ALGA 2018b).

In terms of the technological displacement of workers through technology, the report (ALGA 2018b: 28) suggested that; 'Occupations such as General Clerical Clerks, Numerical Clerks, Other Clerical and Administrative Workers, Inquiry Clerks and Receptionists are expected to disappear with the impact of technology advances and digitization. These are often areas of high female participation and where employment numbers have grown significantly between 2006 and 2016'.

Key Technologies

As the local government sector encompasses a range of occupations and professions and a range of services and functions, it also encompasses all technologies that impact on other industries. However, there are three important differences to consider when evaluating the impact of technology on the sector. The first is that the capacity of the sector to embrace technologies is uneven. Remote and rural councils are limited by their skills and professional capacity, in their financial capability, and by their infrastructure, especially in terms of internet access. Overall, the sector is constrained in its financial capacity. Second, the sector provides public goods that are not priced by the market and they must meet legislative standards imposed by state governments regarding service provision and the quality of services. Third, they are subject to legislative and voter controls and sanctions that mean that choices are constrained.

To highlight the importance of inequalities in capacity and infrastructure across regions the ALGA (2018a: 3) submission to the Senate Reference Committee on Regional Inequalities noted that:

'Experiences cited by the local government sector demonstrating unequal access and/or outcomes in non-metropolitan areas included transport and health, plus:

- access to basic infrastructure such as reasonable road access, clean water supplies and wastewater services, digital technology and telecommunication services, and housing, including housing for employees in remote localities providing social and essential services to the community; and
- declining intellectual capital to support local workforce skills needs, particularly in transforming employment markets'

Employment Impacts

As with other sectors, those occupations that are non-cognitive and routine are subject to replacement through automation and digital technology (Aldeney 2018). The ALGA (2018b) and ASU (2016) identified clerical and administrative positions as most likely to be replaced by technology. The process may be direct or indirect, through outsourcing and contracting out. Automation and digital technology can also support many LG functions such as monitoring the environment; planning and development; parking; the maintenance of parks and gardens; customer feedback; the payment of bills; financial reporting; governance; reporting to State governments; and the maintenance of roads, footpaths, and parks. Technologies including drones; solar energy cells; sensors; satellite technology and cloud computing can support asset management and maintenance; water management; planning and construction management; flood and fire mitigation; traffic management; and improve service delivery.

The following section identifies some of the technologies, the opportunities for implementation, and the challenges for local governments.

Case Studies in Local Government & Employment Impacts

Australian Local Government Association Report Local Government Workforce and Future Skills Report Australia (ALGA 2018b)

The ALGA (2018b) surveyed councils across Australia to identify areas of current and prospective skill shortages. Across all local governments, and across three classifications of local government (rural and rural remote; urban and urban fringe; and urban, regional cities) the major shortages were in the professions – engineers; middle managers; town planners and surveyors. The main challenges faced in recruiting professional staff included the inability to compete with the private sector for remuneration; limited local talent available; remoteness and lack of facilities and infrastructure, for those councils in rural areas; and lack of career progression, especially in small councils.

Many councils reported a skills gap and the difficulties of providing access to training programs to address the skills gap. The constraints included lack of courses and training providers locally, the absence of suitable online programs, the costs associated with attending training programs in capital cities, changing legislative requirements that generate demand for new skills, and the difficulty of freeing up staff to participate in training programs.

In terms of those factors that will impinge on future training needs, the major conditions identified by the survey were changes in external funding from state and federal government, local infrastructure projects, an ageing workforce and community, changes in state government legislation, and technological change and digitisation. Although technological change and digitisation was identified as a factor impacting on future skill needs, 70% of councils reported that they had not conducted an analysis of the likely impact on jobs and skill requirements (ALGA 2018b: 56).

Of those councils that had considered the impact of technological change, the major developments included the application of drones, cloud computing, mobile devices, GPS and mapping, social media platforms, data analytics, and remote working. The technologies have potential application across all council functions and are likely to displace labour, generate the demand for new skills and jobs, augment existing jobs, and change work and workplaces. The key challenge identified in the report is for local governments to develop soft skills within its workforce to accommodate the demands of technological change. The report suggested that, in terms of soft skills development that local governments should address:

> Ability to work productively, drive engagement, and demonstrate presence as a member of a virtual team; novel and adaptive thinking; and the ability to understand concepts across multiple disciplines. In order to address these emerging skills gaps, local governments will be mainly looking to upskill existing staff. To a lesser extent they will look to use shared service arrangements to address these gaps, particularly in the Digital Skills area. (ALGA 2018b: 60)

2016 Federal Government Smart Cities Program

The Smart Cities Program (Australian Government 2016) developed by the Federal Government provides competitive funding for developing infrastructure and deploying technological solutions to support the future development of Australian cities. Under the program, local governments have the opportunity to partner with other organisations, such as universities, to apply for funding for programs that seek to achieve the program objectives in three areas: infrastructure; governance; and technology. On technology, the purpose of the program was to: "embrace new technology with the potential to revolutionise how cities are planned, function, and how our economy grows. Disruptive new technology in transport, communications and energy efficiency are becoming a reality—we will position our cities to take full advantage. We will leverage real time open data driven solutions and support investment in sectors commercialising new innovations to grow Australia's economy." (Australian Government 2016: 4).

The Round 2 programs selected for funding included:

- City of Parramatta Council, NSW – Melrose Park: Smart planning for Climate Responsive Neighbourhoods, $571,000
- Wollondilly Shire Council, NSW, Western Sydney Parkland City Sensor Network Project,
- $700,000
- Logan City Council, Queensland, Flooded Roads Smart Warning System, $250,000
- Cairns Regional Council, Queensland, Smart Urban Irrigation Project, $250,000
- Launceston City Council, Tasmania, Greater Launceston Transformation -Creating our Digital Future,
- $2,904,775
- Mornington Peninsula Shire Council, Victoria, Mornington Peninsula Smart Parking and Amenities for High Demand Areas, $500,000

Technology, jobs, and lifestyle are central to the Smart Cities Program. However, the program has limited funding, the grants are one off, and many of the grants are awarded to councils in capital cities that already benefit from large infrastructure investment by state and federal government.

Australian Services Union Submission to the Human Rights Commission Inquiry into Artificial Intelligence (2019)

The ASU is the union that represents employees in local government. The ASU (2019) submission to the Human Rights Commission Inquiry into Artificial Intelligence set out several key principles associated with what it called a "just transition" to digitalisation and automation of service jobs, including those in local government.

'Just Transition policy framework should address the uncertainties regarding job impacts, risks of job losses, of undemocratic decision-making processes and of lowering rights at work, as well as of regional or local economic downturn, among others. Key principles of a Just Transition should include:

- Research and early assessment of social and employment impacts
- Social dialogue and democratic consultation of social partners and stakeholders
- Active labour market policies and regulation, including training and skills development
- Social protection, including securing of pensions
- Community renewal and economic diversification plans
- Sound investments leading to high quality, decent jobs'

The adjustment and transition process following technological transformation is important for local government since in many regions there are few alternative employment opportunities. The twin effects of unemployment and the degradation of employment conditions will adversely impact local economies and further encourage the concentration of skilled jobs in capital cities. The submission identified the challenges associated with technological change for the sector including local job loss, the growth in insecure employment, and the skill and training requirements for preparing the workforce to apply new technologies to the range of occupations found across local government.

Local Government Libraries

Technology is used to extend and transform service delivery, and at the same time it is utilised to monitor and measure staff and library performance. Local government public libraries are offered as free services to the community and they are expected as part of the service delivered to the local community (Wyatt et al. 2018). The public library sector in Australia operates in the form of branches; mobile libraries; online and outreach services (Leorke and Wyatt 2018). Public access to libraries was not free until 2008 with every council providing free access to the community to access library services (Bundy 2012). According to Mansell (2002), public libraries mediate between the community and the state. Public libraries have undergone organisational transformation from that of book repositories and lending, towards meeting local community functions such as meeting and information services, online access and service delivery, and providing services for targeted groups such as children and retirees (ALGA 2018a). Libraries have moved beyond storing and providing access to physical book collections as libraries are responsible for meeting the information, educational, cultural and recreational needs of the community members and offer variety of services including extensive collection of books, magazines, CDs, DVDs, audio-books, eBooks, electronic sources of information, meeting rooms, and recreational materials. Australian public libraries provide digital access to communities by providing static PCs and free Wi-Fi in branches; programs for all age groups including early childhood literacy, cultural activities, job seeking skills, workforce development and opportunities for lifelong learning (PLV 2018). Library services have been digitalised; can be linked to other regional, state, and national collections; and offer the opportunities for shared services.

Technology has supported the extension of library services within local communities and at the same time the function of libraries has expanded. NPSM principles have resulted in libraries and staff being monitored for performance, and the system of metrics is supported by ICT systems. For example, in Victoria public libraries reporting metrics include the number of service points, opening hours, staff numbers, registered users, loans made, the number of reference enquiries, the number of items in collection/acquisition, the number of public access PCs and all data on usage (Rosenfeldt 2006). The Victorian Public libraries routinely collect performance information that is machine generated and include data on membership numbers, holdings, number of visitors, website traffic, usage rates of PCs, program attendance, and circulation activities (PLV 2018). In order to justify their services, public libraries conduct customer satisfaction surveys to measure the impact of their services on communities (Schwirtlich 2010).

Challenges & Opportunities

The ethical challenges around data storage, surveillance systems, data sharing, and automated decision making in the delivery of public services embodies many ethical challenges. The limits and dangers of using automated systems to deliver public services was demonstrated by the infamous "Robodebt" saga (Hayne and Doran 2020). The Robodebt system demonstrated that using AI to make decisions in the administration of welfare was profoundly flawed as it was based on an incomplete data set, was not subject to close supervision, and decisions were automated and not subject to an independent evaluation.

The Robodebt crisis highlights the ethical and regulatory challenges associated with the deployment of AI in the delivery of public services, not just by the Federal government, but by all tiers of government where automated processes are applied for decision making. The potential areas impacted include: rate evaluations, billing and charges for local services, planning approval processes, disaster mitigation, and environmental assessments. Local government will increase the application of IT systems for service delivery and evaluation. However, behind the use of data systems there are major ethical issues that all tiers of government must carefully consider as more services are being bundled and moved to online delivery. The UK Committee on Standards in Public Life (2020: 6), commented that:

'Artificial intelligence has the potential to revolutionise the delivery of public services, creating an opportunity for more innovative and efficient public service delivery. Machine learning in particular will transform the way decisions are made in areas as diverse as policing, health, welfare, transport, social care, and education'.

The other challenge facing local government will be to accommodate the consequences of COVID19. Since local government delivers local services of a public goods nature, the demand for services will be unaffected by the pandemic. However, the financial capacity to deliver services will be tested. The main income source (rates) will be affected by a downturn in the property market in both the commercial and residential sectors across Australia (Business Insider Australia 2020). Transfers from state and federal governments are also likely to be reduced as the fiscal positions of both levels of government decline for the duration of the pandemic. For local government, the likelihood is that the demand will be to meet its service obligations with reduced revenue. This will support further outsourcing and reductions in employment, and encourage shared services, automation, and multi-tasking of staff. However, there are two challenges to further streamlining of service delivery, especially through IT, that have been noted. First, IT infrastructure is unevenly distributed across the regions. Second, there are skill shortages and difficulties in upskilling staff in remote and regional areas.

Conclusion

Technological applications will be employed in local government for service delivery, cost reductions and efficiencies, and for meeting the various reporting requirements imposed by state governments. As with other industry sectors discussed in this book there is the potential for technological displacement of routine service work and the augmentation of professional work. Ongoing structural changes imposed by state governments and the financial pressures linked to falling property prices will further put pressure on governments to seek technological solutions to reduce costs but maintain services. Within the sector, and before COVID, there were funding challenges linked to the dependence on grants from other tiers of government (ALGA 2017). However, there are limits to the application of technological solutions to structural and financial pressures. First, public services and goods must be provided and of a specified quality under the various state government regulations. Second, the reach of ITC supporting infrastructure is not even across the nation, with local governments in rural and remote regions at a disadvantage. Third, and associated with remoteness, there are skills shortages in non-metropolitan regions and there are challenges in developing skills in existing workforces. Finally, local government occupation and skill profiles are uneven across regions, and the scope for uniform IT and AI solutions is limited since many tasks remain labour intensive and individualised – such as water safety, health inspections and childcare services.

References

Aldeney, R. (2018). *Structural change in the Australian economy*. Reserve Bank of Australia Bulletin. March, 1–18.

ALGA. (2017). ALGA submission to the 2018/2019 Federal Budget. *Invest in Australian Communities, Make it Local*. ALGA.

Australian Local Government Association (ALGA 2018a). *Submission to the senate economics references committee in response to the inquiry into the indicators of, and impact of, regional inequality in Australia*. ALGA.

ALGA. (2018b). *Local government workforce and future skills report Australia*. ALGA.

ASU. (2016). *Our local: A history of local government services and building community resilience*. Carlton: ASU.

ASU. (2019). *Submission to the Senate ASU Submission to Senate Standing Committees Jobs for the Future in Regional Areas, Submission 152*. Carlton: ASU.

Australian Broadcasting Commission (ABC News, 2020). *Balranald Shire Council sacked after NSW Government inquiry hands down report*. Jan 31. https://www.abc.net.au/news/2020-01-31/nsw-balranald-council-placed-under-administration-after-inquiry/11912656

Australian Government. (2016). *Smart cities plan*. Canberra: Department of Prime Minister and Cabinet.

Australian Services Union (ASU 2019). *Submission to the Australian human rights commission inquiry into artificial intelligence*. Carlton: ASU.

Bundy, A. (2012). Better, more accessible, libraries for all in Australia: Progress and potential. *Australasian Public Libraries and Information Services, 25*(3), 138–144.

Business Insider Australia. (2020). *Australian property prices are in freefall, as the coronavirus puts last year's recovery into reverse gear*. https://www.businessinsider.com.au/australian-property-prices-falling-covid19-2020-7

Committee on Standards in Public Life. (2020). *Artificial intelligence and public standards: A review by the committee on standards in public life*. London: UK Government.

Dollery, B., Crase, L., & Byrnes, J. (2006). Local government failure: Why does Australian local government experience permanent financial austerity? *Australian Journal of Political Science, 41*(3), 339–353.

Dollery, B., Kortt, M., & Drew, J. (2016). Fostering shared Services in Local Government: A common service model. *Australasian Journal of Regional Studies, 22*(2), 225–242.

Drew, J., & Kortt, M. (2015). No Aladdin's cave in New South Wales? Local government amalgamation, scale economies, and data envelopment analysis specification. *Administration & Society, 1*(21), 1450–1470.

Hayne, J., & Doran, M. (2020). Government to pay back $721m as it scraps Robodebt for Centrelink welfare recipients. *ABC News*, May 29. https://www.abc.net.au/news/2020-05-29/federal-government-refund-robodebt-scheme-repay-debts/12299410

Hornsby Council. (2019). *Annual Report, 2018/2019*. https://www.hornsby.nsw.gov.au/__data/assets/pdf_file/0011/144587/HSC5185-Annual-Report-2018-19.pdf

Leorke, D., & Wyatt, D. (2018). *Public libraries in the smart city*. Singapore: Springer.

Mansell, R. (2002). From digital divides to digital entitlements in knowledge societies. *Current sociology, 50*(3), 407–426.

Parker, L., & Guthrie, J. (1993). The Australian public sector in the 1990s: New accountability regimes in motion. *Journal of International Accounting Auditing & Taxation, 2*(1), 59–81.

PLV (Public Libraries Victoria). (2018). *Victorian Public Library Directory 2017*. https://docs.wixstatic.com/ugd/1f8737_3c280360c9cf4900bf7d65d94d0a3ab2.pdf

Queensland Government. (2019). *Local government personnel data*. Brisbane: Department of Local Government, Racing and Multicultural Affairs.

Rosenfeldt, D. (2006). *Libraries building communities. Performance measurement and metrics*.

Schwirtlich, A. M. (2010). Public libraries and change: A perspective from Victoria. *Australasian Public Libraries and Information Services, 23*(1), 22–27.

Worthington, A., & Dollery, B. (2002). An analysis of recent trends in Australian local government. *International Journal of Public Sector Management, 15*(6), 496–515.

Wyatt, D., Mcquire, S., & Butt, D. (2018). Libraries as redistributive technology: From capacity to culture in Queensland's public library network. *New Media & Society, 20*(8), 2934–2953.

Chapter 10
Higher Education

Julia Connell and Ashish Malik

Abstract This chapter seeks to explore the impact and influence of the fourth industrial revolution (4IR) and artificial intelligence applications on the Australian Higher Education (HE) sector. Specifically, it explores the real and potential impact of new technologies and their anticipated effects on the sector, its educators, and students. The aim is to provide a broad understanding of the potential challenges and changes within the context of the recent coronavirus global pandemic. Many factors in the higher education system, particularly with the increasing costs of tuition, imply that the higher education sector "is ripe for disruption", and the coronavirus crisis may just have provided that much-needed disruption.

As if one significant wave of technological disruption and restructuring of employment caused by the 4IR was not enough, the world was hit by COVID-19, a global health pandemic bringing economies to a grinding halt. The challenges for the Australian and global higher education sector from early 2020 due to both the technological and health crises form the focus of this chapter. Therefore, the chapter begins by providing a brief background of how 4IR and artificial intelligence (AI) has affected the HE sector in Australia. Next, we analyse the impacts of the significant external changes on the sector, present a review of how the sector has responded, and where the future challenges lie.

Keywords 4IR, artificial intelligence · Ethics · Higher education · Teaching and learning

J. Connell (✉) · A. Malik
Newcastle Business School, College of Human and Social Futures, University of Newcastle, Newcastle, NSW, Australia
e-mail: julia.connell@newcastle.edu.au; Ashish.malik@newcastle.edu.au

A. Nankervis et al. (eds.), *The Fourth Industrial Revolution*,
https://doi.org/10.1007/978-981-16-1614-3_10

Introduction

There are 43 universities in Australia – (40 Australian universities, two international universities, and one private speciality university) undertaking teaching and research (Universities Australia 2020). Along with the 43 universities, there are around 127 other higher education providers offering higher education courses, with the latter unlikely to conduct research (ibid)). Australian universities employ over 130,000 people in academic and professional roles. In regional areas, universities are significant employers and support over 14,000 jobs (Universities Australia 2020). Some staff specialise in teaching or research, while many combine both. Higher education providers have the legal power to issue qualifications, ranging from a diploma to a doctorate. Although AI is, or will most likely impact almost every discipline in some way the disciplines reported in a meta-analysis of AIEd papers were from Computer Science and STEM (Zawacki-Richter et al. 2019). All Australian providers must be registered with the Tertiary Education Quality and Standards Agency (TEQSA). TEQSA ensures that institutions meet conditions set by government – this requires 'supporting free intellectual inquiry; offering teaching and learning that engages with advanced knowledge and inquiry; employing academic staff who are active in scholarship; and issuing qualifications that comply with the Australian Qualifications Framework (AQF)', (Norton and Cherastidtham 2018: 9). AI-enabled education and faster models for competency development are emerging with the algorithmic design of workflow and an increasing number of applications in teaching (Shalini and Tewari 2020) and research.

While the skills that 4IR and AI technologies require are necessarily interdisciplinary, there is also an extensive reliance on individual skills, such as data fluency and digital competence as well as skills needed to undertake the analysis of big data and use of complex computerised algorithms. AI is already being used to enhance productivity in HE, as well as to create new knowledge at a much faster pace. The Grattan Report *Mapping Australian Higher Education 2018* shows that in 2016 a record 41% of Australian 19-year-olds were enrolled in higher education institutions (Norton and Cherastidtham 2018). In addition, Australian higher education institutions have become increasingly international with overseas student enrolments/fees proving to be the single most significant source of university revenue – a factor which has proved to be highly problematic in 2020 due to the COVID-19 pandemic. We provide below an overview of how the changes and implications these disruptive technologies have in reshaping HE in Australia, and globally.

IT Infrastructure Improvements for Online Education

Face-to-face teaching results in all students receiving the same delivery; however, the move to online teaching and learning, which was accelerated further by Covid-19, has meant that some students have struggled to access stable Wi-Fi connections to continue with their educational needs. Ghaffar and Hussain (2019), for example, proposed a system to support verification of HE students' enrolment data using blockchain technology. Nonetheless, online education can exacerbate the digital divide with wealthy students possessing the latest laptops, enhanced bandwidths, stable WIFI connections and more sophisticated audio-visual tools; hence several hardware and software issues need to be addressed before remote learning can be considered adequate and digital inequalities be addressed (Govindarajan and Srivastava 2020).

Online Courses Need Educational Support

Govindarajan and Srivastava (2020) question what training is required for lecturers, designers, trainers, and coaches to support student learning and course completion, and facilitate changes in mindsets and behaviours. The speed with which the move to online learning took place in Australia following the Covid-19 lockdown meant that many academic staff moved their usual teaching materials to platforms such as Zoom or Collaborate, while their teaching style may have failed to take the virtual environment into account. Moreover, these platforms have their limitations when academics have attempted to retain their usual teaching styles using a one-dimensional virtual mode. When reporting on her experiences moving to online teaching enabled by Zoom, Blum (2020) reflects that it is less than satisfactory, noting 'there is constant need to repair, to apologise. People are constantly talking at the same time and interrupting someone else's signal'.

Students May Face Difficulties with Online Courses

Campolo (2019 webpage) proposes that the degree of adjustment required from an AI-enabled world both in Australia and globally may vary considerably, due to the degree of disruption which may either exacerbate or ameliorate present social and educational problems. Attention spans can be shorter, students may feel like they do not belong to a peer group/cohort, and they may also miss face-to-face interactions. Some experts predicted that the massive open online courses (MOOCs) would take over face-to-face education, but until now, it has not occurred (Govindarajan and Srivastava 2020).

4IR and Higher Education

The higher education (HE) sector has witnessed significant disruption caused by technological change with the onset of the 4IR. It is rapidly transforming itself, with the adoption of new technologies to improve reach, access, and experience, as well as driving speed and efficiency in the delivery of education and allied educational services (Gleason 2018a). The 4IR marks the advent of cyber-physical systems (Rajkumar et al. 2010), a set of physical and engineered communication and computing core applications that include, for example, multiple systems based on artificial intelligence (AI) and robotics. These systems will control how humans interact with technology, shaping current and future ways of working and thereby affecting the nature of work and work processes that will influence all walks of life, including HE. In the realm of HE research and practice, the term technology-enhanced learning (TEL) focuses on a combination of social and technological systems integration that leverages AI and data-driven technology. TEL is socially and contextually relevant and sensitive, integrating a range of cognitive and behavioural skills to deliver transformative education (Lytras et al. 2020). The disruptions caused in the technological domain can enable *just-in-time* educational delivery for learners, giving them the necessary cognitive flexibility while providing service providers with cognitive agility (Gleason 2018a). The current hierarchy of learning – progressively moving from simple and less complicated, rule-based instrumental learning through to sophisticated analytical, inter-and intra-personal communicative learning to paradigm changing, critical thinking and complex problem-solving transformative learning (Mezirow 1981, 1994) – is challenged through the ease and availability of metacognitions. The primacy of the learner is becoming ever more critical, as the ability of technology to personalise, hyper-personalise and individualise *just-in-time* educational experiences for learners becomes more accessible.

The support for managing these disruptive technological changes and transitions has to be backed by the dominant coalition of stakeholders, such as industry, the government, HE providers and the learners themselves. The Economist Intelligence Unit (EIU 2018) created the Automation Readiness Index (ARI) comprising three key components: the innovation environment; education policies; and labour market policies. The ARI indicates the relative ability of twenty five countries to develop and apply automated solutions, together with their ability to support the innovation process (through education), and translate it into programs that support workplace adjustment and upskilling, ranking the selected countries against these criteria. Ranked in the top three were: (i) South Korea; (ii) Germany and (iii) Singapore.

Singapore's triple program comprising the Smart Nation, Skills Future, and the establishment of three new universities illustrates Singapore's intentions regarding automation readiness through delivering and shaping the country's technological transformation in HE (Gleason 2018b). As Waring et al. (2018:138) explain:

> The aim of the program is to improve competitiveness by increasing the skills and productivity of the workforce: to develop a strong Singapore-core workforce; to incentivise busi-

nesses to 'go lean'; get more done with less by relying on automation, mechanisation and relying on technological solutions.

Overall, the challenge lies in leveraging the technological opportunities that the 4IR offers to HE which will depend on how well we can employ these new technologies to deliver transformative educational change and outcomes for the learners (Penprase 2018). For this chapter, we now focus on one such key technological trend – the use of AI in HE.

Key Technologies & Applications

Global Trends

Technology has become an indispensable part of every human life with many of the tasks we undertake every day utilising AI across a range of sectors (Jackson 2019). This is particularly the case in the education sector, where technology usage has been highly prominent in a range of disciplines (Luckin et al. 2016). For example, AI can assist with teaching, marking, record-keeping, providing one-to-one tutoring and personalised feedback to students (Dickson 2017). AI has been applied in medicine (Han et al. 2019); music (Holland 2000); mathematics (Gadanidis 2017) and English (Park 2018) education, and many more. The goal of AI in the education sector is to develop systems and AI educational (AIEd) tools that are flexible, inclusive, personalised, engaging, and effective, to support effective teaching and active learning (Luckin et al. 2016).

Different forms of AI have been used in the higher education sector over the past few decades. Applications have taken the form of:

(i) institutional support; marketing and recruiting, admissions and enrolment, curricula, and resource planning such as Intelligent Management Information Systems (iMIS) (Gama et al. 2016);
(ii) student support; guidance, financial aid, early warning – identifying students who may be at risk of failing (through learning management systems, e.g. Pence 2019) or dropping out, such as Ubiquitous e-Teaching and e-Learning (UTiLearn) system (Mehmood et al. 2017);
(iii) instructional support; through self-paced progress, personalised learning, and pedagogical improvement (Zeide 2019). Intelligent Computer-Assisted Instruction (ICAI) systems and Computer-Assisted Instruction (CAI) systems facilitate student learning, and Expert systems assist with educational diagnosis and assessment (Jones 1985). However, in the current turbulent environment, rapid advances are encouraging the introduction of different forms of AI in education, and particularly in the higher education sector (Luckin et al. 2016; Southgate et al. 2019) to facilitate teaching and enhance students' learning. This has included increased use of supercomputers, web-based learning, and educational robots in educational institutions (Adamson et al. 2014).

> Supercomputers have the power to provide interactional and communicative advice to students on almost any area including admissions, enrolment, tuition fees, accommodation, extra-curricular activities, health and safety, employment opportunities and other topics (Deakin University 2015). AI-powered systems such as Intelligent Tutoring Systems (ITS) and Virtual Pedagogical Agents help lecturers in reducing their workload and support active learning for students.

Making use of AI in the education sector has also provided educational institutions with the ability to be more cost-effective and efficient (Luckin et al. 2016). For example, AI-powered tools can result in quick responses and are available anytime and anywhere, with ease of access, such as via mobile phones. Furthermore, teachers and students can benefit from greater levels of personalisation, hyper-personalisation, and individualisation of their preferences through to the design and delivery of learning. The challenges lie, in common with any new technology adoption in upskilling and overcoming individual and institutional inertia, to embrace and fully leverage what new technology offers. Luckin et al. (2016) maintain that authors have difficulty in defining AI due to its continually shifting content and interdisciplinary features (Luckin et al. 2016). Despite the promise AIEd offers, it is still in its infancy – especially as educators need to develop foundational knowledge about AI and other emerging technologies in order to empower students to thrive in a technologically advanced world (Southgate et al. 2019). The HE sector is rapidly absorbing AI in different forms to facilitate teaching, student learning and the administrative tasks of universities (Popenici and Kerr 2017). AI can support work as a virtual chatbot for managing admissions (Jackson 2019) and perform other ancillary and functional tasks such as enhancing HE providers' recruitment practices through expanding searches and removing recruitment bias.

Machine learning can review a résumé, which reduces the burden on university staff when preparing for interviews (Jackson 2019). Moreover, integrated AIEd and Educational Data Mining (EDM) techniques are used by universities to track student behaviours as well as in assisting staff to track class attendance and monitor assignments monitoring, which in turn may improve student retention (Luckin et al. 2016). Applications in medical HE through digitalised health care systems, can enable future physicians to access a vast range of technologically supported resources (Han et al. 2019). The above suggests that, while 'Anytime Anywhere Education' is a reality now, the challenges of overcoming this paradigm change operates at several levels. Foremost amongst these is the individual and institutional inertia concerning the need to communicate the need for change, prepare and support new generations of learners. They need to be provided with the necessary new skills and supporting infrastructure to embed new ways of learning, education, and skills development.

Australian AI Applications

The Australian HE sector has shown a great deal of interest thus far in adopting AI; however, Barnett, the Managing Director of Pearson Australia (2017 webpage) maintains that educators must be central to the design of AIEd tools as 'the future of education will only be in the hands of educators if they embrace and master intelligent technologies'. Further, Southgate et al. (2019) suggest that there is a need for timely assessment regarding where learning with and about AI and emerging technologies can be accommodated within the Australian Curriculum – including the Digital Technologies Curriculum (Southgate et al. 2019).

An example of AIEd in Australian universities is at Deakin University where the Supercomputer IBM Watson was used for providing advice to students in the entire student engagement lifecycle (Deakin University 2015). Watson is a ground-breaking cognitive computing platform that helps to enhance student learning while transforming advisory platforms. Many Australian EdTech companies have used academic research findings to underpin the design and development of their products, and likewise many Australian universities are creating/adopting technologically advanced products and systems to support teaching, learning and administration. A summary is outlined in Table 10.1 below:

Models of AIEd in Specific HE Functions

Pedagogy/Andragogy

The use of AIEd systems involves three models: the pedagogical model; the domain model and the learner model as outlined in Table 10.2. The pedagogical model represents the knowledge and expertise of teaching and effective approaches to teaching. For example, this model consists of knowledge of assessment and feedback provided to students in order to improve their learning. The domain model represents knowledge of the subject being learned, and the learner model represents knowledge of the learner. Virtual Pedagogical Agents can now operate as lecturers or even as student peers (Luckin et al. 2016). Through contemporary AI platforms that use machine learning techniques, self-training algorithms can enable lecturers to decide what content needs to be provided to students and when (Luckin et al. 2016).

According to Luckin et al. (2016:25), a modern, adaptive system is one that is flexible and requires multiple AIEd tools in its architecture. Such a system would include tools such as deep learning and neural networks for developing the knowledge of learners' cognitive and affective states. Additionally, by engaging the learners using Socratic learning principles, the system can learn and deploy discussion-based questioning and answering systems. Additionally, a modern model-based adaptive system would promote reflection and self-awareness among

Table 10.1 Some Technological Applications used in Australian Universities

University	Application	Description
UNSW	The virtual reality simulator AVIE	a world first which casts 360-degree 3D images using a floor-to-ceiling screen and is available for student use and industry training
LaTrobe	a gamified app	Guides students learning capabilities such as innovation and big picture awareness, cultural intelligence, collaboration, communicating and influencing
Range of Australian universities – Australia's response to Groningen Declaration, an international initiative of 56 universities and 20 private sector companies from around the world	My eQuals –	Digital authenticated qualifications system used by universities in Australia to issue electronic transcripts and graduation documents.
Melbourne Polytechnic	Hosts the only academically integrated finance and innovation intelligence system.	The first tertiary education institute to provide students and industry partners access to the world's single largest global repository of innovation and analytics
DeakinDigital	World-first system of independently verified, evidence-based employability credentials	Credentials provide recognition of an individual's skills and capability learned through work and life, benchmarked against globally recognised standards

Source: Adapted from Australian Education Technology (webpage 2020)

learners and in their inquiries and interactions with such a system. In the presence of these tools, it is then engaging the learners through meta-cognitive scaffolding (which focuses on providing dynamic help and support to enhance learner motivation and engagement) and social simulation models, which focus on enabling language learning for students to understand cultural and social norms.

Educational cobots – robots that work alongside humans – mainly support human lecturers to perform their tasks. Cobots can help lecturers differentiate instructions between each learner so that learners receive more tailored teaching (Timms 2016). Cobots are virtual and intelligent technological assistants that have access to the knowledge objects that academic staff use and frequently deploy through a computerised system. Specific algorithms can be developed to assist staff overcome routine administrative operations.

Five Australian universities (Melbourne, Deakin, Edith Cowan, Sydney, and Flinders) have installed a Baxter research and education robot (a cobot) to support research projects across a variety of fields (Training Systems Australia 2019). The Baxter cobot can be used in collaboration with humans to carry out multiple tasks.

Table 10.2 AI-Ed Models and Implications for Staffing and Skills

AI-Ed models	Core emphases	Examples	Skills implications
Pedagogical Model	Imparting rule-based knowledge and skills	Simple, Yes/No, True/False approaches to test knowledge and progress accordingly	Staff need to be comfortable with principles of instrumental learning and planning instruction in a stepped manner using AI technologies
Domain Model	Develop subject matter expertise	Still largely rule-based but with reasoning and proven competencies	Staff need to develop application scenarios to allow the progression of higher-order relational knowledge and skills
Learner Model	Knowing the adult learner	Relational and emotional mental states are explored	Truly engaging with the highest and most sophisticated level requires knowledge of deep and neural networks for engaging with this model

Source: Adapted from Luckin et al. (2016: 19)

Compared to the Baxter "manufacturing" version, the difference is the embedded software. The supplier's webpage (Training Systems Australia 2019) indicates that:

> The Baxter Research robot may advantageously be used to support numerous research and education programs such as human-robot interaction, collaborative robotics, planning, object recognition and object manipulation, computer science, perception, neurosciences, and cognitive sciences.

However, as Taguma et al. (2018) explain, there are limits, including: perceptual and manipulation tasks that cannot yet be adequately performed by mobile robots and cobots;

AI and machine learning cannot deal with creative intelligence tasks, and AI-powered tools cannot work with social intelligence tasks, which require real-time recognition of human emotions and intelligent responses. Besides, as Marr (2018) points out, AI has limitations in some areas of intelligence, as (for example) machine and AI-tools do not have access to the contextualised and subjective knowledge that humans have.

Teaching Efficiency

Academic workloads and costs can be reduced through AI tools such as automated marking, record-keeping and student feedback (Luckin et al. 2016), AI can also assist with the evaluation and relevance of teaching materials, providing insights as to how well assessments fit with course learning objectives, though this needs further work for complex curricula (Dickson 2017). AI-powered tutoring systems have also proved to be useful teaching tools for well-defined courses such as maths and physics (Luckin et al. 2016). AI can provide one-on-one human tutoring and is being considered an effective method to enable the identification of individual student needs (Schroeder et al. 2013).

Although AIEd can provide seamless benefits to educational institutions, some resistance may be evident from instructors who may need to change their behaviours, mindsets, skills and competencies (as outlined in the next section) concerning technical resources that support education (Govindarajan and Srivastava 2020). Several authors have pointed out that AI cannot replace lecturers as they the various tools have no self-awareness or metacognitive regulation and technology lacks empathy (Dickson 2017; Wilson and Daugherty 2018). However, AI can augment lecturers' cognitive skills and creativity, free lecturers from low-level routine tasks, and extend their physical and cognitive capabilities for more productive tasks (Wilson and Daugherty 2018). Wilson and Daugherty (2018) further argue that the main impact of technology in classrooms will be in complementing and augmenting lecturers' capabilities if they are willing to explore the possibilities.

Employment Impact

This section discusses the employment impact of 4IR technologies on six crucial components of HE teaching and learning – namely, lecturer competencies, learner preparedness, learning styles, teaching and learning, assessment and ethics.

Lecturer Competencies

For new technologies to be effective in the classroom, lecturers will need to possess technical skills of data fluency and 'digital savviness' in their repertoire of science, literacy, numeracy and micro-literacy skills, which will enable them to identify and evaluate AIEd systems (Luckin et al. 2016). Consequently, AI platforms can also be used to help lecturers meet their specific needs, so that training can be completed anytime and anywhere, although there are still questions concerning how successful AI is in supporting training. It has been argued that traditional training methods are best suited in providing trainees with direct and personalised feedback in a physical setting where trainees can ask questions and discuss issues (Bratt et al. 2005). Moreover, Wilson and Daugherty (2018) assert that machines can be trained to perform tasks and understand the outcomes of tasks concerning people and be programmed to avoid potential harm to humans. This will require diverse sets of algorithms and databases with negative feedback loops to prevent potential harm for a range of objects.

Lecturer expertise has been proposed as key to the effective achievement of learning objectives where they need to operate as central agents; educated in technological literacy; trained to acquire new skills, and possess the ability to understand how AIEd is functioning and what it offers (Luckin et al. 2016). Specifically, lecturers will also need to have fusion, deep thinking…and big data analysis skills, as well as the capacity to develop questioning skills among learners of the results provided by AIEd tools, and to work with students to analyse the data provided by such tools (Luckin et al. 2016).

Ally (2019) identified nine primary competencies required by digital lecturers for future education – namely, general qualities; being digitally literate; having the ability to develop digital learning resources and re-mix learning resources and to communicate effectively with learners; facilitating learning; using appropriate pedagogical strategies; assessing learning, and having the appropriate personal characteristics. Kaendler et al. (2015) proposed that five lecturer competencies are needed to foster student interaction in collaborative learning. They are the ability to *plan*, *monitor*, *support*, *consolidate*, and *reflect* on student interactions. The UNESCO-ICT-CFT framework identifies a further set of 18 ICT competencies wherein, it emphasises the role of ICT in the curriculum, assessment strategies, pedagogy, digital skills, organisation and administration and on-going development (UNESCO 2019).

Learner Preparedness

In common with their lecturers, students must also rise to the challenges of AIEd, and it has been proposed that this means they should possess three transformative competencies. These are their ability to: *create new value*, *reconcile tensions and dilemmas*, and *take responsibility*. Critical and scientific problem-solving and other higher-order learning skills, such as action orientation, 'helicopter' perceptions and the ability to challenge their own and others' assumptions through critical and Socratic thinking, can help develop these three transformative competencies. Continuous learning is an integral part of graduates' lives (Lelei 2013); however, providing a personalised learning experience can be challenging, which is where AI can assist in improving the learners' learning experiences (Luckin et al. 2016). AI platforms such as intelligent systems can engage student learners in any learning experience to address gaps in understanding or help lecturers in identifying and responding to the specific needs of students (Dickson 2017). Moreover, AI and Big Data tools help learners with competency building and assessment of their personal analytics, which in turn, can help them to become active learners. For examples and applications see Table 5.1 with reference to LaTrobe and Deakin Digital education technologies.

AI can also assist with data providers to develop a model illustrating a real-time understanding of students' learning and engagement with specific topics (Luckin et al. 2016). Using online business simulation exercises, researchers have pointed to opportunities where students can explore, interact, and manipulate aspects of a simulated world for effective knowledge transfer to real scenarios (Luckin et al. 2016). Identifying and analysing learners' emotions is an essential part of active learning as researchers found that students expressed different types of emotions during their first computer programming learning sessions, where confusion, frustration and boredom were the main emotions experienced (Bosch et al. 2013). Harley et al. (2013) found that neutrality, curiosity, and hope, were the most prominent emotions experienced by learners who used MetaTutor. It is anticipated that using robots in the classroom with high definition cameras will help to identify students' facial expressions and gestures as well as their voices while they work (Timms 2016). Affect-sensitive intelligent tutoring systems can offer personalised to hyper-personalised learning experiences for students to maximise their learning through intelligent handling of emotions (Bosch and D'Mello 2013).

Learning Styles

Each student is characterised by different learning styles (Phobun and Vicheanpanya 2010). An objective of the learner model is to provide information that enables an adaptive learning environment, one that incorporates a learner's needs. One of the most popular models is the Open Learner Model (OLM) (Bull and Kay 2010; Luckin et al. 2016), which provides the outcomes of the analysis including the learner's achievements back to the learner and lecturer. This model assists a technology-mediated dyadic interaction to help understand mutual gaps better and enable each to shape future learning experiences effectively. Moreover, such a model can help students in tracking their progress and reflecting on their learning (Luckin et al. 2016).

Bull and Kay (2010) employed three learning styles, based on models by Felder and Silverman focusing on aspects, such as *perception*, *processing* and *understanding*. They found that using Bayesian networks (BN), the e-Lecturer can model both qualitative and quantitative data about students' learning styles. Bayesian networks refers to an approach which generates probabilistic graphical models to depict the variables and contingencies affecting an outcome – factors which support the development of each student's profile as well as suggesting actions that favour a student's learning style (Bull and Kay 2010). Such an e-learning system can help to detect a student's learning style based on their past actions. Thus, an e-Lecturer can use the data obtained from the student profile and other databases to proactively help students by advising him/her personalised courses of action during their learning process (Schiaffino et al. 2008). AI-powered tools can also support collaborative learning by comparing student learner models (Dickson 2017). Other AI-enabled web-based applications can help students learn despite their different learning styles using predictive models to determine the learners' knowledge, skills, and behaviours (Phobun and Vicheanpanya 2010).

Teaching and Learning

AI-enabled tools that can enhance students' learning are agent-based visual programming tools, which allow students to conceptualise and develop computational models of scientific phenomena, implement the models as simulations, conduct experiments to validate the simulation behaviours, and use those models to solve real-world problems (Basu and Biswas 2013). Educational robots are another form of AI-powered tools, which can be employed in practice-based subjects such as physics or chemistry to demonstrate phenomena in a natural way, not as a video or simulation (Timms 2016). Moreover, the use of robots in education can help to enhance interaction with students, as robots can move around the classroom and observe and recognise every individual students' face, expression, and voice (Timms 2016). According to Holland (2000), this has led to different ways of teaching in Music Education as a result of AI application. Examples include music theory, listening, composition and performance. While the above tools have higher cognitive and analytical abilities than humans, the acceptance of humanoids as co-creators and co-workers is still a contested area. The implications for job loss or takeover of certain types of tasks are inevitable as AI bots continue to take over simple, routine, and mundane tasks, freeing up humans for more creative and contextual tasks.

Assessment

According to Luckin (2017), AI can open the' black box' of learning by providing an in-depth and fine-grained understanding of when and how learning occurs. That said, Yuki the first robot lecturer has been delivering lectures to university students at the Philipps University of Marburg in Germany. The robot acts as a teaching assistant during lectures, getting a sense of how students are going academically and what kind of support they need – feedback has been quite positive to date (Ameen 2019). As educational robots become more sophisticated and commonplace this may impact on the academics working with them requiring academics to focus more on research to increase their employability, retention, and career development (Ameen 2019). However, there are caveats related to the use of AI in education as Southgate (2019 webpage) points out:

> The 'black box' opaque nature of AI systems is complicated. AI is 'opaque' because it is often invisibly infused into computing systems in ways that can influence our interactions, decisions, moods, and sense of self without us being aware of this.

Luckin (2017) supports this argument stating AI assessment systems can obtain information about student's achievements, their emotional state, or motivation and this information can be used to analyse and create an Open Learner Model (OLM) which can, in turn, be used to identify student's approaches to learning which can motivate students to track their progress and reflect on their learning (Luckin 2017). Southgate (2019) points out the ethical issues related to integrating facial recognition technology into classrooms to monitor the 'mood' and 'engagement' of students despite research suggesting that inferring affective states from facial expression is fraught with difficulties. China introduced such technologies as a pilot which was halted in 2019 due to privacy and human right concerns among other issues (Shead 2019) although others have reported that the facial recognition technology is continuing (Bala 2020).

Ciolacu et al. (2017) note a wide array of AI-enabled instructional and assessment systems that offer personalised solutions to the learner by leveraging individual learners' learning analytics and deploying a range of AI-applications, chatbots, teletutors, and many more. That said, AI-powered assessment, although it offers productivity gains and frees up academics' time for other research activities, it can be an expensive application to design and implement in the first instance. Other issues, of the nature and transparency of algorithms, need to be vetted by unbiased and objective human agents regarding the assessment tools and ethical implications (Luckin 2017). There are other relational and ethical issues of privacy and social interactions between humanoids and co-workers and the beneficiaries of this exchange, the students. At the moment, we do not have established normative frameworks for managing such exchanges. Hence more work is required, even though the technological capability exists, the human ecosystem may not be fully ready.

Ethics

Mcmurtrie (2018) argues that when AI is in use in the classroom, more attention is needed in terms of ethics and efficacy. Although AI-powered tools provide several benefits to the education sector, there is a need to consider ethical issues such as decision making; whether these systems are accountable, controllable or regulated; and the moral, societal and legal consequences of their actions (Luckin et al. 2016). Taguma et al. (2018) maintain that HE curricula need to include resources on the basic concepts of AI and basic AI programming; how to work with AI systems effectively; digital and data literacy; and ethical reasoning. Further, Taguma et al. (2018) argue that people and organisations need to take careful consideration of the consequences of how they use AI, robotics, and big data. Moreover, the character and integrity of those who create and use AI- tools should be a central concern of education both today and in the future (Campolo et al. 2017).

Luckin (2017) has also advocated that educationalists should work with AI developers, stressing that 'everyone needs to be involved in a discussion about what AI should and should not be designed to do' (p.121). Southgate et al. (2018) proposed an ethical framework for adoption and implementation of AI in education, albeit in primary and secondary school levels, but Southgate (2020) argues that it has relevance for HE as well. The framework employs United Nations principles, which have been further summarised by the Australian Human Rights Commission under the acronym PANEL. The focus is on using PANEL principles of **P**articipation,

Accountability, Non-discrimination and equality, Empowerment and Legality in the design and implementation of AI applications, only then can we achieve awareness, explainability, fairness, transparency and accountability as essential outcomes of this framework.

Challenges & Opportunities

While it is clear that a teacher standing in front of a classroom full of students who respond to direction is becoming a thing of the past (McLaughlin 2020: webpage), implementing new disruptive technologies such as AI in educational settings is not straightforward either. This is because traditional pedagogy and policies need to be adapted, and many resources, including hardware and software, are costly (Southgate et al. 2018). There may also be resistance from lecturers and students to learning and using such technologies. Reasons for resistance could be due to a lack of skills, cultures that resist change and habit among other factors (Chandler 2010). Furthermore, there is significant structural, ethical legal and relational structuration that is needed before AI in 4IR era can realise its full potential (Southgate 2020). As discussed elsewhere in this chapter, there is also a need to for educators to adapt and grow as, 'in light of a shift towards a more personalised learner experience, teachers of the future must be prepared to be data collectors, as well as analysts, planners, collaborators, curriculum experts, synthesisers, problem-solvers and researchers' (McLaughlin 2020: webpage).

Thus, although AI can create new opportunities, there are some serious issues which need to be addressed. (Luckin et al. 2016) argue that there two main challenges. Firstly, AIEd tools and techniques need fine-grained analysis to assess each learner's development of skills and capabilities. Secondly, data collected from AIEd tools need to be used in tracking learner progress against different teaching approaches, as this will help to develop the best teaching practices suited to the development of different skills and capabilities. For example, it has also been argued that lecturers need to spend more time with students, rather than reducing it (Pence 2019).

An additional issue raised in this chapter that needs to be kept at the forefront of AIEd considerations is that of AI and ethics. As Campolo et al (2017) state while citing others in Campolo (2019):

> AI is not impartial or neutral. Technologies are as much products of the context in which they are created as they are potential agents for change. Machine predictions and performance are constrained by human decisions and values, and those who design, develop, and maintain AI systems will shape such systems within their own understanding of the world (p.18).

Further Southgate et al. (2018) point out that transparent and accountable systems of governance need to be considered when adopting AI in education. There is also a need to ensure that all students can gain potential benefits and to comply with ethics, considering when to implement and use such AIEd tools. AI-powered tools can assist global classrooms with making learning available to all – including students who speak different languages or have the problems of visual or hearing impairments, or on any course that is not available in their school. Marr (2018). also explained that in order to bring education into the digital classroom, resources need to be invested, and entire generations of educators need to be upskilled and trained to prepare for the challenges of the twenty-first century and beyond Marr (2018).

Conclusion

Beginning sometime during the last months of 2019 in China, the COVID-19 pandemic is currently experiencing a second wave across the world (Worldometers 2020). The World Bank predicts that the world's economy is on the brink of global depression, and the effects are already being felt by the international and national tertiary education sectors. As Hirst (2020, webpage) points out, 'tertiary education is a vital sector of the Australian economy and the third-largest earner of export income, but it will not soon be bouncing back to business as usual'. The higher education sector has lost close to $5 billion by mid-2020 with losses predicted to be $13 to $15 billion due to a significant decline in demand. Recent reports from QS (an opt-in university ranking system) suggest that almost two-thirds of the international students surveyed believed that COVID-19 had affected their plans to study overseas, and at least half of those surveyed deferred their plans to study overseas (QS 2020a).

Relative to face-to-face learning modes, international students were less interested in studying online (QS 2020a). Although New Zealand and China have been perceived as the top two countries that have best handled the COVID-19 crisis, Australia was only ranked as fifth best (QS 2020b). However, this provides little solace in relation to the downturn in student enrolments that has affected almost all Australian universities to varying degrees, and has led to Universities Australia (2021) reporting huge job losses in higher education. Some universities have already made cuts in 2020, especially in relation to casual academic staff, and others are predicting worse to come in 2021 (Davies 2020). Meanwhile, the Labor Party has been urging the federal government to "act to help universities and save jobs" – Tanya Plibersek (cited in Davies 2020).

Future Challenges

What does this mean for the future of academic jobs? The loss of casual academic staff means that those in permanent academic roles are likely to have to take on more teaching and will therefore be unable to conduct as much research as before. Previously in Australia, international enrolments could bring in more university funding than all government funding streams combined (Ross and McKie 2020). Moreover, the proposed reforms under the current education minister's "Job-ready Graduates" package are likely to threaten the ability of university's to cross subsidise research by using profits from teaching Australian students as domestic bachelor's course revenues are likely to break even if that (Ross and McKie 2020).

Throughout the pandemic and beyond. Govindarajan and Srivastava (2020) maintain that it is vital to examine higher education business models relating to the provision of quality higher education. As discussed earlier, the move to online education exacerbates the digital divide in three main ways:

(i) until Internet infrastructure is stronger in regions that have low speed/no Internet, there will be unequal access to online learning opportunities, thus infrastructure must be in place to provide better access to the Internet before remote learning can be considered adequate and digital inequalities be addressed (Ferri et al. 2020);
(ii) the delivery of online courses needs dedicated education support with training available for lecturers, designers, trainers, and coaches to support student learning and facilitate changes in mindsets and behaviours and;
(iii) students also need support as they adjust to the loss of face to face education and support towards online peer interaction (Govindarajan and Srivastava 2020).

Currently academics are facing challenges such as taking on greater teaching loads – much of it online and they will also need to create new curricula to suit this mode of teaching while facing 'a steep learning curve in new forms of pedagogy' (Ross and Mckie 2020: webpage).

Given the emphasis given to online teaching does the coronavirus pandemic signal the end of the physical campus? It appears that is not the case in Australia where most universities began a gradual return to campus life around mid-2020. Will campus life be the same as before? Probably not – for example some universities at the time of writinglimit face to face teaching to 1 h 40 min for what were previously 3-h classes. The remaining time comprises a hybrid model of teaching either through live streamed classes (offered to both domestic and international students) and/or pre-recorded material. Social distancing in the classroom, copious amounts of sanitiser, Covid related health/warning signs and students employed as 'social distancing marshalls', are all clearly evident however and may just become part of the 'new normal' over time.

Clearly, technology in its various forms has been vital for the continuity of higher education during the pandemic. Chaka (2020:21) considered 85 universities (based in the US and South Africa) to determine what technologies they used during the COVID-19 outbreak and found that they transitioned to tried and tested tools described as 'low-tech versions of 4IR technologies such as video-conferencing, social media technologies, and cloud computing'. Chaka (2020) questions whether the universities used familiar technologies due to the speed required to move to online teaching and whether more sophisticated technologies will be explored in future.

That said Campolo et al (2017) stress that those in the education space must become aware of how AI works, as well as what it can and cannot do. This will require investment in terms of resources and time – as Zeide (2019) points out, 'be cautious and thoughtful about what you are doing with AI' (p. 12).

In summary, COVID-19 has been a major disruptive force which has added to the complexity of designing and implementing AI in the educational space. The role of higher education in society and the economy is changing and will have to transform to offer best practices in online teaching and high-quality online materials appropriate for all student contexts (Bajpai and Biberman 2020; Dahlan et al. 2020).

References

Adamson, D., Dyke, G., Jang, H., & Rosé, C. P. (2014). Towards an agile approach to adapting dynamic collaboration support to student needs. *International Journal of Artificial Intelligence in Education, 24*(1), 92–124.

Ally, M. (2019). Competency profile of the digital and online teacher in future education. *The International Review of Research in Open and Distance Learning, 20*(2).

Ameen, N. (2019). *What robots and AI may mean for university lecturers and students*. https://theconversation.com/what-robots-and-ai-may-mean-for-universitylecturers-and-students-114383, viewed 30/9/2020.

Bajpai, N., & Biberman, J. (2020). *The COVID-19 economy: Building a sustainable future in the shadow of a crisis.* ICT India Working Paper #33, Center for Sustainable Development, Viewed 30/7/2020, https://academiccommons.columbia.edu/doi/10.7916/d8-zd8j-4a62

Bala, N. (2020). The danger of facial recognition in our children's classrooms. *18 Duke Law & Technology Review* (pp. 249–267) (2020) viewed 30/7/2020.

Basu, S., & Biswas, G. (2013). *A computational thinking approach to learning middle school science.* Paper presented at the International Conference on Artificial Intelligence in Education.

Blum, S. (2020). *Why we're exhausted by zoom*. Accessed on 10/6/20: https://www.insidehighered.com/advice/2020/04/22/professor-explores-why-zoom-classes-deplete-her-energy-opinion

Bosch, N., & D'Mello, S. (2013). *Programming with your heart on your sleeve: Analysing the affective states of computer programming students.* Paper presented at the International Conference on Artificial Intelligence in Education.

Bosch, N., D'Mello, S., & Mills, C. (2013). *What emotions do novices experience during their first computer programming learning session?* Paper presented at the International Conference on Artificial Intelligence in Education.

Bratt, E. O., Schultz, K., Peters, S., Chen, T., & Pon-Barry, H. (2005). *Empirical foundations for intelligent coaching systems.* Paper presented at the Proceedings of the interservice/industry Training, Simulation and Education Conference.

Bull, S., & Kay, J. (2010). Open learner models. In *Advances in intelligent tutoring systems* (pp. 301–322). Springer.

Campolo, A. (2019). *Preparing for the Impact of Artificial Intelligence on Education in Australia.* https://cpl.asn.au/sites/default/files/journal/Kalervo%20Gulson%20-%20For%20Your%20Future%20-%20Preparing%20for%20the%20Impact%20of%20Artificial%20Intelligence.pdf

Campolo, A., Sanfilippo., Whittaker, M., & Crawford., K. (2017). *AI Now 2017 Report.* AI Now Institute. New York: New York University. https://ainowinstitute.org/AI_Now_2017_Report.pdf

Chaka, C. (2020). *Higher education institutions and the use of online instruction and online tools and resources during the COVID-19 outbreak-An online review of selected US and SA's universities*. https://assets.researchsquare.com/files/rs-61482/v1/ea822947-e8f3-4708-81e5-a2b24dafb6f8.pdf

Chandler, N. (2010). Reasons and forms of organizational resistance to change in the higher education sector. *Practice and Theory in Systems of Education, 5*(1), 87–104.

Ciolacu, M., Svasta, P. M., Berg, W., & Popp, H. (2017). *Education 4.0 for tall thin engineer in a data driven society*. Paper presented at the 2017 IEEE 23rd International Symposium for Design and Technology in Electronic Packaging, SIITME 2017 – Proceedings.

Dahlan, A., et al. (2020). *Journal of Information Systems and Digital Technologies, 2*(1), 48.

Davies, A. (2020). *Australian universities to close campuses and shed thousands of jobs as revenue plummets due to Covid-19 crisis*. https://www.theguardian.com/australia-news/2020/jun/04/australian-universities-to-close-campuses-and-shed-thousands-of-jobs-as-revenue-plummets-due-to-covid-19-crisis

Deakin University. (2015). https://www.deakin.edu.au/about-deakin/media-releases/articles/ibm-watson-helps-deakin-drive-the-digital-frontier. Accessed 12 Dec 2019.

Dickson, B. E. N. (2017). HOW artificial intellgence is shaping the future of education. *PC Magazine, 105*.

Economist Intelligence Unit (EIU) Ltd. (2018). *The automation readiness index: Who is ready for the coming wave of automation?* Commissioned by the ABB (ASEA Brown Boveri). https://www.automationreadiness.eiu.com/. Accessed 1/7/2019.

Gadanidis, G. (2017). Artificial intelligence, computational thinking, and mathematics education. *The International Journal of Information and Learning Technology, 34*(2), 133–139.

Gama, J. A. P., Caro, R., Hernan, C., Alvarado, D. B., Gomez, C. L. C., Gomez, G. H., & Mena, A. M. (2016). *Work in progress – New education model based on competencies of higher education and iMIS with architectures*. Paper presented at the IEEE Global Engineering Education Conference, EDUCON.

Ghaffar, A., & Hussain, M. (2019). *BCEAP – A blockchain embedded academic paradigm to augment legacy education through application*. Paper presented at the ACM International Conference Proceeding Series.

Gleason, N. W. (2018a). *Higher education in the era of the fourth industrial revolution* (p. 229). Springer.

Gleason, N. W. (2018b). Singapore's higher education systems in the era of the fourth industrial revolution: Preparing lifelong learners. In *Higher education in the era of the fourth industrial revolution* (pp. 145–169). Singapore: Palgrave Macmillan.

Govindarajan, V., & Srivastava, A. (2020). What the shift to virtual learning could mean for the future of higher Ed, *Harvard Business Review*. Accessed on 10/6/20. https://hbr.org/2020/03/what-the-shift-to-virtual-learning-could-mean-for-the-future-of-higher-ed

Han, E.-R., Yeo, S., Kim, M.-J., Lee, Y.-H., Park, K.-H., & Roh, H. (2019). Medical education trends for future physicians in the era of advanced technology and artificial intelligence: An integrative review. *BMC Medical Education, 19*(1), 460.

Harley, J. M., Bouchet, F., & Azevedo, R. (2013). *Aligning and comparing data on emotions experienced during learning with MetaTutor*. Paper presented at the International Conference on Artificial Intelligence in Education.

Hirst, M. (2020). *University staff pressuring government in a fight for their jobs*. https://independentaustralia.net/life/life-display/university-staff-pressuring-government-in-a-fight-for-their-jobs,13895

Holland, S. (2000). Artificial intelligence in music education: A critical review. In E. R. Miranda (Ed.), *Readings in music and artificial intelligence. Contemporary music studies* (pp. 239–274). Routledge.

Jackson, S. S. (2019). Using artificial intelligence to improve access to and success in higher education. *INSIGHT into Diversity, 92*(4/5), 34–36.

Jones, M. (1985). Applications of artificial intelligence within education. *Computers & Mathematics with Applications, 11*(5), 517–526.

Kaendler, C., Wiedmann, M., Rummel, N., & Spada, H. (2015). Teacher competencies for the implementation of collaborative learning in the classroom: A framework and research review. *Educational Psychology Review, 27*(3), 505–536.

Lelei, D. E. K. (2013). Supporting lifelong learning: Recommending personalized sources of assistance to graduate students. In *International conference on artificial intelligence in education* (pp. 912–915). Berlin/Heidelberg: Springer.

Luckin, R. (2017). Towards artificial intelligence-based assessment systems. *Nature Human Behaviour, 1*(0028).

Luckin, R., Holmes, W., Griffiths, M., & Forcier, L. B. (2016). *Intelligence unleashed: An argument for AI in education*. UCL: Pearson Publishing.

Lytras, M., Sarirete, A., & Damiani, E. (2020). Technology-enhanced learning research in higher education: A transformative education primer. *Computers in Human Behaviour, 109*, 106350.

Marr, B. (2018). https://www.forbes.com/sites/bernardmarr/2018/07/25/how-is-ai-used-in-education-real-world-examples-of-today-and-a-peek-into-the-future/#b9bd453586e8

McLaughlin, T. (2020). *The future of learning and teaching: Big changes ahead.* Accessed on 19/6/20 https://www.rmit.edu.au/study-with-us/education/discover-education/the-future-of-learning-and-teaching-big-changes-ahead-for-education

Mcmurtrie, B. (2018). How artificial intelligence is changing teaching. *The Chronicle of Higher Education*.

Mehmood, R., Alam, F., Albogami, N. N., Katib, I., Albeshri, A., & Altowaijri, S. M. (2017). UTiLearn: A personalised ubiquitous teaching and learning system for smart societies. *IEEE Access, 5*, 2615–2635.

Mezirow, J. (1981). A critical theory of adult learning and education. *Adult Education, 32*(1), 3–24.

Mezirow, J. (1994). Understanding transformation theory. *Adult Education Quarterly, 44*(4), 222–232.

Norton, A., & Cherastidtham, I. (2018). *Mapping Australian higher education 2018*. https://grattan.edu.au/wp-content/uploads/2018/09/907-Mapping-Australian-higher-education-2018.pdf

Park, S. (2018). Virtual pedagogical agents for English language teaching and learning. *The TESOL Encyclopedia of English Language Teaching*, 1–9.

Pence, H. E. (2019). Artificial intelligence in higher education: New wine in old wineskins? *Journal of Educational Technology Systems, 48*(1), 5–13.

Penprase, B. E. (2018). The fourth industrial revolution and higher education. In *Higher education in the era of the fourth industrial revolution* (p. 207).

Phobun, P., & Vicheanpanya, J. (2010). Adaptive intelligent tutoring systems for e-learning systems. *Procedia-Social and Behavioral Sciences, 2*(2), 4064–4069.

Popenici, S. A., & Kerr, S. (2017). Exploring the impact of artificial intelligence on teaching and learning in higher education. *Research and Practice in Technology Enhanced Learning, 12*(1), 22.

QS. (2020a). *How COVID-19 is impacting prospective international students across subject areas*. Report Published in July 2020.

QS. (2020b). *The outlook for university admissions: The impact of COVID-19*. Report Published in July 2020.

Rajkumar, R., Lee, I., Sha, L., & Stankovic, J. (2010). Cyber-physical systems: The next computing revolution. In *Design automation conference* (pp. 731–736). IEEE.

Ross, J., & McKie, A. (2020). *Will Covid kill off the teaching-research employment model?*. https://www.timeshighereducation.com/news/will-covid-kill-teachingresearch-employment-model, viewed 30/9/2020.

Schiaffino, S., Garcia, P., & Amandi, A. (2008). eTeacher: Providing personalised assistance to e-learning students. *Computers & Education, 51*(4), 1744–1754.

Schroeder, N. L., Adesope, O. O., & Gilbert, R. B. (2013). How effective are pedagogical agents for learning? A meta-analytic review. *Journal of Educational Computing Research, 49*(1), 1–39.

Shalini., & Tewari, A. (2020). *Sustainable education in India through artificial intelligence: Challenges and opportunities*, 12th ACM Conference on Web Science Companion (pp. 41–47).

Shead, S. (2019). *Chinese residents worry about rise of facial recognition*. https://www.bbc.com/news/technology-50674909, viewed 30/7/2020.

Southgate, E. (2019). *Artificial intelligence in schools: An ethical storm is brewing*, viewed 30/7/20 https://www.aare.edu.au/blog/?p=4325

Southgate, E. (2020). *Artificial intelligence, ethics, equity and higher education: A 'beginning-of-the-discussion' paper*. National Centre for Student Equity in Higher Education, Curtin University, and the University of Newcastle.

Southgate, E., Blackmore, K., Pieschl, S., Grimes, S., McGuire, J., & Smithers, K. (2018). *Artificial intelligence and emerging technologies in schools: A research report*. Newcastle: University of Newcastle, Australia.

Southgate, E., Smith, S.P., Cividino, C., Saxby, S., Kilham, J., Eather, G., Scevak, J., Summerville, D., Buchanan, R., & Bergin, C. (2019). Embedding immersive virtual reality in classrooms: Ethical, organisational and educational lessons in bridging research and practice. *International Journal of Child-Computer Interaction, 19*, 19–29.

Taguma, M., Feron, E., & Meow Hwee, L. (2018). *Future of education and skills 2030: Conceptual learning framework*. http://www.oecd.org/education/2030/Education-and-AI-preparing-for-the-future-AI-Attitudes-and-Values.pdf, viewed 30/7/2020.

Timms, M. J. (2016). Letting artificial intelligence in education out of the box: Educational cobots and smart classrooms. *International Journal of Artificial Intelligence in Education, 26*(2), 701–712.

Training Systems Australia. (2019). *Five Australian Universities Purchase & Install Baxter Research Robot*, viewed 24/9/29 http://www.trainingsystemsaustralia.com.au/news/five-australian-universities-purchase-install-baxter-research-robot/

UNESCO. (2019). *ICT Competency Framework for Teachers harnessing Open Educational Resources*, Viewed 30/7/2020. https://en.unesco.org/themes/ict-eduction/competency-framework-teachers-oer

Universities Australia. (2020). *The Voice of Australia's Universities*, https://www.universitiesaustralia.edu.au, viewed 24/9/20.

Universities Australia. (2021). *17,000 UNI JOBS LOST TO COVID-19*, https://www.universitiesaustralia.edu.au/media-item/17000-uni-jobs-lost-to-covid-19, viewed 8/4/21.

Waring, P., Vas, C., & Bali, A. Z. (2018). Work-readiness in Singapore. In R. Cameron, S. Dhakal, & J. Burgess (Eds.), *Transitions from education to work* (pp. 124–144). Oxon: Routledge.

Wilson, H. J., & Daugherty, P. R. (2018). Collaborative intelligence: Humans and AI are joining forces. *Harvard Business Review, 96*(4), 114–123.

Worldometers. (2020). *Coronavirus cases*. Accessed on 14th Aug 2020 from https://www.worldometers.info/coronavirus/

Zawacki-Richter, O., Marín, V. I., Bond, M., & Gouverneur, F. (2019). Systematic review of research on artificial intelligence applications in higher education–where are the educators? *International Journal of Educational Technology in Higher Education, 16*(1), 39.

Zeide, E. (2019). Artificial intelligence in higher education: Applications, promise and perils, and ethical questions. *EDUCAUSE Review, 54*(3) (Summer 2019).

Chapter 11
Healthcare

Narges Kia, Jillian Cavanagh, Hannah Meacham, Beni Halvorsen, Patricia Pariona Cabrera, and Timothy Bartram

Abstract The use of Artificial intelligence (AI) has grown dramatically across various industries around the world, especially in the healthcare sector where AI supports patients, nurses, and doctors to complete tasks with greater precision, speed and safety. Although countries such as the USA and China are the most advanced in their use of AI, interest in AI use has grown in Australia, especially in healthcare facilities such as nursing homes and hospitals. Despite predictions of AI related job losses across the Australian economy, we argue that within the Australian healthcare sector the picture is much more complex, and that AI may create more jobs overall and enable clinicians and health care organisations to more efficiently and effectively support the needs of patients and communities in the future. That said, the growth of AI is not without its challenges and negative effects on clinicians, healthcare organisations and patients, especially where it is not managed ethically or strategically by healthcare organisations. This chapter focusses on the significance of AI in the Australia healthcare system and its impact on the work organisation and employment of the healthcare workforce.

Keywords Artificial intelligence · Australia · Healthcare · Doctors · Nurses

Introduction

Artificial intelligence (AI) continues to break ground in the healthcare sector addressing clinical challenges by assisting clinicians, such as doctors and nurses caring for patients in healthcare organisations (Mindfields 2018). The number of organisations within the healthcare sector utilising AI has increased dramatically

N. Kia (✉) · J. Cavanagh · H. Meacham · B. Halvorsen · P. P. Cabrera · T. Bartram
School of Management, College of Business and Law, RMIT University,
Melbourne, Australia
e-mail: narges.kia@rmit.edu.au; jillian.cavanagh@rmit.edu.au;
Hannah.meacham@monash.edu.au; beni.halvorsen@rmit.edu.au;
patricia.pariona-cabrera@rmit.edu.au; timothy.bartram@rmit.edu.au

A. Nankervis et al. (eds.), *The Fourth Industrial Revolution*,
https://doi.org/10.1007/978-981-16-1614-3_11

over the last decade due to awareness, availability and the reduced costs of the technology (Davenport and Kalakota 2019; Mindfields 2018). AI is defined as 'technology designed to perform activities that normally require human intelligence' (Luxton 2014: 2). Globally, an increasing population is witnessing a decline in the number of healthcare workers, "and the gap is seen to be widening over time" (Mindfields 2018: 7). According to the World Health Organisation (WHO), in 2035 the world will be short of approximately 13 million healthcare workers. In developed countries such as Australia, the US, Canada, Germany, and the UK a large proportion of their Gross Domestic Product (GDP) is spent in healthcare. As a result, the adoption of new technologies such as AI has become increasingly important to their health systems to increase labour productivity and the quality of patient care, and alleviate clinician and budget shortages (Mindfields 2018).

In recent years there has been increasing interest in the field of AI and its applications to healthcare (Reddy 2018). AI is used to enhance the effectiveness of the delivery of healthcare and to address intractable healthcare challenges (Gambhir et al. 2016; Ramesh et al. 2004). The hundreds of AI-based healthcare applications covering assisted surgery, preliminary diagnosis, and administrative workflows that have been presented in recent years are testimonials to its importance. The AI science field is 'concerned with the computational understanding of what is commonly called intelligent behaviour and with the creation of intelligent agents that exhibit such behaviour' (Shapiro 1992: 89). AI involves machines assuming human-like capabilities via computer programming and displaying aspects of human intelligence, such as learning, adapting and self-correction, as well as thinking and acting like humans and displaying rationality. Using computer programming, AI tries to emulate intelligent behaviour (Kok et al. 2009; Ramesh et al. 2004; Reddy 2018; Warwick 2013).

Within healthcare, AI uses advanced algorithms to decipher relevant information from a large volume of healthcare data to assist nurses in clinical practice. AI may also reduce human error in clinical practice and identify diseases such as cancers more accurately in their initial stages (Dilsizian and Siegel 2014; Lee et al. 2013; Patel et al. 2009). For example, according to the American Cancer Society (Wilson 2017), a high percentage of mammograms yield false results, leading to errors. The use of AI enables mammograms to be reviewed and translated 30 times faster and with greater accuracy than before (Wilson 2017). Another example is the attention paid to the field of radiology. The ability to interpret imaging results using AI technology can help clinicians identify a minute change that they may unintentionally miss (Abhinav and Subrahmanyam 2019), thus decreasing the human error rate. AI allows medical digital devices to see and recognise objects, identify and respond to identifiable messages, make decisions, and even learn to change its behaviour and thinking by analysing data points in a distributed memory known as the cloud (Abhinav and Subrahmanyam 2019), all contributing to the increased accuracy of medical diagnoses.

Although AI has many benefits, it also has its challenges. The impact of AI on the workforce (for example, job design, deskilling), and the potential for job loss is a major concern (Frey and Osborne 2013; Smith and Anderson 2014). Frey and Osborne (2013) predict that half of the jobs in the USA will be automated within the next decade. Moreover, Lee (2018) noted that a quarter of Asian countries, such as Singapore, will be at high risk from automation. It is predicted that in Australia, AI and automation will replace 20% of occupations in the public sector, such as those in health and education, by 2030. In the Australian healthcare sector, around 100,000 jobs are likely to be displaced; however, approximately 190,000 new jobs will be created for nurses and medical specialists due to the changes in technology (for example, the emergence of new jobs in areas such as nanotechnology, engineering and design – Taylor et al. 2019). At this stage, in the healthcare industry there are contradictory signs as to how the growth in AI will play out in terms of employment. What is certain is that the jobs of clinicians, and the organisation and management of health care facilities will be transformed by AI in the future.

Industry Overview

This chapter focusses on the healthcare industry in Australia, which is the largest employing industry. The sector employed 1.7 million healthcare workers in 2019 and is expected to increase to 1.9 million by 2024 (Australian Bureau of Statistics 2018). AI is one of the ongoing trends driving change in the Australian healthcare sector that has impacted jobs, and as a result, healthcare workers have needed to improve the skills required to work with this technology (ABS 2018). The COVID-19 pandemic has impacted healthcare workers physically and psychologically. Healthcare workers such as nurses, and doctors are vulnerable as they work face to face with affected patients (Ku et al. 2020). Due to the current pandemic, healthcare professionals need to work under pressure in very difficult circumstances which may lead to mental health issues, burnout and even turnover. Therefore, using AI is critical in this sector to assist healthcare workers in their routine jobs.

There are many factors driving the development of AI in healthcare. In the US, demand has increased due to its rising and ageing population and financial pressures on the healthcare sector (Trump 2019). The use of AI in medicine has increased by 40% and its expenditure is estimated to reach $6.6 billion by 2021 around the world. However, in Australia there is minimal investment in AI in comparison with 'superpower countries' such as China and the USA (Williams 2019). This chapter discusses the significance of AI in the healthcare sector. Further, it will outline how AI assists healthcare professionals such as doctors, nurses, people who work in Australian health care. Finally, the influence of AI on employment and deskilling will also be discussed.

Key Technologies

Machine learning and deep learning are two types of AI that allow healthcare organisations to analyse a huge volume of different data (Davenport and Kalakota 2019). Machine learning fits models to data and allows technology to "learn" by training these models with the data (Davenport and Kalakota 2019: 94). In the healthcare sector, the primary application of machine learning is in precision medicine, predicting the best treatment for patients based on their situation and treatment context. Davenport & Kalakota (2019, 94) argue that 'the most complex forms of machine learning involve deep learning, or neural network models with many levels of features or variables that predict outcomes. The most significant application of deep learning in healthcare is 'recognition of potentially cancerous lesions in radiology images' (Davenport and Kalakota 2019: 94).

AI can increase the quality of patient care through deep learning in an automatic system for the recognition of diabetic retinopathy (Gulshan et al. 2016). Gulshan et al. (2016) investigated the significance of deep learning algorithms for the detection of diabetic retinopathy in the US. For the purpose of this study, fifty four US licensed ophthalmologists and ophthalmology senior residents were trained in its use. They found that the identification of diabetic retinopathy or diabetic macular oedema in retinal fundus images with high sensitivity and high specificity of deep neural networks can be trained, using large data sets and without the need to specify lesion-based features. This finding leads to the provision of high-quality outcomes in medical imaging tasks. Contreras and Vehi (2018) reviewed recent papers on AI from 2010 to 2018 and found that AI plays a significant role in clinical daily practice and the self-management of diabetes.

Jha and Topol (2016) discussed the theoretical importance of AI in the radiology and pathology area. They argued that the use of deep learning AI helps in the detection of diseases such as lung and breast cancer, and that the role of AI in pathology is important in some tasks such as Papanicolaou tests, cell counts, typing, and the screening of blood, have been automated by this technology. Similarly, Chang et al. (2019: 4) found that using AI assists in 'diagnostic pathology involves segmentation, detection, and classification, as well as quantification and grading'. Pearce et al. (2019) noted in their study that the POLAR Diversion Plan resulted in an automated decision-support tool (DST) driven by AI which was developed in an emergency department of a large Australian health service. The implication is that 'it can be delivered automatically to the GP when the patient is sitting with them, which enables immediate intervention that may reduce risk' (p. 538).

While AI has some benefits, it is not without its challenges. For instance, it has been shown that diagnostic applications should not be embedded in integrated environments such as electronic medical records as they have limited clinical acceptance. The application of AI may be challenging as healthcare professionals face ethical dilemmas in their practice, and AI is unable to provide ethical judgments, thinking, and reasoning (Luxton 2014). The challenges of AI are not just experienced by providers, but by patients themselves. Information is available for patients via the internet, creating the potential for healthcare to be democratised (Schulz and Nakamoto 2013). Moreover, in the context of the COVID-19 pandemic we have seen the emergence of tele-health consultations with healthcare practitioners. At the same time, there is evidence that a growing number of patients are not keeping their appointments, or are not making appointments with their doctors, or are having difficulty in accessing and using the technology, which in some circumstances may compromise their health and wellbeing (Hope 2020).

One of the most significant benefits of AI is helping people to manage their own health (Arnold and Wilson 2017). The use of AI in different healthcare applications allows people to manage their own health by healthier living, keeping themselves well and thus reducing the strain on healthcare services. For instance, 'the *Smart belt – welt* has a built-in mechanism that alerts a person when they overeat. It relies on a magnetic sensor to track waist size and tension to determine when the users may have over eaten and alerts the wearer' (Arnold and Wilson 2017: 3).

Such applications assist people to engage in healthier behaviour and manage their lifestyle. In fact, such technology may prompt patients to think about their wellbeing and health and improve their lifestyle choices. Moreover, AI has the potential to increase the understanding of healthcare professionals regarding the needs of people they care for. This understanding supports healthcare workers to guide and support patients, and to provide enhanced and often in-time feedback regarding their health outcomes (for example, using smart technology such as in-time health information from smart watches and similar technology) (Arnold and Wilson 2017).

In their study, Arnold and Wilson (2017) surveyed more than 11,000 people across twelve countries (Europe, the Middle East and Africa) to investigate people's willingness to use AI and robots in healthcare, as well as the advantages and disadvantages of using this technology in the healthcare system. The study reported that, up to 73% of all respondents (from 11,000 in total) were willing to have minor surgeries such as eye laser or cataract surgery undertaken by robots instead of human doctors. Moreover, the researchers found that 37% of participants were happy for their health records to be checked by robots, and 32% had no problem with blood test results being provided by robots. Moreover, respondents in Nigeria, Turkey and South Africa were the most willing to have minor surgery performed by robots (73%, 66% and 62% respectively), with the UK the least willing (36%). Based on their findings in Belgium, the UK, Germany and Sweden, respondents were generally not willing to be patients in surgeries undertaken by robots. However, one-third of the participants agreed that such surgeries were important. The participants were generally unwilling to be patients of robots undertaking procedures in major surgeries such as the removal of a tumour, or heart surgery.

Medical Applications

In the healthcare sector, AI is used for electronic medical records, clinical algorithms and image data analysis in pathology and radiology (Köse et al. 2018). For instance, AI assists healthcare professionals in the management and analysis of large amounts of data, reduces repetitive work procedures, and decreases human error. It can even go beyond those processes helping healthcare professionals to interpret radiological images such as mammography, ECG analysis, and the interpretation of arterial blood gas (Köse et al. 2018). In surgery, the use of AI can support decision-making and the application of surgical techniques during surgical procedures. However, complex surgical procedures, instantaneous complications, and the personal solutions offered by the surgeons to patients may hinder or even prevent the full use of AI in surgery at the current time (Mirnezami and Ahmed 2018).

The most powerful application of AI is through its human-like performance. Specifically, 'artificial intelligence systems can perform certain tasks very well that normally require human intelligence' (Ho et al. 2019: 9). For example, with this technology, the error rate in the detection of cancer-positive lymph nodes reduced from 3.4 to 0.5% in samples used (Wang et al. 2016). The deep learning system errors were not connected with human pathologist errors. Therefore, while a pathologist may be better than a deep learning system alone in terms of quality, incorporating a deep learning system and a human pathologist reduced the error rate in pathology testing. The smart tissue autonomous robot is the first example of robots that can help surgeons perform intestinal anastomoses, a surgical procedure that 'involves connecting the tubular loops of the intestine' (Shademan et al. 2016:1), as they are more accurate and faster than surgeons, but it is still under the surgeon's control (Shademan et al. 2016). Robot assistance can also control all vital signs during operations, provide verbal warnings when needed, information analysis and pathological testing, and can determine surgical margins in solid organ tumours (Camarillo et al. 2004).

Minimally invasive surgical (MIS) techniques have been developed to support surgeons to perform their surgery without any need to place their hands on the patient's body during an operation (Camarillo et al. 2004). This technique has revolutionised the concept of surgical procedures (Camarillo et al. 2004). In MIS, small incisions are made on the patient's body to insert observation tools and instruments. Long manipulators are used to conduct operations under physical control (Camarillo et al. 2004). It is, therefore, clear that the surgical damage in these methods is reduced and the recovery of the patient is faster. These methods have many advantages, but there are difficulties in some areas, such as conventional endoscopic instrumentation (Camarillo et al. 2004). The advantage of robotics is to reduce many of these barriers, while at the same time improving tremor filtration and motion scaling (Camarillo et al. 2004), which concerns the movement of the surgeon's large hands to smaller movements and has a major role in increasing accuracy in robotic surgical systems (Prasad et al. 2004). Surgeons may now teleoperate a robot in skilful, comfortable and intuitive ways Satava (1999). Ballantyne and Moll (2003) have reported that laparoscopic surgery 'transitional' technology has led to substantial improvements in robotic surgery use and clinical results.

Nursing & Allied Healthcare Applications

Human-like robot nurses (or nurse-bots) can be used to support healthcare professionals in Australia due to the shortage of healthcare workers and an increasingly ageing population, which is expected to increase to around 8.1 million in 2050 (ABS 2018).

Robot nurses help patients to perform their daily tasks such as dressing, bathing and assisting them to engage in social activities such as simple conversations. Using nurse-bots allows hospitals to provide nursing resources to other significant areas such as critical care or emergency rooms. They are also beneficial for the aged care sector and supporting elderly patients. For instance, in Australia a social robot named Matilda supports elderly people in nursing homes, providing entertainment and group activities. Matilda was designed to have various attributes, such as emotions, a voice, gestures, music, and movement, including dance (Khosla et al. 2012a).

According to the McKinsey Global Institute report, by 2030, 400 to 800 million employees across all sectors will be replaced by robots around the world (Lost 2017). It is predicted that 2.7 million Australians who now have jobs could be completely replaced by automation by 2034 (Taylor et al. 2019). Robotic nurses around the world are the revolution in the healthcare sector making tasks and procedures more efficient and safer. In recent years, the advancement of technology in nursing has occurred; however, none is comparable with the effect of AI in the healthcare sector. AI is used in nursing in different areas such as developing treatment plans, medication management and the simplification of repetitive jobs (Bini 2018). Therefore, some nurses are concerned that the increasing implementation of AI may render them jobless (Pepito and Locsin 2019). In Australia, it is predicted that using AI in the healthcare sector will also lead to job loss for people such as radiologists who carry out automatable activities (Taylor et al. 2019).

While using AI has some benefits for nurses, it also has downsides. Robot nurses can only perform those tasks they were designed to do and they lack the emotional intelligence of human beings, rendering it impossible for such nurse-bots to communicate with patients on an emotional level (at least with current technology). Patient privacy might also be jeopardised if there are insufficient standards of protection, as robots often collect patients' personal data from different departments, such as blood test and x-ray results and other examination outcomes (Liang et al. 2019b).

In hospitals, nurse robots work as supplementary healthcare workers. For example, the Da Vinci Surgical Robot is a robot used in more than 3600 hospitals around the world (Kelly n.d.). In Australia, a lifting robot is an example of a nursing robot used in elderly care. They assist elderly people by lifting and moving bed-bound patients and carrying medication and meal trays (Khosla et al. 2012b; Sparrow and Sparrow 2006). Pepper is the name of a social robot with emotion recognition and is used in trials in Australian hospitals to study how robots could support the quality of care of patients (Forbrig 2019). Robear is another example of a nurse robot that has been used in Japan (Szondy 2015). In addition, another robot named Tug is now being utilised in numerous hospitals for prescription dispensing. According to the International Data Corporation (2017), around the world \$91.5 billion was spent on robotics which will be increased to \$188 billion in 2020 (Croce et al. 2017), suggesting that the use of robotics in the healthcare sector is set to increase. In Australia, the 2018–19 Australian Federal budget announced an AU\$29.9 million investment over 4 years to support the development of AI (Williams 2019).

Technology advancements may make it easier for nurses to care for patients and perform their jobs safely (Pepito and Locsin 2019; Pepito and Locsin 2018). As examples, robotic-assisted surgery may one day replace nurses in operating rooms (Criss and Gadepalli 2018) and nurse-bots are replacing human nurses in some hospital departments (Eriksson and Salzmann-Erikson 2017). They also have increasing responsibilities such as supporting elderly patients, children with autism and people with disabilities. AI robots are also helping nurses in medication administration, which coupled with the major advancement of technology and AI, enables machines to coordinate patient care (Saraee et al. 2017), and make critical decisions in healthcare. As a result, nurses are facing challenges in the advancement of such technologies, especially in relation to their nursing practice. Resistance to change can often be found within the nursing fraternity amid these new technologies threatening and undermining their employment (Pepito and Locsin 2019). However, according to Healthcare Workforce, by 2025, all healthcare workers including nurses, doctors and midwives are expected to remain in the workforce even in situations of supply exceeding demand (Healthcare Workforce 2012).

Robot nurses learn to undertake nursing roles such as the measurement of vital signs, ambulation support, infectious disease protocols, medication administration and they augment the role of nurses in the delivery of care. Previous research indicates that, between 8% and 16% of nurses spend most of their time on non-nursing activities and duties that should be assigned to others. The challenge of AI assisted robot nurses is their lack of knowledgeable and complicated decision-making capabilities that are integral to the nursing role. For example, robots designed to remind patients to take medication are required to know the reason for patients refusing medications and need to have the ability to respond accordingly. Human nurses have knowledge, expertise, values and the ability to communicate and perform clinical roles effectively. In response to this, AI companies have developed machine learning applications to simplify daily tasks and computerise organisational processes to support nurses during patient treatment. To find the correct balance between AI support and personalised patient care, it is imperative that healthcare organisations balance their business needs by providing high quality care to patients and supporting clinicians to carry out their tasks efficiently.

Employment Impact

As discussed earlier in this chapter, the advancement of technology and the use of AI have major implications for the workforce (Wisskirchen et al. 2017). In Australia, with growing AI applications, different skills are required of employees even in healthcare. Advanced technology skills, high cognitive skills – such as applying specialist knowledge, social skills and emotional intelligence will be required by the healthcare workforce. In Australia, it is predicted that by 2030 there will be a shortage of 600,000 university graduates in the health sector (Taylor et al. 2019). However, it has also been suggested that the adoption of AI leads to increased employment opportunities and demand for new-age skills (Thrall et al. 2018). AI impacts 25% of jobs across the country, but this differs depending on occupation. For example, it is predicted that in the healthcare sector, more doctors and nurses will be needed, but there will be lower demand for radiologists (Taylor et al. 2019).

The use of AI in healthcare may lead to the assumption that greater use of artificial technologies and robotics, as explained earlier, might lead to a reduction of jobs in this sector (Montemanni et al. 2019). For example, based on a survey in Norway (Nordlander et al. 2016) participants perceived that the healthcare system would be changed by 2035 and that consequently, individuals would not see this sector as a viable employment option (Montemanni et al. 2019). Healthcare is however a critical sector that will absorb more and more resources soon; hence, AI and new technologies should be adopted to increase efficiency. This situation could shift the workforce to more specialised employment roles capable of dealing with the advancement of technology (Montemanni et al. 2019). Furthermore, the over-usage of technology could have negative effects on clinical practices, such as communication and the socio-emotional aspects of patient care. In addition, the communication skills of physicians may deteriorate due to reliance on technology, hindering them from sharing information with their patients (without human interactions) (Verghese 2008). Physicians might spend most of their time reading information from assessments of technology, and therefore less time interacting with their patients, which leads to decreased communication skills (Gallagher and Payne 2015). In the clinical field, previous studies have found that electronic medical systems could be a barrier to communicating with patients because doctors need to type the electronic medical records of patients when interacting with them (Cummings 2013).

Another concern may be the deterioration of bedside or physical examination skills. With the advancement and prevalence of technology, physicians are performing fewer physical examinations (Verghese and Horwitz 2009). For example, it is reported that the number of physicians using an electronic health record system has increased by 16.9% to 33.8% since 2008. It predicted that this number would increase in the next few years as hospitals and physicians' rooms have the willingness to provide high-quality services to patients (Graham-Jones et al. 2012). In clinical practice, the use of medical technology may blunt doctors' examination skills. Moreover, the Electronic Health Record (EHR) could also reduce clinical knowledge and narrative note-taking skills and abilities. In a study of 78 primary care physicians in New York, it was found that most clinicians, when they wanted to write patient visit reports, tended to cut and paste some parts from other patients (Lu 2016). Hoff also found that physicians progressively lost their ability to understand and abstract information, believing that patient information should be rich and unique in the standardised electronic health record format, thus undercutting their ability to make informed decisions around diagnosis and treatment (Hoff 2011).

Challenges & Opportunities

There are implications for management practice around how employees relate to AI, management-employee communication and how best to deploy AI to increase the efficiency, labour productivity and overall quality of patient care. Management must establish clear lines of communication that integrate AI in day-to-day work activities which must be underpinned by strict adherence to human resource management (HRM) policies and ethical guidelines. We argue that organisations need to consider the recruitment and selection of staff who may be open to AI, and also ensure that all employees receive training and development to better support them to work alongside AI interventions both ethically and operationally. More research needs to be carried out in organisations that compare what is happening for workers across the healthcare sector when they are required to engage with AI. We encourage further research that compares how AI is implemented and evaluated across different healthcare professional groups and different health care organisations. It is also important to conduct research into its impact on the quality of patient care, safety and clinician mental health and wellbeing, as well as work-related attitudes such as organisational commitment, resilience and intention to leave.

Conclusion

In conclusion, the use of AI in healthcare settings has important implications for medical practice, the quality of patient care, employment, the types of jobs in the sector, and the wellbeing of clinicians. The support AI offers doctors and nurses may significantly lighten the burden of caring for patients in a fast-paced and underfunded sector. The use of such technology in offering accurate diagnosis, drug dispensary and minor surgery, not only supports healthcare workers but can also offer positive effects on the quality of patient care, such as reduced waiting times and decreased mortality rates. The support AI offers healthcare staff may increase their perceived wellbeing, by freeing up their time from administrative tasks and allowing them to spend more time with patients supporting their socio-emotional needs.

The concern surrounding deskilling and unemployment may be warranted in some circumstances, as some clinical tasks, such as minor surgeries, can be undertaken through AI. However, AI creates opportunities for new job roles, upskilling through the utilisation of data generated by AI, and more individualised patient centred care by reducing administration and tedious manual labour. AI should be celebrated and embraced in healthcare, although carefully managed ethically and systematically, to ensure that it is used to improve the quality of clinician jobs, enhance the quality of patient care, and build healthier communities.

References

Abhinav, G., & Subrahmanyam, S. N. (2019). Artificial intelligence in healthcare. *Journal of Drug Delivery and Therapeutics, 9*(5-s), 164–166.

Arnold, D., & Wilson, T. (2017). *What doctor? Why AI and Robotics will define new health.*

Australian-Bureau-of-Statistics. (2018). *Population by age and sex, regions of Australia.* Australian Bureau of Statistics.

Ballantyne, G. H., & Moll, F. (2003). The da Vinci telerobotic surgical system: The virtual operative field and telepresence surgery. *Surgical Clinics, 83*(6), 1293–1304.

Bini, S. A. (2018). Artificial intelligence, machine learning, deep learning, and cognitive computing: What do these terms mean and how will they impact health care? *The Journal of Arthroplasty, 33*(8), 2358–2361.

Camarillo, D. B., Krummel, T. M., & Salisbury, J. K. (2004). Robotic technology in surgery: Past, present, and future. *The American Journal of Surgery, 188*(4), 2–15.

Chang, H. Y., Jung, C. K., Woo, J. I., Lee, S., Cho, J., Kim, S. W., & Kwak, T. Y. (2019). Artificial intelligence in pathology. *Journal of Pathology and Translational Medicine, 53*(1), 1–12. https://doi.org/10.4132/jptm.2018.12.16.

Contreras, I., & Vehi, J. (2018). Artificial intelligence for diabetes management and decision support: Literature review. *Journal of Medical Internet Research, 20*(5), 1–24.

Criss, C. N., & Gadepalli, S. K. (2018). Sponsoring surgeons: An investigation on the influence of the da Vinci robot. *The American Journal of Surgery, 216*(1), 84–87.

Croce, C., Goepfert, J., Zhang, J., & Soohoo, S. (2017). *International Data Corporation, worldwide semiannual robotics and drones spending guide.* Retrieved from https://www.idc.com/getdoc.jsp?containerId=IDC_P33201.

Cummings, C. L. (2013). Communication in the era of COWs: Technology and the physician–patient–parent relationship. *Pediatrics, 131*(3), 401–403.

Davenport, T., & Kalakota, R. (2019). The potential for artificial intelligence in healthcare. *Future Healthcare Journal, 6*(2), 94–98.

Dilsizian, S. E., & Siegel, E. L. (2014). Artificial intelligence in medicine and cardiac imaging: Harnessing big data and advanced computing to provide personalized medical diagnosis and treatment. *Current Cardiology Reports, 16*(1), 1–8.

Eriksson, H., & Salzmann-Erikson, M. (2017). The digital generation and nursing robotics: A netnographic study about nursing care robots posted on social media. *Nursing Inquiry, 24*(2), e12165.

Forbrig, P. (2019). Challenges in multi-user interaction with a social humanoid Robot Pepper. In *EICS Workshops* (pp. 10–17).

Frey, C. B., & Osborne, M. (2013). *The future of employment* (pp. 1–77). University of Oxford.

Gallagher, S., & Payne, H. (2015). The role of embodiment and intersubjectivity in clinical reasoning. *Body, Movement and Dance in Psychotherapy, 10*(1), 68–78.

Gambhir, S., Malik, S. K., & Kumar, Y. (2016). Role of soft computing approaches in healthcare domain: A mini review. *Journal of Medical Systems, 40*(12), 1–20.

Graham-Jones, P., Jain, S. H., Friedman, C. P., Marcotte, L., & Blumenthal, D. (2012). The need to incorporate health information technology into physicians' education and professional development. *Health Affairs, 31*(3), 481–487.

Gulshan, V., Peng, L., Coram, M., Stumpe, M. C., Wu, D., Narayanaswamy, A., & Cuadros, J. (2016). Development and validation of a deep learning algorithm for detection of diabetic retinopathy in retinal fundus photographs. *JAMA, 316*(22), 2402–2410.

Health Workforce Australia. (2012). *Health workforce 2025: Doctors, nurses and midwives.* Australia.

Ho, S. B., Yang, X., Quieta, T., Krishnamurthy, G., & Liausvia, F. (2019). On human-like performance artificial intelligence: A demonstration using an Atari game. In *Proceedings of the IEEE Conference on Computer Vision and Pattern Recognition Workshops* (pp. 9–12).

Hoff, T. (2011). Deskilling and adaptation among primary care physicians using two work innovations. *Health Care Management Review, 36*(4), 338–348.

Hope, Z. (2020, September 5). Doctors concerned people with stroke are staying away from hospital. *The Age*. Accessed 09 Sept 2020. https://www.theage.com.au/national/victoria/doctors-concerned-people-with-stroke-are-staying-away-from-hospital-20200904-p55sjg.html

Jha, S., & Topol, E. J. (2016). Adapting to artificial intelligence: Radiologists and pathologists as information specialists. *JAMA, 316*(22), 2353–2354.

Kelly, S. (n.d.). *New surgical robots may get a boost in operating rooms*. Retrieved July 19, 2018, from Scientific American: https://www.scientificamerican.com/article/new-surgical-robots-may-get-a-boost-in-operating-rooms/.

Khosla, R., Chu, M. T., Kachouie, R., Yamada, K., Yoshihiro, F., & Yamaguchi, T. (2012a). Interactive multimodal social robot for improving quality of care of elderly in Australian nursing homes. In *Proceedings of the 20th ACM international conference on Multimedia* (pp. 1173–1176).

Khosla, R., Chu, M. T., Kachouie, R., Yamada, K., & Yamaguchi, T. (2012b, January). Embodying care in Matilda: an affective communication robot for the elderly in Australia. In *Proceedings of the 2nd ACM SIGHIT International Health Informatics Symposium* (pp. 295–304).

Kok, J. N., Boers, E., Kosters, W. A., Van der Putten, P., & Poel, M. (2009). Artificial intelligence: Definition, trends, techniques, and cases. *Artificial Intelligence, 1*, 270–299.

Köse, E., Öztürk, N. N., & Karahan, S. R. (2018). Artificial intelligence in surgery. *European Archives of Medical Research, 34*, S4–S6.

Ku, M., Brown, T., Malbon, A., Bartram, T., Cavanagh, J., & Halvorsen, B. (2020). Provision of a consistent national approach to Radiation Therapy workforce protection measures in Australia during the COVID-19 pandemic, *Australian Health Review* (in press).

Lee, J. D. (2018). Perspectives on automotive automation and autonomy. *Journal of Cognitive Engineering and Decision Making, 12*(1), 53–57.

Lee, C. S., Nagy, P. G., Weaver, S. J., & Newman-Toker, D. E. (2013). Cognitive and system factors contributing to diagnostic errors in radiology. *American Journal of Roentgenology, 201*(3), 611–617.

Liang, H., Tsui, B. Y., Ni, H., Valentim, C. C., Baxter, S. L., Liu, G., & He, L. (2019b). Evaluation and accurate diagnoses of pediatric diseases using artificial intelligence. *Nature Medicine, 25*(3), 433–438.

Lost, J. (2017). Jobs Gained: Workforce transitions in a time of automation. McKinsey & Company.

Lu, J. (2016). Will medical technology Deskill Doctors?. *International Education Studies, 9*(7), 130–134.

Luxton, D. D. (2014). Artificial intelligence in psychological practice: Current and future applications and implications. *Professional Psychology: Research and Practice, 45*(5), 1–12.

Mindfiels. (2018). *Artificial intelligence in healthcare*. Retrieved from https://www.cpaaustralia.com.au/-/media/corporate/allfiles/document/employers/ai-in-healthcare-.

Mirnezami, R., & Ahmed, A. (2018). Surgery 3.0, artificial intelligence and the next-generation surgeon. *British Journal of Surgery, 105*(5), 463–465.

Montemanni, R., Guzzi, J., & Giusti, A. (2019). Artificial intelligence for healthcare and rescuing technology: Technical developments and thoughts about employment impacts. *Millenium*, (10), 77–82.

Nordlander, T. E., Lamorgese, L., Nguyen, T. V. L., & Montemanni, R. (2016). Homecare planning, a challenging task in a growing market. *Lecture Notes in Management Science, 8*, 67.

Patel, V. L., Shortliffe, E. H., Stefanelli, M., Szolovits, P., Berthold, M. R., Bellazzi, R., & Abu-Hanna, A. (2009). The coming of age of artificial intelligence in medicine. *Artificial Intelligence in Medicine, 46*(1), 5–17.

Pearce, C., McLeod, A., Reinhart, N., Whyte, R., Deveny, E., & Shearer, M. (2019). Artificial intelligence and the clinical world: A view from the front line. *The Medical Journal of Australia, 210*(6), 38–40.

Pepito, J. A., & Locsin, R. (2018). Can nursing drive technological advances in healthcare in the Asia-Pacific? *Asian/Pacific Island Nursing Journal, 3*(4), 190–198.

Pepito, J. A., & Locsin, R. (2019). Can nurses remain relevant in a technologically advanced future? *International Journal of Nursing Sciences, 6*(1), 106–110.

Prasad, S. M., Prasad, S. M., Maniar, H. S., Chu, C., Schuessler, R. B., & Damiano, R. J., Jr. (2004). Surgical robotics: Impact of motion scaling on task performance. *Journal of the American College of Surgeons, 199*(6), 863–868.

Ramesh, A., Kambhampati, C., Monson, J. R., & Drew, P. (2004). Artificial intelligence in medicine. *Annals of the Royal College of Surgeons of England, 86*(5), 334–338.

Reddy, S. (2018). Use of artificial intelligence in healthcare delivery *eHealth-Making Health Care Smarter*. IntechOpen.

Saraee, E., Joshi, A., & Betke, M. (2017). *A therapeutic robotic system for the upper body based on the Proficio robotic arm.* Paper presented at the 2017 International Conference on Virtual Rehabilitation (ICVR).

Satava, R. M. (1999). Emerging technologies for surgery in the 21st century. *Archives of Surgery, 134*(11), 1197–1202.

Schulz, P. J., & Nakamoto, K. (2013). Patient behavior and the benefits of artificial intelligence: The perils of "dangerous" literacy and illusory patient empowerment. *Patient Education and Counseling, 92*(2), 223–228.

Shademan, A., Decker, R. S., Opfermann, J. D., Leonard, S., Krieger, A., & Kim, P. C. (2016). Supervised autonomous robotic soft tissue surgery. *Science Translational Medicine, 8*(337), 337ra364–337ra364.

Shapiro, S. C. (1992). *Encyclopedia of artificial intelligence* (2nd ed., pp. 1229–1234). New York: John Wiley & Sons, Inc.

Smith, A., & Anderson, J. (2014). AI, robotics, and the future of jobs. *Pew Research Center*, 1–77.

Sparrow, R., & Sparrow, L. (2006). In the hands of machines? The future of aged care. *Minds and Machines, 16*(2), 141–161.

Szondy, D. (2015). Robear robot care bear designed to serve Japan's aging population'.

Taylor, C., Carrigan, J., Noura, H., Ungur, S., van Halder, J., & Singh Dandona, G. (2019). *Australia's automation opportunity: reigniting productivity and inclusive income growth* (pp. 1–111). Mckinsey & Company.

Thrall, J. H., Li, X., Li, Q., Cruz, C., Do, S., Dreyer, K., & Brink, J. (2018). Artificial intelligence and machine learning in radiology: Opportunities, challenges, pitfalls, and criteria for success. *Journal of the American College of Radiology, 15*(3), 504–508.

Trump, D. (2019, February 11). Executive order on maintaining American leadership in artificial intelligence. *Executive Order, US White House.*

Verghese, A. (2008). Culture shock — Patient as icon, icon as patient. *New England Journal of Medicine, 359*(26), 2748–2751.

Verghese, A., & Horwitz, R. I. (2009). In praise of the physical examination. *British Medical Journal Publishing Group.*

Wang, D., Khosla, A., Gargeya, R., Irshad, H., & Beck, A. H. (2016). Deep learning for identifying metastatic breast cancer. *arXiv preprint arXiv:1606.05718.*

Warwick, K. (2013). *Artificial intelligence: The basics.* Routledge.

Williams, M. A. (2019). The artificial intelligence race: Will Australia lead or lose? *Journal of Proceedings of the Royal Society of New South Wales, 152*(1), 105–114.

Wilson, T. (2017). *No longer science fiction, AI and Robotics are transforming healthcare.*

Wisskirchen, G., Biacabe, B. T., Bormann, U., & Muntz, A. (2017). *Artificial intelligence and robotics and their impact on the workplace* (pp. 2–120). IBA Global Employment Institute.

Chapter 12
Utilities

Chi-Tsun Cheng, Nuwan Ganganath, Tsz-Kwan Lee, and Kai-Yin Fok

Abstract In this chapter, the authors focus on the impact of artificial intelligence (AI) and associated technological changes on work and jobs in Australia's utility sector. The chapter comprises extensive commentary on the collective effects of AI incorporating machine learning, big data, blockchain, and other technological advances. The aim is to attempt to predict vocational areas in this industry sector that may diminish, noting that it is a demanding task amidst a plethora of differing views. The analysis mainly focuses on disruptive technology in a relatively broad context that is intended to complement knowledge contributed within other chapters that focus on different industry sectors.

Keywords Artificial intelligence · Disruption · Jobs · Utility sector

Introduction

This chapter focuses on the impact of artificial intelligence on the utility sector in relation to employment. The utility sector provides basic amenities, such as water, sewage services, electricity, natural gas, and renewable energy. In this chapter, an industry overview is outlined, along with prominent new technologies that impact on productivity and the workforce as well as relevant challenges and opportunities. The chapter ends by outlining the key issues identified in the research.

C.-T. Cheng (✉)
RMIT University, Melbourne, VIC, Australia
e-mail: ben.cheng@rmit.edu.au

N. Ganganath
The University of Western Australia, Perth, WA, Australia
e-mail: manganganath@gmail.com

T.-K. Lee
Deakin University, Melbourne, VIC, Australia
e-mail: glory.lee@deakin.edu.au

K.-Y. Fok
An Independent Researcher, Hong Kong, China
e-mail: kyfok@ieee.org

A. Nankervis et al. (eds.), *The Fourth Industrial Revolution*,
https://doi.org/10.1007/978-981-16-1614-3_12

Industry Overview

The energy industry overlaps with the utility industry in terms of the overall responsibility for the production and distribution of energy, water, and gas throughout Australia. The utility industry sector comprises companies participating in the exploration and development of coal, uranium, oil and gas and renewable energy assets (Australian Stock Exchange 2013).

Australia has rich natural resources and possesses extensive energy assets (Australian Stock Exchange 2013; Australian Renewable Energy Agency 2018). Australia is also the world's largest coal exporter and a major supplier of LNG (Liquefied Natural Gas) and Uranium to world markets, in particular Asia. Companies in the utility sector are generally involved in water, electricity, and gas distribution, generation, and infrastructure. The utility industry is charged with responsibility for the infrastructure used to provide public services, sewerage systems, power line distribution, stormwater drains, and more. The utility sector, including energy, has major employers among its ranks in all states creating approximately 155,000 jobs for electrical engineers, civil engineers, chemical engineers, and many other professionals (Nichols n.d.).

Many other occupations feature in this sector and as illustrated in Table 12.1, the jobs included range from professions to trades, semi-skilled and unskilled jobs. These will be outlined with estimations on the level that AI is expected to impact on jobs and the future of employment in this sector. In 2013 Bloomberg estimated the

Table 12.1 Impact of AI on jobs in utility industry sector

Occupations	Susceptibility to automation % (Source: Byrds et al. 2017)	Future growth (Source: Job Outlook 2020)	Skill level (Source: Job Outlook 2020)
Chemical and Materials Engineers	Both 10%	Moderate	Very high skill
Chemical, Gas, Petroleum & Power Plant Operators	All 56%	Stable	Medium skill
Civil Engineering Professionals	All 10%	Very strong	Very high skill
Electrical Distribution Trades Workers	Both 36%	Stable	Medium skill
Electrical Engineers	10%	Moderate	Very high skill
Electricians	All 41%	Moderate	Medium skill
Environmental Scientists	All 44%	Strong	Very high skill
Other Stationary Plant Operators	All 68%	Strong	Lower skill
Recycling and Rubbish Collectors	46%	Moderate	Lower skill
Truck Drivers	All 48%	Moderate	Lower skill

Source: Created by the authors using occupations listed in the information media and telecommunication industry by (Job Outlook 2020) and job susceptibility due to automation forecasts by (Byrds et al. 2017)

market capital worth of the top 100 stocks in the energy and utilities field to be worth a sizeable AUD $130.5 billion (Australian Stock Exchange 2013).

In the next decade, it is anticipated by (Nichols n.d.) that this industry sector will alter significantly (Lauterbach and Bonime-Blanc 2018). The research points to three main challenges. These include: (i) growing demand for renewable energy sources, (ii) a mounting need to invest in Australia's energy infrastructure, and (iii) the pressure to adapt to revised policies and public expectations, as private and public organisations meet environmental changes and challenges aided by artificial intelligence which is having a considerable impact on the utility sector (Lauterbach and Bonime-Blanc 2018).

Employment Impact

Industry 4.0 (I4.0) technologies, including automation and artificial intelligence (AI), may cause some labour-intensive jobs to become obsolete (Skilton and Hovsepian 2018; Susskind 2020; World Economic Forum 2020). However, at the same time, the transformation process brings in new business opportunities to the market, which creates new jobs (Furness 2019). Most of the tools and equipment in the utility sector are designed to be operated and maintained by the workforce and most likely, technological developments will continuously augment the workforce. Vocational fields under threat of abolition due to automation in all industries involve repetitive and routine work (Frey and Osborne 2017; Manpower Group 2018; O'Neill 2017; Susskind 2020; World Economic Forum 2016). As pointed out previously many people work in semi-skilled and unskilled positions work in the utility industry sector (Job Outlook 2020). To further substantiate the notion that many routine/repetitive jobs are at risk, (Manyika et al. 2017) cite copious largescale studies which claim such occupations were at risk. They contend that in all industries, including the utility sector, there will be change that is propelled by emerging technologies in the 4th industrial revolution (4IR) that will eliminate activities that involve routine vocational tasks – including physical work and many other jobs – that reduce the need to employ people (Manyika et al. 2017). Currently, however, humans are good at handling complex problems and, with interpretations of sensory perception, while machines are better with repetitive tasks that require high precision and speed (Susskind 2020).

Apart from processes that involve physical machines, automation can also bring transformations to paper-based and management workflows that exist in all businesses (Susskind 2020; Manyika et al. 2017). Filing robots can undertake and data entry tasks at high speed and with a low error rate (Susskind 2020; Manyika et al. 2017). With an effectively designed AI algorithm, relatively fairer judgements can be made in some day-to-day decision-making processes. Businesses can also reduce their expenditure on recruiting and training management personnel (Dignan 2020).

The utility industry, which was considered a slow mover in technology adoption, needs to increase its competitive edge by undertaking digital transformation while facing new challenges – including competition from new sources driven by technology and by changes in consumer demand (ABI Research 2019). In some countries the utility industry has been upgrading its infrastructure by conducting digital transformation (ABI Research 2019) with projects costing US$14 billion being spent on modernising the infrastructure of the utility industry in the United States. In addition, an estimated 55% of the total expense on security measures will be spent on securing smart infrastructure to tackle the rising cybersecurity risk (ABI Research 2019).

New technologies such as the Internet of Things (IoT) and big data enable new perspectives on renewable energy, storage, and distributed energy resources (DERs). In 2015, more than 250 million IoT devices were installed in utilities, globally (APEC 2015). IoT spending in 2019 is expected to be US$726 billion, and it is anticipated that US$1 trillion will be exceeded in 2022 (IDC 2019). Moreover, big data plays a vital role in making use of unstructured data to enhance competitive advantage and the efficiencies of the utility industry. It is expected that 65% of power, gas, and water companies will deploy edge computing to optimise their assets in the United States (Villali 2018).

Table 12.1 indicates the proportion of jobs in the utility sector that are susceptible to automation. Numerous occupations in the utility sector are listed using job forecasting by (Byrds et al. 2017; Job Outlook 2020) for a balanced perspective. Table 12.1 indicates that low skill occupations will require considerably fewer staff given the impact of artificial intelligence on these occupations.

The increasing adaptation of high-speed machines and intelligent controllers in workplaces indicates a major disruption to the vocational job market. Specifically, data (see Byrds et al. 2017) suggests that lower skilled jobs (truck drivers, recycling and rubbish collectors, "other" stationary plant operators), and chemical, gas, petroleum and power plant operators are all in vocational fields destined to experience significant susceptibility to automation. However, jobs which require medium to very high skill levels are also not immune to disruption. In the utility sector, electrical distribution trades workers possess medium skills, but the susceptibility to automation is ranked at 36% which suggests that one person in three in the occupations in this category may lose their jobs. Environmental scientists, despite having high-level skills, are also likely to be susceptible to automation which indicates many job losses as AI encroaches on the professions in this category (see Table 12.1–46%).

Key Technologies

Energy

Electricity generation companies are upgrading their infrastructure by adopting new technologies such as the industrial internet of things (IIoT), machine learning, and Cloud computing on asset monitoring (Rebolini et al. 2017), smart metering

(Gordon 2019; T&D World Staff 2019), predictive maintenance, and the operations of distributed energy resources (DERs) (Darrell 2019). The implicit risk in adopting the new technologies in developed countries has raised awareness in various arenas as the changes in demand could affect the self-sustainability of the existing utility networks, thus influencing the reliability standards in the industry (Sotter 2019).

The cost of electricity transmission can be significantly reduced with the help of AI (T&D World 2020). Solutions adopting IIoT and machine learning can collect behavioural information concerning asset depreciation and maintenance and support preventive maintenance programs. IIoT can be employed in utilities such as electricity-generating coal plants where, with the aid of sensor networks and AI, a new control operating platform can be developed to increase the efficiency of the plant. Also, operational faults and maintenance issues can be predicted in advance.

IIoT devices have outperformed their counterparts in monitoring applications. Compared to traditional sensing devices, IIoT devices are low-cost and easily installed. These devices can be widely deployed to legacy machines or equipment that was not previously monitored. Also, IIoT devices can communicate through the internet, which helps to establish a sensor network within a short timeframe (West 2018).

Drones enable the utility sector to extend their sensing capabilities at a relatively low cost significantly. Overhead transmission cables (Nichols 2019) and other utility assets can now be inspected via drones rapidly and regularly, which allows service providers to perform predictive maintenance and avoid nationwide outages. However, drones and other autonomous vehicles operating in the working environment can be a hazard to other human workers within proximity. Those issues can be handled with smart sensors and motion capture technologies (Vicon 2019). With the help of machine learning, drones can estimate motions of moving subjects in the environment and avoid them.

To reduce capital expenses, utilities are likely to cooperate with third-party companies to establish, upgrade, and maintain a communication network (Grijpink et al. 2018). Instead of developing a new communication infrastructure, Dakota Valley Electric Cooperative, an electric company in North Dakota, USA, cooperated with a national cell phone service provider to establish a sensor network with 9300 smart meters over a short timeframe. Such partnerships help the company in saving millions of dollars (Verizon 2017).

In an ordinary power generation system, energy is generated from various power sources, including coal, hydro, and nuclear power plants. These sources can fulfil most of the energy demand throughout the day. The key drawback is that they involve large overheads in cranking them up after a complete shutdown (Ganganath et al. 2017), so they are normally left in continuous operating modes. To cope with the demands during peak hours, peaker plants, such as gas turbines, which can operate almost instantly but less efficiently, are used to top up the supply. However, the introduction of renewable energy sources has imposed new challenges to the system as they introduce fluctuations to energy supply, such as through wind turbines and solar panels. Extra energy storage and sensing units are needed for storing and releasing energy dynamically depending on the needs. In most existing power grids, sensing devices have been installed at major branches and leaf nodes to continuously collect system parameters at the hundred-millisecond time resolution (Faheem et al. 2018).

With the development of DERs, buyers and sellers will begin to merge in the electricity market. Buildings, including residential, can generate and store electricity resulting in excess energy being generated which can be released to the market. Electric vehicles (EVs) can also function as mobile DERs, and buyers can thus introduce dynamic factors that add to the grid. Still, in the process, since the generation is uneven, it can jeopardise its stability (Furukawa 2019). With the emergence of distributed power generation units like rooftop solar panels, power retailers need a mechanism to pay households who contributed power to the grid but, more importantly, the system has to regulate the quality of the power by monitoring and to compensate all the fluctuations introduced by different power sources and loads continuously (Hinson 2019). IIoT-based platforms (Connected Technology Solutions 2019) allow users to optimise their energy usage and reduce their carbon footprint.

To eliminate the impact introduced by the increasing number of DERs to the grid, explicitly monitoring and controlling the power flow at every node in the grid can be achieved with IIoT devices and Cloud computing (Vidhyalakshmi and Kumar 2016). Not only new tools on the Cloud are available, but new business opportunities are also created at the same time (Amazon Web Services 2017). To maintain their competitive edge and self-sustainability, electric companies must adapt to the changing electricity market. Nonetheless, rising issues such as cybersecurity, service availability and data ownership must also be tackled.

Water, Oil, and Gas

By employing sensor networks to the aging water infrastructure, water scarcity and loss can be dealt with efficiently. For example, corroding pipes can be inspected by using sensors, and leaks can be traced. Smart technologies provide a track record to not only the utility companies but also the consumers about their water usage. For example, Sydney Water has applied IIoT technologies on upgrading its service by deploying low-cost sensors to gather data and conduct further data analytics (Prackwieser et al. 2019). Service faults can be detected beforehand, which help to establish better maintenance plans. It is reported that water interruptions to over 100,000 properties were avoided, and water interruptions were detected in advance for over 50,000 customers within 1 year. To support developing countries to employ water-monitoring equipment, a smart low-cost device was created (IEEE IoT Tech Expo 2019). Also, this low-cost device diverts water storage during drier phases by enabling better planning for the drainage systems (Fell et al. 2019).

Recent advancements in IIoT technologies provide new ways to conduct asset integrity management (AIM) promptly and continuously in the oil and gas industry (Maguire 2019a). The integrated system allows business operators to schedule an inspection and perform preventive maintenance in a cost-effective manner, which can ultimately reduce their cost due to downtimes and possibly enhance productivity. Integrating IIoT systems with AIM allows data to be aggregated with minimum human interventions and thus reduces data-entry errors and potential security risks (Maguire 2019b).

AI technologies have been used in the oil and gas sector for classifying types of rock while drilling to improve efficiency (Pallanich 2019). Digital twin models have been developed to indicate the status of machines and the condition of the environment in real-time, which enables continuous optimisation. Autonomous robots, including unmanned aerial vehicles (UAVs) and unmanned underwater vehicles (UUVs), will be digitally coordinated with surveillance systems to perform asset integrity management (AIM), which allows the human workforce to be "redistributed" to tasks that are too costly to be automated (Lu et al. 2019).

The adoption of AI not only allow businesses in the oil and gas sector to perform maintenance tasks predictively and avoid downtimes it also enables predictive maintenance and introduces new business opportunities for selling lubricants and other oil by-products (Michu 2020). Consumable suppliers can help other companies to monitor the health condition of their machines, proactively provide maintenance suggestions, and arrange the delivery of the right amount of consumables in time.

The oil and gas sectors are reluctant to store their data off-site. However, while having on-site data can have advantages such as higher security and having a more rapid data access rate, the cost to own and maintain a state-of-the-art business and IT system for more than 10^{23} bytes of data annually is high (Sharma 2019). The elastic storage and computational power offered by modern Cloud and I4.0 systems make it attractive for the industry to consider data storage and processing off-premises, as partnering with a Cloud service provider allows access to industrial-graded security measures at a low cost (Michu 2020). It also opens new opportunities as the data is accessible throughout an organisation, which enables the synchronisation among departments and the whole value chain (Michu 2020).

Challenges and Opportunities

In this section, eight fundamental challenges in the utility sector are identified that are linked with developments in new technologies.

Lack of Talent and Appropriate Training

Like many tech giants, utility companies are aware of the importance and the power of their data. However, as indicated in Vigliarolo (2020), very few of them analyse and make effective use of the data. Many employees are not aware of how to use the data to assist their decision making in their daily tasks, which means most of the efforts in data collection are being wasted. Training is required to help employees to realise what data they need and to equip them with the skillsets and tools for working with data.

Even though many job titles may become obsolete as they could be replaced with AI-based and I4.0 systems, many new job positions are likely to emerge as intelligent information systems where regular updates and fine-tuning are needed to keep up with their dynamic production environment (Dawson et al. 2019). In time these newly created positions will be absorbed in the technological advances stemming from the enduring or continually recurring changes induced by AI (Susskind 2020). Programmers are needed to monitor the correctness of AI-algorithms in terms of accuracy and fairness and to ensure the consistency of the autonomous decision-making process under different intrinsic and extrinsic influences. For applications where discretion and exceptions apply, expert-systems should only be used to assist human decision-makers. Auditors with engineering backgrounds are required to regularly assess the intentional and non-intentional impacts imposed by intelligent algorithms. Professional consultants will also be needed to regularly review algorithms and system architectures to ensure they comply with Australian and International laws and regulations. Strong demand in data scientists/analysts is expected as they are essential for ensuring attributes in data have been handled by AI-based information systems in an unbiased manner and to help prevent potential privacy breaches. To enhance the transparency of Utility 4.0 systems, technical writers are necessary to convert sophisticated algorithms into layman readable documentations. To prepare the workforce for the upcoming challenges, experienced trainers are critical to the development of training programs for AI developers and users, on ethical AI practices and standards. The lack of training personnel and resources could slow the growth of Utility 4.0 technology adoption in the utility sector.

Cyber-Physical Attacks

Utility networks comprise tremendous numbers of sub-systems, which are geographically distributed within and across nations. Fully integrating them with Utility 4.0 technologies can improve their overall utilisation, while at the same time make them more vulnerable and fragile to supply and demand fluctuations (Zhang et al. 2017). Interconnecting utility infrastructure using communication networks also exposes the system to software glitches and cyber-attacks (Faheem et al. 2018). With utility networks connected online, cyber-physical attacks have become a potential challenge. The Department of Energy in the US have been steering the development of roadmaps in deploying countermeasures into their energy delivery systems (Energy Sector Control Systems Working Group 2011). A cyber-physical attack often begins with gaining access to network-level parameters. From there, the weakness of a utility network can be spotted, and attackers will initiate attacks to bring a set of nodes offline which could trigger a system-level failure with minimum effort. In SRIVASTAVA et al. (2018), network science techniques have been developed to assess and quantify the vulnerability of a utility network. The outcomes allow early detection and blocking of cyber-physical attacks.

Security

Security and privacy issues related to Utility 4.0 are significant concerns of service providers and end-users. Smart meters and Cloud clusters need to authenticate each other's identities before exchanging customers' usage information. Password-based authentications have demonstrated many shortcomings in IIoT and other applications that comprise massive volumes of connected entities with limited capabilities (World Economic Forum 2020). Alternatives, including password-less authentications, can address both the security and scalability issues at a lower cost. The effort and time saved from managing passwords can bring better user experience and help companies generate new revenue (World Economic Forum 2020).

I4.0 or IIoT devices require regular software updates to fix programming bugs and tackle new security exploitations. Unlike consumer electronics, which commonly have an average of 5-year of technical support from their release dates (Perlow 2020), industrial devices are expected to operate for 10+ years and with a very high expectation on their reliabilities under harsh operating environments. Apart from relying on the support commitments from the II4.0 solution providers over the lifetime of the products, a more sustainable approach for utility companies is to have their in-house application developers work on open-source platforms, which introduces a strong demand for programmers and security experts.

Artificial Intelligence, Privacy, and Ethics

While AI is good at revealing hidden correlations in data, it is worth noting that we are still years or even decades from Artificial General Intelligence, which refers to AI that can be applied to an arbitrary context without special training or fine-tuning. Most of the AI implementations that are operating in the field today are adopting the "human-in-the-loop approach" (Gopalakrishna et al. 2017). In this process, the crucial role of a human operator is to safeguard the decision-making process by resolving biases, ethical issues, and vague interpretations in AI training processes (Gopalakrishna et al. 2017). A typical example is panic buying behaviour in the recent pandemic outbreak. The sudden surge in demands for masks and hygiene products due to freak events can cause an AI system to act irrationally as it has no or inadequate contextual information (Heaven 2020). Training processes in ordinary AI implementations often require access to massive volumes of data collected from assets including sensors and cameras. For understanding and predicting the behaviours of a target group, personal data can be involved which is likely to lead to privacy and ethical issues (Heaven 2020). The major obstacles are often the difficulty in seeking consensus from the subjects due to poor communication and lack of trust between the parties (Wilson 2019).

Social Responsibility

Apart from focusing on the economic benefits that Utility 4.0 technologies can bring to the industry, the rising public concerns on the impact of these technologies on the environment and social sustainability have stressed the expectation for the industry to develop scientific ways to quantify their impact. One possible solution is to adopt the assessment method proposed in (Bai et al. 2020) which involves a non-linear mapping between performance parameters and evaluation metrics which measure the corresponding influences on the United Nations Sustainable Development Goals. The same approach can be applied to Utility 4.0 solutions.

Electric Vehicles and Distributed Energy Resources

The rapid adoption of EVs and DERs have imposed stress and fluctuations on energy networks. EVs' owners, who are likely to perform charging in the evening, are likely to trigger power surges in the network, especially at times of the year when the demands for air conditioning and heating are also high. DERs, which primarily comprise solar panels, on the other hand, will inject extra power into the system during the daytime. Such a mismatch induces the demand for energy storage units and pricing policies to steer the behaviours of the end-users. (Patil and Kalkhambkar 2019) showed that, by coordinating the charging schedules of EVs via an information system, the charging cost of each EV could be minimised and help to flatten the power peaks in the network. The same can be applied with regard to coordinating gas-powered water boilers and wet electric appliances within the same water distribution network. Moreover, in the study conducted by the National Renewable Energy Laboratory of the United States (Ardani et al. 2018), it has been shown that instabilities in a power grid can be mitigated by coordinating DERs in the area via an information system.

An Open Utility Market

Blockchain is the enabling technology behind many popular cryptocurrencies, including Bitcoin (Nakamoto 2014) and Ethereum (Wood 2015). The abstract ideas of blockchain and its first application, Bitcoin, were introduced in Nakamoto's white paper in 2014 (Nakamoto 2014). Blockchain is a distributed database with an irreversible nature whereby new data can only be appended to the end of the chain. As each block contains a hashed version of its previous block, modifying the data in a single block requires the modification of all the blocks built on top of the underpinning blocks. The chain is replicated and stored on multiple nodes on the blockchain network, which makes the database immune to a single-point-of-failure and virtually impossible to shut down. Transactions among individuals are broadcast and verified by blockchain nodes on the network in a fully distributed manner such that a central regulatory authority is not necessary. Cryptocurrencies and utility systems share similarities, including many data exchanges among individuals (Christidis and Devetsikiotis 2016). By integrating utility networks with blockchains, machine-to-machine (M2M) communications can be executed freely and securely without the need for a centralised system (Pureswaran and Brody 2015). The deployment and maintenance costs of a Utility 4.0 network can, therefore, be vastly reduced. With the tamper-proof nature of blockchains, less computational resources are required to secure the transactions. Dong et al. (Dong et al. 2018) discussed the application of blockchain technologies in future utility systems. As Utility 4.0 systems will be primarily based on Industrial IoT devices and Cloud systems, blockchain serves as a secure platform for data storage and verification. Smart contracts can be issued and executed autonomously among utility companies, individual DER operators, and end-users, which allow a more open utility market.

Marching Into the Post-pandemic era

The Coronavirus outbreak crisis in 2020 has triggered utility industries to reassess their day-to-day business practices and reposition their technology adoption strategies to adapt to the post-pandemic era. Maintaining social distancing at the workplace is essential for slowing down the future waves of the contagious virus before a vaccine becomes widely available. On the bright side, by incorporating the workforce into the digital-twin model, Utility 4.0 technologies can help the utility sector to remain competitive and agile in such a difficult time (Javaid et al. 2020). In this section, three cases of Utility 4.0 technologies are outlined which can tackle issues in the sector during a pandemic.

Redesign Workflows to Minimise Human Contacts

Workflows and the layouts of the workplace need to be redesigned to minimise human-to-human contacts in day-to-day businesses. Virtual reality (VR) technologies can be used to quickly evaluate workflows and structures to identify the underlying biohazards. Hundreds and thousands of designs and their combinations can speedily be realised in the virtual space at low cost. Once a design has been chosen,

VR can then be used for training the workforce to adapt to the new setup (Ulmer et al. 2019). The utilisation of VR technologies in the training process allows human instructors to provide supervision remotely to reduce physical contacts further.

Maintenance tasks that required technical support personnel to work face-to-face with operators on-site in the past can now be accomplished with the support team assessing the situation remotely using Augmented Reality (AR) technologies. Live video streams captured by operators on site allow the remote support team to conduct accurate situational assessments. The support team can then provide suggestions and instructions to the operators by interactively annotating in the augmented space. The AR technology allows a single supportive team to manage multiple sites.

Contact Tracing

The workforce in the utility sector, particularly for those involved in routine maintenance tasks, are often required to work in confined spaces such as maintenance holes, which imposes challenges in enforcing social distancing rules. Nevertheless, due to poor ventilation, social distancing needs to be carried out both spatially and temporally. That is space should not be used by other personnel within a fixed duration of time, which would be determined by the size of the space and the ventilation condition.

In mid-July 2020, the World Health Organization (WHO) changed its guidance on the airborne transmission of COVID-19 to "cannot be ruled out". While maintaining social distancing and personal hygiene remain the commonly adopted approaches in slowing down the pandemic, for places where social distancing cannot be maintained, wearing surgical masks, and keeping the space well ventilated are recommended. By integrating sensing and monitoring systems into the Utility 4.0 systems, utility companies can have real-time information on their workforce, which allows them to make dynamic plans in minimising the possibility of airborne transmissions. By integrating video technologies and machine learning algorithms, existing surveillance systems can be used to detect if the staff have worn the appropriate safety gear before entering a workspace (Kamoona et al. 2019).

Besides, airflow meters and revolution sensors can be installed in air ducts and fans, respectively to continuously monitor ventilation conditions. To ensure the sustainability of the system, the airflow of a room should be regulated proportionally to its number of occupants. Kurihara et al. (2016) have demonstrated a cost-effective way of monitoring and regulating in-door pressure. Their design utilises a single low-cost aeration fan to act as both a sensor and an actuator. When the indoor-outdoor air pressure difference has exceeded a certain threshold, the fan will act like a windmill and start spinning. Such an action will cause the fan to generate electricity which triggers the fan circuitry to turn on and keep the air pressure difference within a desirable range. Controlling air pressure in confined workspaces is crucial in containing highly contagious respiratory droplets.

Shifting Utility Demand under COVID-19

As more people are required to work or study from home due to the pandemic, demands have been shifted from commercial districts toward residential districts. This makes load shifting even more critical as residential districts often, by design, have comparatively lower energy reserve margins. Ali et al. (2019) have performed a simulation study on the effect of load shifting in Australia's residential areas. According to their research, Australia's energy demands can be accomplished with its renewable energy sources by shifting the utilisation window of electric water boilers in residential areas by as little as an hour. With Utility 4.0 systems, utility prices will be adjusted dynamically. Smart appliances will intelligently pick the right time to turn on to reduce the overall cost and ultimately yield a more stable system (Elham and Shahram 2017).

Conclusion

Existing challenges in the industry, together with new challenges due to the adoption of modern i4.0 concepts and technologies in their day-to-day businesses, have been discussed. Their corresponding solutions proposed in the literature in recent years have been reviewed. From there, several fundamental research gaps and business opportunities have been identified. Several emerging demands in the utility sector due to the outbreak of COVID-19 have also been identified and practical solutions have been introduced. It is argued that Utility 4.0 technologies are not disrupting but instead are transforming the job market in the utility sector. While vocational jobs could become obsolete with the further adoption of intelligent systems, the complexity of these new systems has generated new job opportunities for establishing, maintaining, and futureproofing them. In general, the utility sector is highly applicable for digitalisation as it involves extensive physical assets that continuously generate valuable data. However, apart from direct data usage in production control in the upstream, such as power plants and oil refineries, and in fault detections in the midstream, which covers the transmission and distribution networks, there is a lack of any business case to involve the massive volume of end-users. Opening the proprietary utility networks to the public can bring economic benefits, while at the same time introduce new technical issues such as security and system integrity. Advanced sensing technologies and intelligent control mechanisms in Utility 4.0 systems can facilitate coordination among users with heterogenous equipment and needs. AI can be used under human supervision to process big data collected from utility assets and support better decision making. However, privacy and ethical issues must be appropriately addressed whenever personal data is involved. Utility 4.0 technologies can shape a utility company to become more lean and agile, which is essential for it to maintain its competitiveness for the post-pandemic era and what is likely to be a very challenging future.

References

ABI Research. (2019). *Warning: Undetected unauthorized activity in critical systems is the number 1 cybersecurity risk to utilities*. Retrieved from https://www.abiresearch.com/press/warning-undetected-unauthorized-activity-critical-systems-number-1-cybersecurity-risk-utilities

Ali, S. M. H., Lenzen, M., & Tyedmers, E. (2019). Optimizing 100%-renewable grids through shifting residential water-heater load. *International Journal of Energy Research, 43*(4), 1479–1493.

Amazon Web Services. (2017). *Pacific gas & electric company case study*. Retrieved from https://aws.amazon.com/solutions/case-studies/pacific-gas-electric

APEC. (2015). *Internet of Things (IoT) development for the promotion of information economy*. Retrieved from https://www.apec.org/Publications/2015/12/Internet-of-Things-IoT-Development-for-the-Promotion-of-Information-Economy

Ardani, K., O'Shaughnessy, E., & Schwabe, P. (2018). *Coordinating distributed energy resources for grid services: A case study of pacific gas and electric*, National Renewable Energy Laboratory.

Australian Renewable Energy Agency. (2018). *Australian energy resource assessment*. Retrieved from https://arena.gov.au/assets/2018/08/australian-energy-resource-assessment.pdf

Australian Stock Exchange. (2013). *Energy & utilities sector profile*. Retrieved from https://www.asx.com.au/documents/professionals/ASX_Energy_and_Utilities.pdf

Bai, C., Dallasega, P., Orzes, G., & Sarkis, J. (2020). Industry 4.0 technologies assessment: A sustainability perspective. *International Journal of Production Economics, 229*, 1–15. https://doi.org/10.1016/j.ijpe.2020.107776.

Byrds, J., Spraggon, B., O'Neill, M., & Liddy, M. (2017). *Could a robot do your job?, Australian Broadcasting Commission News Sydney*. Retrieved from https://www.abc.net.au/news/2017-08-08/could-a-robot-do-your-job-artificial-intelligence/8782174?nw=0

Christidis, K., & Devetsikiotis, M. (2016). Blockchains and smart contracts for the internet of things. *IEEE Access, 4*, 2292–2303.

Connected Technology Solutions. (2019). *EDF Energy deploys PTC's ThingWorx for innovative energy management solution*. Retrieved from http://connectedtechnologysolutions.co.uk/remote-monitoring-capabilities-to-increase-value-to-customers-whilst-reducing-carbon-footprint

Darrell, P. (2019). *Innovative Microgrid Will Power Finnish Distribution Center*, POWER. Retrieved from https://www.powermag.com/innovative-microgrid-will-power-finnish-distribution-center

Dawson, D., Schleiger, E., Horton, J., McLaughlin, J., Robinson, C., Quezada, G., Scowcroft, J., & Hajkowicz, S. (2019). *Artificial intelligence: Australia's ethics framework*. Data61 CSIRO, Australia.

Dignan, L. (2020). *Your manager, or 69% of what that person does, will be automated, says Gartner*, ZD Net. Retrieved from https://www.zdnet.com/article/your-manager-or-69-of-what-that-person-does-will-be-automated-says-gartner

Dong, Z., Luo, F., & Liang, G. (2018). Blockchain: A secure, decentralized, trusted cyber infrastructure solution for future energy systems. *Journal of Modern Power Systems and Clean Energy, 6*, 958–967. https://doi.org/10.1007/s40565-018-0418-0.

Elham, S., & Shahram, J. (2017). Cost reduction and peak shaving through domestic load shifting and DERs. *Energy, 124*, 146–159.

Energy Sector Control Systems Working Group. (2011). *Roadmap to achieve energy delivery systems cyber security*. US Department of Energy.

Faheem, M., Shah, S. B. H., Butt, R. A., Raza, B., Anwar, M., Ashraf, M. W., Ngadi, M. A., & Gungor, V. C. (2018). Smart grid communication and information technologies in the perspective of industry 4.0: Opportunities and challenges. *Computer Science Review, 30*, 1–30. https://doi.org/10.1016/j.cosrev.2018.08.001.

Fell, J., Pead, J., & Winter, K. (2019). Low-cost flow sensors: Making smart water monitoring technology affordable. *IEEE Consumer Electronics Magazine, 8*(1), 72–77.

Frey, C., & Osborne, M. (2017). The future of employment: How susceptible are jobs to computerisation? *Technological Forecasting and Social Change, 114*(C), 254–280.

Furness, D. (2019). *Robots aren't coming to steal your job. They're coming to improve it, Digital Trends*. Retrieved from https://www.digitaltrends.com/cool-tech/dont-fear-the-robot-automation-threat-overblown

Furukawa, K. (2019). *Honda, GM blockchain project to examine how EV owners could earn revenue from smart grids*, Nikkei Asian Review. Retrieved from https://asia.nikkei.com/Business/Automobiles/Honda-and-GM-join-in-smart-grid-and-electric-car-research

Ganganath, N., Wang, J. V., Xu, X., Cheng, C.-T., & Tse, C. K. (2017). Agglomerative clustering-based network partitioning for parallel power system restoration. *IEEE Transactions on Industrial Informatics, 14*(8), 3325–3333.

Gopalakrishna, A. K., Ozcelebi, T., Lukkien, J. J., & Liotta, A. (2017). Relevance in cyber-physical systems with humans in the loop. *Concurrency and Computation, 29*(3), 1–18.

Gordon, P. (2019). *Swedish telco to connect 900,000 IoT-enabled smart meters*. Smart Energy International. Retrieved from https://www.smart-energy.com/industry-sectors/smart-meters/swedish-telco-to-connect-900000-iot-enabled-smart-meters

Grijpink, F., Ménard, A., Sigurdsson, H., & Vucevic, N. (2018). *The road to 5G: The inevitable growth of infrastructure cost*. Mckinsey & Company. Retrieved from https://www.mckinsey.com/industries/telecommunications/our-insights/the-road-to-5g-the-inevitable-growth-of-infrastructure-cost

Heaven, W.D. (2020). *Our weird behavior during the pandemic is messing with AI models*. MIT Technology Review. Retrieved from https://www.technologyreview.com/2020/05/11/1001563/covid-pandemic-broken-ai-machine-learning-amazon-retail-fraud-humans-in-the-loop

Hinson, S. (2019). Microgrid in a box: A plug-and-play microgrid will make rooftop solar grid-friendly. *IEEE Spectrum, 56*(12), 28–33.

IDC. (2019). *Worldwide internet of things spending guide*. Retrieved from https://www.idc.com/getdoc.jsp?containerId=IDC_P29475

IEEE IoT Tech Expo. (2019). *Using IoT to improve water quality in developing countries*. Retrieved from https://innovate.ieee.org/innovation-spotlight/low-cost-water-iot

Javaid, M., Haleem, A., Vaishya, R., Bahl, S., Suman, R., & Vaish, A. (2020). Industry 4.0 technologies and their applications in fighting COVID-19 pandemic. *Diabetes & Metabolic Syndrome, 14*(4), 419–422. https://doi.org/10.1016/j.dsx.2020.04.032.

Job Outlook. (2020). *Explore careers, national skills commission, Australian Government Canberra*. Retrieved from https://joboutlook.gov.au/careers/explore-careers?keywords=&industry=4&skilllevel=0

Kamoona, A. M., Gostar, A. K., Tennakoon, R., Bab-Hadiashar, A., Accadia, D., Thorpe, J., & Hoseinnezhad, R. (2019). Random finite set-based anomaly detection for safety monitoring in construction sites. *IEEE Access, 7*, 105710–105720.

Kurihara, Y., Kaburagi, T., & Watanabe, K. (2016). Room ventilation control by a self-sensing fan. *IEEE Sensors Journal, 16*(7), 2094–2099.

Lauterbach, A., & Bonime-Blanc, A. (2018). *The artificial intelligence imperative: A practical roadmap for business*, ABC-CLIO.

Lu, H., Guo, L., Azimi, M., & Huang, K. (2019). Oil and gas 4.0 era: A systematic review and outlook. *Computers in Industry, 111*, 68–90. https://doi.org/10.1016/j.compind.2019.06.007.

Maguire, D. (2019a). *How to secure oil & gas assets in the age of the IIoT*. Engineer Live. Retrieved from https://www.engineerlive.com/content/how-secure-oil-gas-assets-age-iiot

Maguire, D. (2019b). *How to secure oil & gas assets in the age of the IIoT- part two*. Engineer Live. Retrieved from https://www.engineerlive.com/content/how-secure-oil-gas-assets-age-iiot-part-two

ManpowerGroup. (2018). *Skills Revolution 2.0.: Robots need not apply: Human solutions for the skills revolution*. Retrieved from https://www.manpowergroup.com/wps/wcm/connect/59db87a7-16c6-490d-ae70-1bd7a322c240/Robots_Need_Not_Apply.pdf?MOD=AJPERES

Manyika, J., Chui, M., Miremadi, M., Bughin, J., George, K., Willmott, P., & Dewhurst, M. (2017). *A future that works: Automation, employment, and productivity*. New Jersey: McKinsey Global Institute, MGI McKinsey & Company. Retrieved from https://www.mckinsey.com/~/media/mckinsey/featured%20insights/Digital%20Disruption/Harnessing%20automation%20for%20a%20future%20that%20works/MGI-A-future-that-works-Executive-summary.ashx.

Michu, S. (2020). *Shell lubricants digitises its customers services to meet industry 4.0, Express Computer*. Retrieved from https://www.expresscomputer.in/artificial-intelligence-ai/shell-lubricants-digitises-its-customers-services-to-meet-industry-4-0/38147

Nakamoto, S. (2014). *Bitcoin: A peer-to-peer electronic cash system.* Retrieved from https://bitcoin.org/bitcoin.pdf

Nichols, G. (2019). *Drones that weave through workers in factories.* ZD Net. Retrieved from https://www.zdnet.com/article/drones-that-weave-through-workers-in-factories/#ftag=RSSbaffb68

Nichols, P. (n.d.). *Energy and utilities in Australia: an overview.* Gradate Careers Association Melbourne. Retrieved from https://gradaustralia.com.au/career-planning/energy-and-utilities-in-australia-an-overview

O'Neill, M. (2017). *Explainer: What is artificial intelligence?*. Australian Broadcasting Commission Sydney. Retrieved from http://www.abc.net.au/news/2017-08-07/explainer-what-is-artificial-intelligence/8771632

Pallanich, J. (2019). *ADNOC Embraces Digital to Reduce Offshore Personnel.* OE Digital. Retrieved from https://www.oedigital.com/news/470082-adnoc-embraces-digital-to-reduce-offshore-personnel

Patil, H., & Kalkhambkar, V. N. (2019). Charging cost minimisation by centralised controlled charging of electric vehicles. *International Transactions on Electrical Energy Systems, 30*(12226). https://doi.org/10.1002/2050-7038.12226.

Perlow, J. (2020). *How IoT betrays us: Today, Sonos speakers. Tomorrow, Alexa and electric cars?*. ZD Net. Retrieved from https://www.zdnet.com/article/sonos-abandoning-its-legacy-customers-is-precisely-what-is-wrong-with-iot

Prackwieser, C., Cash, D., & Wassell, M. (2019). IoT as a digital enabler of a hyper-connected water utility. *Water e-Journal, 4*(3), 1–10. Retrieved from http://ozwater.org/Watersource/wp-content/uploads/2019/09/001-Prackwieser-Christoph_v1.pdf.

Pureswaran, V. & Brody, P. (2015). *Device democracy: Saving the future of the internet of things.* IBM Institute for Business Value. Retrieved from http://www-935.ibm.com/services/us/gbs/thoughtleadership/internetofthings

Rebolini, M., Valant, A., & Pepe, F. M. (2017). *Terna's approach for on-line monitoring system Intelligent management of Assets in a large scale infrastructures*. Paper presented at AEIT International Annual Conference (AEIT), Cagliari, Italy, (pp. 1–6).

Sharma, G. (2019). *Oil, gas industry is embracing its 'Big Data Tsunami'*. Rigzone. Retrieved from https://www.rigzone.com/news/oil_gas_industry_is_embracing_its_big_data_tsunami-22-jul-2019-159366-article/?all=HG2

Skilton, M., & Hovsepian, F. (2018). *The 4th industrial revolution: Responding to the impact of artificial intelligence on business* (1st ed.). Springer International Publishing.

Sotter, E. (2019). *Energy 4.0, revolution or fad*. Electric Energy Online. Retrieved from https://electricenergyonline.com/energy/magazine/1233/article/Energy-4-0-Revolution-or-Fad-.htm

Srivastava, A. K., Ernster, T. A., Liu, R., & Krishnan, V. G. (2018). Graph-theoretic algorithms for cyber-physical vulnerability analysis of power grid with incomplete information. *Journal of Modern Power Systems and Clean Energy, 6*, 887–899. https://doi.org/10.1007/s40565-018-0448-7.

Susskind, D. (2020). *A world without work: Technology*, automation and how we should respond. Henry Holt and Company.

T&D World. (2020). *Transmission system operator uses AI to reduce costs.* Retrieved from https://www.tdworld.com/test-and-measurement/article/21119870/transmission-system-operator-uses-artificial-intelligence-to-reduce-costs

T&D World Staff. (2019). *Ameren Missouri to Deploy 1.4 million advanced meters.* IoT World Today. Retrieved from https://www.iotworldtoday.com/2019/04/30/ameren-missouri-to-deploy-1-4-million-advanced-meters

Ulmer, J., Braun, S., Lai, C. Y., Cheng, C.- T., & Wollert, J. (2019). *Generic integration of VR and AR in product lifecycles based on CAD models.* Paper presented at the 23rd World Multi-Conference on Systemics, Cybernetics and Informatics (WMSCI 2019), Orlando, Florida, USA, pp. 109–114.

Verizon. (2017). *Dakota valley electric cooperative combines traditional service values with a modern grid.* Retrieved from https://16966c0d02ae8ddc176e-a393fe9355878ef10df79e27f1add196.ssl.cf5.rackcdn.com/files/case_studies/10808573_Dakota_Valley_Written_CS_f1a_sb.pdf

Vicon. (2019). *Helping robots and humans work hand-in-hand.* Retrieved from https://www.vicon.com/resources/case-studies/tu-dortmund-helping-robots-and-humans-work-hand-in-hand

Vidhyalakshmi, R., & Kumar, V. (2016). Determinants of cloud computing adoption by SMEs. *International Journal of Business Information Systems, 22*(3), 375–395.

Vigliarolo, B. (2020). *Businesses understand the value of big data, but employees aren't being trained to use it.* TechRepublic. Retrieved from https://www.techrepublic.com/article/businesses-understand-the-value-of-big-data-but-employees-arent-being-trained-to-use-it

Villali, J. (2018). *Top 10 worldwide utilities 2019 predictions.* IDC. Retrieved from https://www.idc-community.com/2018/11/28/top-10-worldwide-utilities-2019-predictions

West, A. (2018). *Duke energy leverages IIoT for predictive maintenance applications.* IHS Markit Technology. Retrieved from https://www.insight.tech/industry/duke-energy-leverages-iiot-for-predictive-maintenance-applications

Wilson, R. (2019). *In advance of a priority service register data-sharing programme being rolled out nationwide by April 2020, what have United Utilities and Electricity North West learnt from piloting the scheme.* Utility Week. Retrieved from https://static.utilityweek.co.uk/app/uploads/2019/10/03164133/fleX-Oct-Dec-2019.pdf

Wood, G. (2015). *Ethereum: A secure decentralised generalised transaction ledger EIP-150 revision.* Ethereum & Ethcore. Retrieved from http://gavwood.com/Paper.pdf

World Economic Forum. (2016). *The future of jobs: employment, skills and workforce strategy for the fourth industrial revolution.* WEF Geneva.

World Economic Forum. (2020). *Passwordless authentication the next breakthrough in secure digital transformation.* World Economic Forum in collaboration with the FIDO Alliance. Retrieved from http://www3.weforum.org/docs/WEF_Passwordless_Authentication.pdf

Zhang, X., Liu, D., Zhan, C., & Tse, C. K. (2017). Effects of cyber coupling on cascading failures in power systems. *IEEE Journal on Emerging and Selected Topics in Circuits and Systems, 7*(2), 228–238.

Chapter 13
Conclusion and Comparisons

Alan Nankervis, John Burgess, Julia Connell, and Alan Montague

Abstract The final chapter of this book reflects on the key aspects of 4IR technologies identified amongst the eleven industry sectors featured in relation to both the production and service sectors. Key implications for Australia's governments and industry are outlined. These include: the need for a national technology policy; significantly increased investment in AI development and training programs offered in both formal educational settings and inhouse by industry to upskill both current and future employees. The authors stress the necessity to urgently address these implications for Australia to make a positive impact in an era where technological advances are having and will continue to have an unprecedented impact even with the recent COVID-19 challenges taking place.

Keywords 4IR sector impacts · Australia · COVID-19 challenges · National technology policy

A. Nankervis (✉)
Centre for Organisational Change and Agility (COCA), Torrens University, Adelaide, SA, Australia

School of Management and Law Curtin University, Perth, NSW, Australia
e-mail: a.nankervis@curtin.edu.au

J. Burgess
Torrens University, Adelaide, SA, Australia
e-mail: john.burgess@torrens.edu.au

J. Connell
Newcastle Business School, College of Human and Social Futures, University of Newcastle, Newcastle, NSW, Australia
e-mail: julia.connell@newcastle.edu.au

A. Montague
School of Management, RMIT University, Melbourne, VIC, Australia
e-mail: alanjmontague@gmail.com

A. Nankervis et al. (eds.), *The Fourth Industrial Revolution*,
https://doi.org/10.1007/978-981-16-1614-3_13

Revisiting the Purpose of the Book

This book was created in response to a gap in knowledge concerning the application of the transformative technologies associated with the 4IR across nations, regions, and industries. The 4IR has raised the widespread possibility of job loss, due to the dominance of robotics and artificial intelligence displacing humans. Such scenarios include the extension of control and surveillance in the home and workplace, a situation further enabled during the COVID-19 global crisis. Positive outcomes suggest the phasing out of work that is physically demanding, safer workplaces, new jobs and skills, improved work-life balance, increased earnings, and new career paths. Although the advent of the 4IR has attracted rhetoric, hype, and unsubstantiated predictions, the new technologies associated with it are real, and they are being applied across the globe albeit with uneven applications and impacts due to the contextual conditions determining the speed and scope of the changes taking place.

A national and industry context frames the discussion and analysis of the impact of 4IR technologies on work, jobs, and skills in industry settings in order to examine the extent to which these technologies have transformed production, employment, skills, and training. An industry broadly represents a collection of enterprises (private, public, and non-government organisations) that produce similar goods and services. Associated with goods or services, similar production processes and requirements for labour, capital, and technology permeate many industry sectors. In an industry context the purpose of the book is to address the following questions:

(a) What are the characteristics of each industry sector, and its current strengths and weaknesses?
(b) What key technologies are currently impacting on the sector and what technologies are likely to have a future impact on the sector?
(c) What is the impact of technological change on the size and composition of the sector's workforce?
(d) What is the impact of technological change on the skill requirements of the sector?
(e) Are there active programs in place to support organisations and workers to accommodate the predicted technological changes? and
(f) What programs and policies are required to address the predicted changes within the sector?

Paralleling the research questions explored within each chapter, the key responses to these questions are summarised in the appendix of this chapter by sector.

The research findings outlined in this book represent eleven of the key industry sectors in the Australian economy – construction, mining and agriculture; manufacturing; retail; accommodation and food services; transport and logistics; media; financial and insurance services; local government; higher education; healthcare; and utilities. This list does not include all industries but is sufficiently diverse to indicate the range and application of technologies that are being applied across Australian workplaces. Two of the studied industries – the healthcare and retail sectors – are the largest employers in Australia, and coincidentally, are also the sectors which have best survived or even grown during the COVID-19 crisis. Two other sectors – higher education and tourism – have been decimated by the crisis wrought by the pandemic, enduring significant revenue losses and redundancies. However, in both sectors, future business models will most likely be transformed using 4IR technologies towards virtual learning or travel experiences for their clients and customers. In the other sectors, there have been both challenges and opportunities provided by the unexpected (and unwanted) confluence of the COVID-19 virus and the development of 4IR technologies, together with the adverse effect on exporters posed by the strained relationship between Australia and China (Chan 2020). However, in almost all industry sectors the quantity and quality of the workforce will probably change irrevocably. These changes are expected to require governments, industry associations, individual employers, education and training institutions, unions and employees themselves, to undertake collaborative, comprehensive and strategic human resource planning processes to ensure that the employees who remain are adequately supported, trained and retrained; and effectively rewarded to ensure that they are equipped and motivated to perform new roles in their future workplaces and industrial environments (Deloitte Access Economics (2018a). A summary of the findings relating to the featured Australian industry sectors follows. The summary mirrors the structure of the book and is divided into two sections – production and services.

Technological Changes and Challenges in the Production Sectors

In the *Construction, Mining & Agriculture (CMA) sector* (Chap. 2) each component has its challenges and opportunities. Thus, while employment in construction has generally maintained its employment levels since the advent of the 4IR, it is likely to displace some workers with the implementation of building information modelling, prefabrication, offsite manufacturing, and 3D printing technologies. Arguably, this circumstance may also disrupt the current large building corporations-small contractor nexus which has been a key structural characteristic for many decades in Australia. Mining, on the other hand, has experienced significant boom and bust periods and is threatened by the growing trade war with China and the frequent use of a fly-in-fly-out (FIFO) workforce which is currently hampered by COVID-19. Mining employers have been relatively eager to adopt new technologies such as autonomous vehicles and haulage trains; robots for processing hazardous materials; automated drilling and centralised remote monitoring systems. That said, the pace of implementing these technologies is likely to increase further in the future for both efficiency, profitability and occupational health and safety reasons. Jobs such as truck operators, geologists and surveyors, drill operators, miners and earth moving operators are poised to decline. Agriculture has been challenged not only by

COVID-19 and new technologies, but also by climate change, bushfires, drought, and the inadequacy of the water supply in parts of Australia. The sector has also experienced a slow general decline in employment over the last few decades. This is due to its ageing workforce and youth migration to the cities, exacerbated by the recent dearth of a seasonal vegetable and fruit picking workforce due to the Australian COVID-19 lockdown. For these long-and shorter-term reasons, employers are likely to welcome new cropping technologies, automated food production and packaging, drones for livestock, plant monitoring and maintenance, and blockchain technologies to track food production and supply chains.

Chapter 3 focuses on *manufacturing* which has experienced a long-term decline in terms of employment and contribution to GDP due partly to the 'resources curse' and the preference for low-cost overseas manufacturers in China and India. However, a glimmer of hope for a return to limited local manufacturing has been provided by both the short-term imperative to produce large quantities of personal protective equipment (PPE) and ventilators for COVID-19 protection and treatment. This has been coupled with the possible benefits of low-cost manufacturing from 4IR technologies such as 3D printing; better connectivity between customers and supply chains through real-time access to production information, logistics and monitoring; and enhanced workplace safety. However, the adoption of these technologies will come at the cost of significantly reduced workforces, and the adverse effects on apprenticeships and employee reskilling from the decimation of the Vocation Education & Training (VET) sector (Deloitte Access Economics (2018b).

Technological Changes and Challenges in the Services Sectors

Conversely, the *retail sector* (Chap. 4) has benefitted from the COVID-19 crisis due to the transition of many customers from face-to-face to online purchasing. It is highly likely that many employers in this sector will expedite the implementation of 4IR technologies, such as blockchain inventory management, robotic warehouse and store cleaners, hazard identification and reduction and shelf-stacking, to replace its majority low-skill, low-wage, casual and contract workforce. However, of all the industry sectors discussed in this book, the *accommodation and food services* (AFS) component of the tourism and hospitality sector (Chap. 5) has arguably borne the brunt of the COVID-19 pandemic, with most hotels, restaurants, cafes, travel agents and airlines closed or only partially operational, with the consequent reduction or redundancy of many employees. It has also been considered to be the sector with the highest level of 'automation susceptibility' due to technologies such as AI reservation systems; keyless entry and hotel check-in systems; virtual reality tourism experiences; robot baristas and room cleaners; and online food ordering with home delivery. In common with the retail sector, the AFS sector has a mostly female, low-paid, low-skill and precarious workforce. It is also likely to become one of the highest future adopters of 4IR technologies with its associated deep impact on the quantity and quality of its workforce. Automation and digital transformation have reportedly had a significant effect on the *transport sector* (Chap. 6); however, disparate forms and degrees of implementation have been experienced in its different sub-components. Expertise in robotics, systems, and electronics engineering, as well as digital literacy, digital business, business analytics and computer science skills will be required in its future workforce. As with other industry sectors, the workforce challenges are likely to include job displacement and/or reconfiguration, and the emergence of new skills and competencies.

Perhaps the industry sector which has made the most significant progress towards the widespread application of 4IR technologies in Australia is the *media and communications* sector (Chap. 7). The Australian Information Media & Telecommunications sector comprises newspaper and internet publishing, journalism, film production, television and radio broadcasting, together with the telecommunications infrastructure and networks; and as such, is probably the most globalised and competitive of all sectors discussed in this book. Although the sector experienced strong employment growth between 2015 and 2020, future challenges are apparent, as trends indicate the increased prominence of large global media conglomerates in the media market. Unlike some other sectors, media production now relies totally on information technology to drive media for screens, laptops, I-pads and mobile telephones and media networks have begun gathering points for these data flows. AI technologies are used in robot-controlled newsrooms; virtual, computer-generated, non-human screen 'actors' and AI algorithms are used in the selection and promotion of story material in publishing and screen story-telling. The impact of these 4IR technologies on employment in this sector has been, and will remain, profound. On the positive side, occupations such as film and television production and direction are likely to have their roles augmented by 4IR technologies, together with jobs involving 3D printing design and Big Data analysis; whereas, on the negative side, human roles in screen, literary and arts production such as camera operators, journalists and news reporters are most likely to be supplanted by such technological advances.

The *finance and insurance sector* (Chap. 8) also lends itself to significant automation, given its heavy reliance on data collection and analysis. Its activities include raising funds; receiving deposits; issuing securities incurring liabilities, investments, and a broad range of financial assets: and pooling risks by underwriting insurance and annuities. Central banking, regulation and monetary control of financial activities are all embedded in this sector, which in turn are heavily regulated by state and federal government agencies. The AI applications currently in use, or predicted for the future, include (inter alia) robo-advisors for customer investment advice; credit-scoring algorithms using standard programmed machine learning; and other applications which predict investment risk or default, assist in fraud prevention and mitigation; and software that assesses compliance with government regulations and improves system efficiencies and effectiveness. It is anticipated that future applications of these technologies will significantly reduce current workforces, not only in repetitive jobs but also those which involve analytical and decision-making capabilities, including insurance brokers, financial investment advisors, bank managers, insurance risk surveyors and insurance investigators.

However, some observers have suggested that comprehensive workforce planning may be able to augment, rather than replace, some of these positions, and still allow the Australian finance and insurance sector to thrive and grow in an increasingly competitive local and international marketplace.

Whilst there are government players in many of the industry sectors already discussed, the *local government sector* (Chap. 9) stands alone as an entirely public entity, different in its aims, structure, management, and operations from all the others. Given its history, traditions, structure, and relatively high union density compared to some of the other sectors, it is likely that its trajectory towards the adoption of 4IR technologies will also be different. Local government in Australia is the third tier of government, sitting underneath the federal and state government sectors, and there are more than five hundred local councils with nearly 200,000 employees in approximately 390 different occupations. Despite the similarity of their services, they have substantial diversity in terms of their financial capacities, employment profiles, demographic and geographic characteristics. The 4IR technologies most relevant to their future operations and priorities include the digitisation of records; automation of property maintenance, traffic and parks management, and waste management; online delivery of such community services such as libraries, planning and the billing of council rates. The sector also uses satellite technology, drones, smart meters, CCTV and smartphone applications for parking and traffic management, and for land-care, animal management, and emergency plans. The impact of 4IR technologies on local government occupations is anticipated to include a combination of the displacement of semi-skilled jobs (for example, maintenance and clerical) and the augmentation of higher-skilled positions (town planners, architects, and financial managers). Potential obstacles to the widespread adoption of AI include uneven access to the IT infrastructure (especially in rural and remote areas), different levels of funding between councils, digital skills shortages, and diverse opportunities for workforce reskilling in these competencies.

Whilst most *higher education* institutions (Chap. 10) in Australia are public universities financed by a combination of government, student and research funding; there is also a small number of private institutions as well. New 4IR technologies have affected every part of the higher education (HE) system, ranging from human resource management processes for staff to all aspects of student learning and administration, and research activities. Whilst online learning has been a feature of HE for several decades, the COVID-19 pandemic has necessarily enhanced this learning option, resulting in both decline in the number of lecturers (especially casual and contract ones) and the need for many staff to acquire new skills, including (but not limited to) data fluency, digital competence, big data analysis and the use of complex computerised algorithms. It has been predicted that job losses in the sector could rise to more than 21,000 staff Australia-wide, and although this was initially caused by the pandemic, it is likely that many (if not most) institutions will choose to maintain largely online learning technologies in their efforts to reduce the funding debts caused by the dramatic decline in international student income. Not only will this severely reduce the numbers of full-time academics, but it will also curtail the career paths of casual, fixed term contract teaching and research staff.

In contrast to HE, the *healthcare sector* (Chap. 11) received a significant boost from COVID-19 as its services were in great demand. However, some allied occupations (for example, dentistry, cosmetic surgery and physiotherapy) suffered due to the closure of their services for several months during the height of COVID-19's impact in Australia. As in other sectors, the adoption of 4IR technologies has been growing in a myriad of healthcare occupations over the last few decades. For example: AI is employed to identify potentially cancerous lesions in radiology images; deep learning is used in the treatment of diabetic retinopathy; a robot called 'Matilda' supports elderly people in aged care homes; and 'Pepper', a social robot with emotion recognition abilities, is being trialled in Australian hospitals to study how robots could improve the quality of patient care. With respect to the employment impact of these technologies, there are likely to be both positive and adverse consequences – increased specialist employment opportunities, new skills and competencies, and opportunities for re-skilling, on the one hand; and job losses and a reduction in the socio-emotional aspects of patient care on the other.

Finally, the *utilities sector* (Chap. 12) has recognised that it needs to increase its competitive edge by conducting a digital transformation whilst facing new challenges, including an increase in competition and changes in customer demands. As examples: energy companies are upgrading their infrastructure by adopting new technologies such as the Industrial Internet of Things (IIoT), machine learning, Cloud computing, smart meters, and predictive maintenance amongst many other initiatives. In the water management space, remote sensors have been employed to monitor the ageing water infrastructure, water scarcity, corroding pipes and leaks; and in the oil and gas sector, to conduct asset integrity management, reduce costs and minimise human interventions to reduce data-entry errors and potential security risks. The key challenges faced in the sector include talent shortages, cyber-physical attacks, and security; and achieving an appropriate balance between traditional and renewable energy sources whilst maintaining profitability without compromising ethical and social responsibilities. As in most other sectors, the utilities sector will inevitably be forced to reduce low-skilled occupations as well as enhancing their higher-skilled counterparts.

The key challenges and opportunities associated with the 4IR in all the sectors discussed above are summarised in Appendix 13.1 at the end of this chapter. The key technologies that contribute to the 4IR, as identified in Chapter one, have the potential to impact on all sectors in terms of production, productivity, employment, skills, and training. As previously mentioned in chapter one the technologies have the potential to restructure sectors internally and to break down the barriers between sectors. As internet networks roll out across the economy massive changes are afoot as all sectors will have access to cloud computing, big data, the internet of things and machine learning. The Cisco/Oxford Economics report (2019) analysis on the impact of technological and structural change in Australia suggested that those occupations most at risk of displacement were found in the trades and routine workers, especially in manufacturing, construction, transport, agriculture, and mining. Those sectors that are capital-intensive such as agriculture, mining, transport, construction, and manufacturing can access robotics and artificial intelligence to increase productivity and augment and displace labour. For more labour-intensive sectors that depend on the direct personal provision of services such hospitality, education, entertainment, healthcare, and retailing, there is scope for the displacement of labour engaged in routine activities through different modes of service delivery such as online entertainment, online retailing, online education, and online food delivery. Across all sectors, routine jobs that have limited autonomy and independent decision-making, are likely to be replaced by technology. The 4IR technologies will augment many jobs, but at the same time, require skills development, especially in soft and IT skills. The Cisco/Oxford Economics (2019) analysis suggested that skills shortages were present across all occupations and industries in terms of IT skills, soft skills, and elementary skills such as verbal and written communication, and teamworking. The implication is that for all vocations and professions there is a need for continuous skill upgrading to accommodate the new technologies.

Implications for Governments and Industry

The challenges for government (Federal and States) are linked to supporting technological implementation and managing the current and future workforce needs for the respective sectors. The 4IR technologies require supporting infrastructure that covers mobile and internet networks; logistics and transport networks; sustainable and renewable energy networks; and a skilled workforce that can employ the new technologies at the workplace. Preparing for the challenges and opportunities afforded by the 4IR requires policy action in many areas including industry, trade, security, education, training, R&D, migration, infrastructure, labour regulation, and regional development. For this reason, a national technology policy that incorporates these areas is required to map the challenges and develop an integrated policy program. The challenges and opportunities identified in this book refer to industry perspectives. For the Federal government the challenge is to develop a holistic national program that incorporates planning for both the opportunities and challenges, and strategies directed not only towards technological solutions but also addressing potential adverse consequences including job loss, deskilling and inequality in the impact of technology across regions, occupations and age groups. Any national program must accommodate not only immediate challenges but also consider the longer-term challenges of technological change in concert with other changes in demography, climate, and workforce skills.

The scope of the technologies is extensive in their application and impact and poses challenges to existing regulatory systems. For example, the digital online economy generates new jobs and opportunities for firms, and the potential for mobile and homework. However, for governments there are challenges to labour and product market regulation, taxation, and dealing with dominant international tech companies. A joint Australia and New Zealand inquiry into the digital economy (Productivity Commission 2019) commented that regulations currently in place were designed for a previous technological epoch and are continually challenged by the online economy.

The WEF (2018) regarded reskilling and retraining the workforce as the priority for organisations, industries, occupations, and government to respond to the 4IR technologies. However, while the need for action is apparent, the execution of strategies from the workplace to the national domains is constrained by a lack of information and detailed forecasting of future jobs and skill requirements, as well as a short-term focus across all key stakeholders. The Cisco/Oxford (2018: 43) report commented that 'the faster the rate of change, the greater the disruption imposed on the workforce, and the steeper the challenge for workers and businesses to reskill and adapt'. Given the uneven impact of technological change, the Cisco/Oxford (2018) Report recommended several policy actions as follows:

> 'In the medium term, this may have implications for fiscal policy, as a matter of redistributing the economic gains to ensure a smooth transition for those who lose out. In the longer term, it also means understanding the impact on the trajectory of the earnings and wellbeing of different cohorts of society. As part of this challenge, policymakers are also charged with facilitating the skills transition the economy needs to take advantage of the opportunity's technology will bring. This means understanding the multifaceted nature of the skills challenge that technological change presents, and the training vehicles to meet it' (p. 43).

In terms of education and training, the Australian Industry & Skills Commission (AISC 2017) mapped the implications for more TAFE education and training in Australia. It suggested that: there will be a greater need for collaboration between industry and education; lifelong learning should be part of the training agenda; disciplinary boundaries should be reduced through cross disciplinary education and that the learning models need to become more fluid, capable of on line delivery and provide courses on demand to any location. Hence, education and training systems need to be transformed, and the assumptions that supported the current model of curriculum, design, and delivery are no longer relevant in the context of ongoing structural and technological changes. Similarly, the Pearson (2019) international survey of learning indicated that the construct of a stable, long-term career was no longer applicable, and that future learning processes would be dependent on digital and virtual learning, with greater emphasis on soft skill development.

The chapters in this book demonstrate that there are uniform challenges across all sectors that require a national policy approach. The key national issues are as follows:

1. *Job displacement needs to be addressed.* Jobs will be lost, and government should be proactive in supporting programs that retrain and upgrade skills for displaced workers. Job losses are predicted to occur in low skilled, routine, and non-cognitive employment. However, many skilled and professional jobs will also be lost or transformed in the trades and professions. National workforce planning requires a re-alignment of training and education programs towards continuous and lifelong learning.
2. *Skills and competencies across all occupations and professions need to be reviewed and qualifications upgraded.* This national task addresses point 1 above.

Throughout the chapters a recurring theme is that the 4IR will require new skills and the re-design of these skills would be required for many existing jobs. There was an identified need for soft skills and for education and training institutions to incorporate soft skill development into training and degree programs.

3. *Address the skills shortages*. The third objective is that of addressing the skills shortages that are projected to be present across all sectors. This can be dealt with in part through the first two objectives, but also requires an ongoing evaluation of the size and composition of the skilled migration program. Part of the response is, as the WEF (2018) indicated, to make sure that there are opportunities for women and older workers to access skills, jobs, and careers.
4. *Ethical challenges*. Data storage, data sharing and automated decision-making processes raise important ethical challenges. These ethical and regulatory challenges are present across all the sectors surveyed, are of importance in the public and financial sectors and have been highlighted by recent cases in the banking and government sectors (for example, the banking royal commission and the Robodebt scandal).
5. *Equity challenges*. Finally, there are distributive and equity challenges in terms of not having equal access to opportunities and protections and being adversely impacted by the consequences. Digitally supported work such as crowd working, online working and gig work offer new job opportunities and flexible employment,. although some evidence suggests ambiguous employment status, invisible employers, and eroded employment conditions (de Stefano 2016). In particular, the contours of division emerge – those with limited skills and education are at risk of displacement or exclusion from the workforce; those living outside of capital cities are at risk from exclusion from access to the internet, and those with established skills and vocations are at risk of being displaced by automation and AI; and in terms of age, youth and older workers at different ends of the age spectrum, face transitional challenges in accessing careers.

In Search of a National Technology Policy

According to the Australian Trade and Investment Commission (2017: 1–2), Australia is in an excellent position to capitalise on the opportunities presented by AI technologies. One initiative, for example, is the Australian Department of Industry, Science, Energy & Resources (DISER) which commissioned CSIRO's Data 61 to develop a roadmap entitled *Artificial Intelligence: Solving problems, growing the economy and improving our quality of life* (Hajkowicz et al. 2019: 2–3) which included three key objectives:

1. highlighting areas of focus to advance the development and adoption of AI technologies in Australia including skills, infrastructure, research, regulation and data governance;

2. identifying three areas where Australia could build on its existing strengths and capabilities, with opportunities to solve national problems and export AI-driven solutions, and
3. framing policy discussion to maximise the benefits for Australia.

The roadmap included industry grants, the creation of a Digital Technologies Hub to provide online educational resources and a Data 61 PhD Scholarship Program to promote studies in AI, machine learning and other data-driven technologies. Asserting that robotics and machine learning are imperative for any future manufacturing sector, Hajkowicz et al. (2019, p47) also argued that Australia needs a strategic plan focussing on AI and ML to remain globally competitive in "all industries" with agriculture and bio-sciences requiring priority consideration' (p. 47). Post COVID-19, some observers, such as Davidson (2020: webpage) encapsulated the message from CSIRO through Hajkowicz et al. (2019) stating: 'Australia urgently needs to figure out a national AI strategy if it is to even keep up with the rest of the world'.

Davidson (2020) was forthright in claiming that state and federal government AI strategies and funding have to date fallen significantly short in attempting to reach these objectives or goals. For example, in its statement to its broad membership the Australian Information Computer Technology (ICT) industry signalled problems with the Australian government's current 4IR strategy and policy, asserting that 'currently {Australia} lacks access to relevant local skills, and is not supported by an effective Research and Development Taxation Incentive (R&DTI) Program that fosters an environment of innovation, commercialisation and export of high-quality Australian AI products and services' (Anonymous 2019: webpage).

While there is not yet a dedicated national AI strategy, the government recently published *Australia's Tech Future*. The plan touches upon the economic importance of AI, as well as skills shortages in AI and data science, as part of a broader discussion of opportunities presented by digital technologies. The 2018–19 national budget included an allocation of AU$29.9 million over four years to boost the country's AI capabilities, including the development of a technology road map and frameworks for standards and AI ethics. However, AI experts are issuing warnings that greater levels of spending will be needed for Australia to keep up with other countries that are lavishing public funds on AI initiatives (Loucks et al. 2019: 10).

Deloitte (2020: webpage) explained the lack of effective government policy bluntly maintaining that there is 'no national strategy or proper funding.' It further claimed that Australia did not have a 'dedicated national AI strategy' despite several 'prominent Australian business and industry leaders ... urgently pushing for {a} national debate on the policies needed to address AI risks'. Further they cited industry leaders' comments that were critical of the meagre '2018-19 federal budget' allocation of 'AU$29.9 million over four years to boost the country's AI capabilities' (Deloitte 2020: webpage). It also suggested that AI experts have warned that significantly increased levels of spending are required for Australia to keep pace with other countries. 'China for example ... has a comprehensive national AI strategy and plans to spend billions to become a world-leading AI innovator. Specifically,

Beijing announced a US$2.1 billion AI-centric technology park, and Tianjin plans to set up a US$16 billion AI fund (Deloitte 2020: webpage).

Smith (2019) reflected the concerns expressed by Deloitte (2020) and Loucks et al. (2019), stating that 'Australia's funding for AI-related initiatives has been comparatively thin' when compared with other developed countries' (Smith 2019: 5). The lack of policy on the 4IR in terms of expenditure is contrary to the fiscal context, as Hajkowicz et al. (2019) argue 'digital technologies, including AI, are potentially worth AU$315 billion to the Australian economy by 2028 and AI could be worth AU$22.17 trillion to the global economy by 2030' (p. v). The $29.9 million in artificial intelligence development under the 2018–2019 budget spread over four years represents such a small fiscal commitment that Australia may be destined for an economic state of disadvantage compared with other global and regional competitors. As comparative examples, France has committed €1.5 billion ($2.4 billion Australian) over five years leading up to 2022; the South Korean government committed to 2.2 trillion won ($2.7 billion) over the same period; India and the European Union also published ambitious AI strategies; Canada pledged $C125 million ($131 million) over five years starting in 2017′ and Singapore committed $S150 million ($155 million) from 2017 to 2022 (Seo 2019: webpage).

Furthermore in Australia, there is an absence of discussion on some of the big issues linked to the 4IR, specifically around how to distribute the productivity gains of the 4IR as efficiency gains could be potentially translated into job losses, higher wages, lower product prices, reduced working hours, and increased profitability. Some key questions posed by the ILO (2017) are also worthy of note. For example, the ILO raised these questions: should there be a social dividend to compensate the losers in the process and should new technology, especially if it displaces labour, be subjected to a new form of tax for industry? (ILO 2017).

Industry Strategies

As apparent from the chapters in this book, specific industry challenges differ but there are shared challenges linked to skill shortages, skills development, and the management of structural adjustments to the industries linked to 4IR technologies. All industry sectors need to significantly increase their support for investment and ongoing research into 4IR technologies to reap the potentially enormous benefits to the economy and their own businesses. Blumenstein (a fellow of the Australian Computer Society), predicted that AI could contribute around $22.17 trillion to the global economy by 2030 according to the Australian Computer Society (ACS) (2020). However, to participate, Australia must boost AI investment according to Blumenstein, quoted by ACS (2020):

> 'I believe we have a long way to go to increase our investment in AI, said Blumenstein. It's really great to look at roadmaps because they are a snapshot of the current status. By ranking of the number of scientific publications and the research output we create in this country, we are number one by capita. The challenge there is the translation of that research. We

have the top ranking by research in the world in AI – the next big step is investing and growing that pie' (webpage).

The Australian Trade & Industry Commission (2017: 1) stated that Australia's transition from a resource-based to a services-based economy is 'driving opportunities in disruptive technologies across multiple sectors, including advanced manufacturing, agriculture, services, health, infrastructure, and resources and energy' (sectors that are included in this book). The Australian Trade & Industry Commission (2017:1) argued that the key strengths for Australian industry to capitalise on due to the 4IR include 'niche solutions and proven capability in additive manufacturing, artificial intelligence, automation, big data and analytics, blockchain, cloud, cybersecurity, immersive simulation, the Internet of Things and systems integration.'

The CSIRO Roadmap (Hajkowicz et al. 2019: 47–51) suggested seven priorities for government and industry to focus on for the effective future management of 4IR technologies in Australia, including government policy issues. These strategies include:

1. Developing an AI specialist technical workforce to meet the operational needs of industry;
2. Helping workers whose jobs are likely to be positively or negatively impacted by AI and related digital technologies make early and strategic career transitions;
3. Ensuring effective data governance and access as AI is typically data hungry and machine learning algorithms need "training data" to be developed and tested;
4. Building trust in AI by ensuring high standards and transparency for all applications developed and applied in Australia;
5. Increasing the activity within the science, research and technology development pipeline to ensure advanced AI capabilities for government and industry in the future;
6. Improving digital infrastructure (for data transmission, storage, analysis and acquisition) and cybersecurity so that AI can be safely and effectively used across Australian cities and regions, and
7. Developing appropriate systems and standards to ensure safe, quality-assured, interoperable and ethical AI is developed and applied within Australia'.

These priorities indicate that 4IR technologies should be a focus for policymakers and government for some time to come. Of course implications will vary across different sectors and this will need careful management as the government and educators work to ensure that the skills required by businesses as they endeavour to adopt new technologies can be delivered quickly.

Conclusion

The WEF (2018) survey of large corporations revealed a split between industries that saw future skill requirements being stable, and those that saw them as being disrupted. Those industries considered to have stable skill needs include health, energy, retail, media, and professional services. Skill disruptions were forecast in the financial services, ICT, logistics, and infrastructure sectors. The future strategies that were seen to be effective in addressing skill needs and shortages included: investment in reskilling current employees; support for mobility and job rotation; collaboration with educational institutions; targeting female talent; attracting foreign talent and offering increased apprenticeships (WEF 2018).

This book has drawn on the expertise of several Australian based academics to examine how new technologies are either impacting industry sectors, or how they may do so in the future. The impact on workplaces due to technical change is an issue that should concern everyone. Underemployment or unemployment can induce economic problems for individuals and the broader society. As a result, there is a need for policy interventions and significant investment and planning to hold a society together and build a robust economy. This concluding chapter, and elsewhere suggests that currently a policy vacuum is apparent as far as the Australian Federal Government policies are concerned, which is in stark contrast to the investments being made by other countries within the competitive global marketplace. The impact of technological change on the skill requirements of the industry sectors covered in this book has been signalled throughout. Unfortunately, we were able to identify little in terms of active programs in place to support organisations and workers to accommodate the predicted technological changes. The development of skills to address the 4IR technologies is more promising in our tertiary institutions, although more policy intervention is undoubtedly needed in the educational domains as well as the need for informal and formal training for current employees. In addition to relevant programs and policies to meet predicted changes within all the Australian industry sectors, broader policy development is vital. Australia certainly has the potential to make a positive impact in a new era where technological advances have unprecedented impact even with the recent COVID-19 challenges considered.

As outlined in chapter one, although this book addresses draws on multiple data sources, the analysis is exploratory in nature, mainly drawing on secondary sources from the key stakeholder groups associated with each industry sector. As the assimilation of 4IR technologies, government policies and education/training programs matures in Australia it is recommended that future research may include broader and deeper research that may focus for example on just one sector, or on a particular aspect across sectors such as skills to provide important insights for strategic planning and more. As the Cisco/Oxford Economics report (2019: 44) points out 'How well the stakeholders in Australia's future can capitalise on those opportunities, for the net benefit of the whole population, will depend on how well it deals with the skills transition'.

Appendix 13.1: Summary of Chapter Findings

Chapter	Industry Overview	Key Technologies (KT)	Impacts of KT on employment/ occupations/productivity	Challenges & Opportunities
2. Agriculture, Construction & Mining	Contributing more than $63 billion or 2.3% to Australia's GDP, Australia is already the 12th largest exporter of agricultural products in the world. Impacted by consequences of climate change: drought, bushfires pressure on river systems and over fishing.	Cropping technologies, automated food production/ packaging; drone livestock maintenance and blockchain, to track food production and supply chains.	Slow decline in employment. Ageing workforce & youth migration out of rural and regional areas. Some manufacturing may be brought back onshore as capabilities such as 3D printing help Australian manufacturers meet demand for highly customised products.	**Challenges:** Without coordinated reskilling efforts, the automation of low-skilled positions could see a large proportion of the agricultural workforce facing unemployment. **Opportunities:** FishTech and 'aquabotics', aquaculture, cell cultured meat and cellular agriculture.
3. Manufacturing	The share of GDP derived from manufacturing fell from 10.7% in 1991–1992 to 5.8% in 2017–2018. While manufacturing and agriculture were dominant industries in the past, service industries are now increasingly important for employment.	Artificial intelligence (AI), digital sensors, big data analytics, additive manufacturing (i.e. 3D-printing), virtual reality (VR), augmented reality (AR) and machine learning (ML).	Improved manufacturing innovation and output, market share and competitiveness. High-value employment in 4IR will require the integration of technical skills with personal skills.	**Challenges:** A downturn in apprenticeships as a result of COVID-19 could present labour shortfalls. **Opportunities:** The 'deglobalisation' implications of COVID-19 may facilitate a resurgence in manufacturing.

(continued)

Appendix 13.1 (continued)

Chapter	Industry Overview	Key Technologies (KT)	Impacts of KT on employment/ occupations/productivity	Challenges & Opportunities
4. Retail	The retail sector is the largest employer in Australia. It ranks 8th of all industry sectors in terms of revenue and employment growth and first by employee numbers. Much employment is in unskilled or low-skilled occupations.	Virtual assistants, augmented reality, algorithms, data-driven insights, AI-enabled chatbots and biometric payments system.	Jobs likely to be 'augmented' by 4IR technologies include software developers, process improvement specialists, data engineers and infrastructure service analysts. New digital technologies and the transition to greater online selling will reduce employment at the lower end of the occupational spectrum. Revenues and profits may surge, accompanied by structural changes favouring large international and domestic retailers.	**Challenges:** The shift in emphasis away from semi-skilled or skilled jobs to highly-skilled professional roles is likely to specifically disadvantage women, transitional workers and retail employees in rural and remote areas of Australia. **Opportunities:** Many retailers may benefit from significantly reduced production, delivery, product promotion and infrastructure costs, enhanced competitiveness and profitability.
5. Accommodation & Food Services	Tourism industries collectively contributed over $100 billion to Australia's GDP and employed nearly one million people in 2019. One-third of AFS sector related jobs were lost due to disruptions caused by COVID-19.	Industrial and social robots, self-service kiosks, artificial intelligence, chatbots, face recognition technology, voice-controlled technologies, wearable and implanted technologies, 3D printing, the internet of things, and other automation technologies that are used instead of human employees.	Innovations such as accommodation providers adopting a fully automated online business model without any face-to-face contact with customers at the time of bookings, making payments for the services and during the stay. The increasing adoption of technologies will increase the demand for digital competencies in the AFS workforce. The hospitality sector has one of the highest levels of automation susceptibility in Australia.	**Challenges:** The lack of 4IR readiness and growing shortage of skilled and semi-skilled labour. The COVID-19 pandemic, and deteriorating diplomatic relations with China, will reduce the number of tourists visiting Australia. **Opportunities:** The lack of overseas travel means that post COVID-19 domestic tourism is likely to get a boost.

6. Transport & Logistics	The transport industry accounts for about 4.6% of GDP. The Australian freight logistics industry accounts for 8.6% of GDP. The sector's workforce is characterised by an ageing workforce, and struggles to attract younger workers.	Automation (such as driverless trains and trucks), Connected and Automated Vehicles (CAVs), robotics, artificial intelligence, human-machine interfaces, advanced computer systems and big data to create 'smart' processes and products.	New occupations have emerged because of these disruptive technologies. Increased demand for expertise in robotics, systems and electronics engineering, as well as digital literacy, digital business, business analytics and computer science. CAVs will see existing drivers replaced with employees with new skills in cybersecurity and automated systems. Technological advances are reducing new infrastructure cost, improving road safety, and improving the efficiency of freight transport. Collaborative electronic platforms will replace many administrative staff. There will be an increase in short-term contracts or freelance work as opposed to permanent jobs.	**Challenges:** As government policy on workforce digital transformation in Australia is lacking, employers must not only implement extensive in-house re-and up-skilling for their workers but also actively develop a sustainable pool of workers for the 4IR. Without an effective and sustainable response to the skills question in the sector, the economy faces significant challenges since efficient transport services are critical to Australia's access to domestic and international markets. **Opportunities:** Future growth in the land freight sector will be facilitated by automation, such as driverless trains and trucks. Automation of stevedoring operations will continue to improve the operational efficiency of major transport and logistic hubs in Australia.

(continued)

Appendix 13.1 (continued)

Chapter	Industry Overview	Key Technologies (KT)	Impacts of KT on employment/ occupations/productivity	Challenges & Opportunities
7. Media & Communications	Digital platforms, such as Facebook and Google, have resulted in significantly reduced advertising revenue within traditional media. In the last decade, the print media have experienced a decline in revenue of 45% to AU$3 billion, and television revenue has also fallen considerably.	Artificial intelligence as a news-gathering tool, automated advertising, automated news systems, robo-writing, machine learning, AI in the scripting, shooting, post-production and distribution of media materials.	Many employees who previously worked within complex workflows have now been superseded by digital production processes. Workers, such as journalists and screen producers, may benefit from further specialist training in areas that enhance their digital literacy, such as programming, data analytics, virtual or 360 production skills, web or software design.	**Challenges:** Citizens, who are elderly, lowly-paid, in precarious employment, or lacking tertiary education, are less likely to be "digitally" included. **Opportunities:** AI-driven processes can achieve a high level of technical precision and organisation which promises a positive future for them as augmenting agents which assist the work of humans in the field. There will be increased demand for analysts and machine trainers to detect and disclose biases that may be inherent in the processes of machine learning.
8. Financial & Insurance Services	4% of the workforce is employed in the sector. The 'Big 4' banks together account for 40% of total sector employment.	AI-aided customer- and self-service, automation, robo-advisors, machine learning for lending decisions and credit scoring.	15–30% of employment will be in the risk zone due to automation. Jobs most threatened include those that are described as routine, repetitive tasks conducted physically and cognitively (such as, accounts and bank clerks, secretaries, receptionists, call centre staff, credit and loans officers and debt collectors).	**Challenges:** Due to the economic effects of COVID-19, the profitability and net interest margins of lenders are likely to be squeezed with a significant impact on employment **Opportunities:** There is potential for automation to be utilised more in back-office activities, assisting employees in customer interactions that require emotional intelligence.

9. Local Government	Total employment in the local government (LG) sector is around 190,000 and it manages non-financial assets valued at over $400 billion.	Automation and digital technology, drones, solar energy cells, sensors, satellite technology and cloud computing.	Automation and digital technology can support many LG functions such as monitoring the environment, planning and development, customer feedback, parking, the maintenance of parks, gardens, roads and footpaths. Clerical and administrative positions are most likely to be replaced by technology.	**Challenges:** Ethical challenges around data storage, surveillance systems, data sharing, and automated decision making in the delivery of public services. Due to the economic effects of COVID-19, the financial capacity to deliver services will be negatively affected. **Opportunities:** Technology has supported the extension and accessibility of services within local communities.
10. Higher Education	Australian universities employ over 130,000 people in academic and professional roles. Downturn in student enrolments due to COVID-19 has led to widespread job losses.	Blockchain technology, artificial intelligence and robotics, virtual reality simulations, supercomputers, web-based learning, and educational robots.	Academic workloads and costs can be reduced through AI tools such as automated marking, record-keeping and student feedback. The loss of casual academic staff means that those in permanent academic roles are likely to have to take on more teaching and will therefore be unable to conduct as much research as before. Academics are taking on greater teaching loads - much of it online.	**Challenges:** AI and machine learning cannot deal with creative intelligence tasks, and AI-powered tools cannot work with social intelligence tasks. When AI is in use, more attention is needed in terms of ethics and efficacy. Moreover, transparent and accountable systems of governance need to be considered when adopting AI in education. **Opportunities:** Educational cobots - robots that work alongside humans - can help lecturers differentiate instructions between each learner so that learners receive more tailored teaching.

(continued)

Appendix 13.1 (continued)

Chapter	Industry Overview	Key Technologies (KT)	Impacts of KT on employment/ occupations/productivity	Challenges & Opportunities
11. Healthcare	The health sector is the largest employing industry. The sector employed 1.7 million healthcare workers in 2019.	Machine learning in precision medicine, AI-based healthcare applications covering assisted surgery, preliminary diagnosis, and administrative workflows. Healthcare, such as blood tests, provided by robots.	AI and automation will replace 20% of occupations in the public sector, such as those in health and education, by 2030. However, by 2025, all healthcare workers including nurses, doctors and midwives, are expected to remain in the workforce. There will be a shift in the workforce to more specialised employment roles capable of dealing with the advancement of technology It is predicted that by 2030 there will be a shortage of 600,000 university graduates in the health sector. One of the most significant benefits of AI is helping people to manage their own health.	**Challenges:** The over-usage of technology could have negative effects on clinical practices, such as communication and the socio-emotional aspects of patient care. In addition, the communication skills of physicians may deteriorate due to reliance on technology. **Opportunities:** The support AI offers healthcare staff may free up their time from administrative tasks and allow them to spend more time with patients supporting their socio-emotional needs. AI creates opportunities for new job roles, upskilling through the utilisation of data generated by AI.

12. Utilities	The utility industry has the overall responsibly for the production and distribution of energy, water, and gas throughout Australia. The utility sector includes approximately 155,000 jobs.	Distributed energy resources (DER), Industrial internet of things (IIoT), blockchain, machine learning, and Cloud computing on asset monitoring, drones, smart metering, sensor networks and predictive maintenance.	Lower skills jobs (truck drivers, recycling and rubbish collectors, "other" stationary plant operators), and chemical, gas, petroleum and power plant operators, are most susceptible to automation. Some medium skill jobs, such as electrical distribution trades workers, are also susceptible to automation. More highly-skilled roles, such as programmers, auditors and professional consultants, will be required.	**Challenges:** Training is required to equip employees with the skillsets and tools for better utilisation of data. Privacy and ethical concerns are associated with personal data being collected. Digital technologies can improve the overall utilisation of utilities, while at the same time making them more vulnerable and fragile to supply and demand fluctuations, software glitches and cyber-attacks. **Opportunities:** The deployment and maintenance costs of a Utility 4.0 network can be vastly reduced by the use of blockchain technologies.

References

ACS. (2020). *Australia must boost AI investment*. www.acs.org.au/insightsandpublications/digital-pulse-2020.html

Anonymous. (2019). Digital Skills Shortages and R&D Tax Incentives Remain Obstacles to Artificial Intelligence Development in Australia, Says AIIA. *Targeted News Service*. https://www.aiia.com.au/documents/aiia-news/2019/digital-skills-shortages-and-r-and-d-tax-incentives-remain-obstacles-to-artificial-intelligence-ai-development-in-australia,-says-aiia. Accessed 14 Dec 2020.

Australian Industry and Skills Committee. (2017). *Future skills and training*. Canberra: Commonwealth of Australia.

Australian Trade & Industry Commission. (2017). *Australian disruptive technologies* (pp. 1–2). Canberra: Commonwealth of Australia.

Chan, L.-H. (2020). Strategic hedging: A "third way" for Australian foreign policy in the Indo-Pacific. *Asia Policy, 15*(3), 87–112.

Cisco and Oxford Economics. (2019). *Technology and the Future of Australian Jobs, What will be the impact of AI on workers in every sector?* www.cisco.com/c/dam/m/en_au/cda/cisco-future-of-australian-jobs-report2019.pdf. Accessed 30 Oct 2020.

Cisco/Oxford. (2018). *Technology & the Future of ASEAN jobs: The impact of AI on workers in ASEAN's six largest economies*, September. www.cisco.com/c/dam/global/en_sg/assets/csr/pdf/technology-and-the-future-of-asean-jobs.pdf accessed 11th December 2020

Davidson, J. (2020). *Australia faces a pandemic-led crunch in AI, industry warns*. Australian Financial Review. Nine Group. Sydney, https://www.afr.com/technology/australia-faces-a-pandemic-led-crunch-in-ai-industry-warns-20200709-p55aiy. Accessed 14 Dec 2020.

De Stefano, V. (2016). *The rise of the «just-in-time workforce»: On-demand work, crowdwork and labour protection in the «gig-economy»* (Geneva, ILO). Available at: www.ilo.org/wcmsp5/groups/public/%2D%2D-ed_protect/%2D%2D-protrav/%2D%2D-travail/documents/publication/wcms_443267.pdf. Accessed 14 Dec 2020.

Deloitte. (2020). *Australia unprepared for AI risks. Australian businesses are the most concerned but least prepared for AI risks*. Deloitte Melbourne. https://www2.deloitte.com/au/en/pages/media-releases/articles/australia-unprepared-for-ai-risks-070519.html. Accessed 14 Dec 2020.

Deloitte Access Economics (DAE). (2018a). *Report for ACS Australia's Digital Pulse Driving Australia's international ICT competitiveness and digital growth 2018*. DAE Sydney, https://www.acs.org.au/content/dam/acs/acs-publications/aadp2018.pdf accessed and downloaded 14 December 2020.

Deloitte Access Economics. (2018b). *The future of work: Occupational and education trends in human resources in Australia*. www2.deloitte.com/au/en/pages/economics/articles/future-of-work-occupational-education-trends.html. Accessed 14 Dec 2020.

Hajkowicz, S., Karimi, S., Wark, T., Chen, C., Evans, M., Rens, N., Dawson, D., Charlton, A., Brennan, T., Moffatt, C., Srikumar, S., & Tong, K. (2019). *Artificial intelligence: Solving problems, growing the economy and improving our quality of life*. CSIRO Data 61, Australia.

ILO. (2017). *The future of work we want: A global dialogue*. Geneva: ILO.

Loucks, J., Hupfer, S., Jarvis, D., & Murphy, T. (2019). *Future in the balance? How countries are pursuing an AI advantage*. Deloitte Touche Tohmatsu Limited.

Pearson. (2019). *The Global Learner Survey*. https://www.pearson.com.au/insights-and-news/pearson-news/global-learner-survey/. Accessed 14 Dec 2020.

Productivity Commission. (2019). *Growing the digital economy in Australia and New Zealand Maximising opportunities for SMEs*. Canberra: Australian and New Zealand Governments.

Seo, B. (2019). Fears Australia will be left behind with minimal AI spending. *The Australian Financial Review*, Melbourne. https://www.afr.com/technology/fears-australia-will-be-left-behind-with-minimal-ai-spending-20190116-h1a4oo. Accessed 28 July 2020.

Smith, E. (2019). Artificial intelligence could be worth $315b. *The Australian Financial Review*, p. 5. 15 November 2020. Fairfax Media Sydney.

World Economic Forum {WEF}. (2018). *The future of jobs report 2018*. Geneva: World Economic Forum.

Glossary

Acronyms

4IR	Fourth Industrial Revolution
ABS	Australian Bureau of Statistics
ACCC	Australian Competition and Consumer Commission
AI	Artificial Intelligence
AIM	Asset Integrity Management
AISC	Australian Industry and Skills Committee
AMGC	Advanced Manufacturing Growth Centre
ANZIC	Australian New Zealand Standard Industry Classification
APEC	Asia-Pacific Economic Cooperation
ARI	Asia Research Institute
ATM	Automatic Teller Machine
BNPL	Buy Now, Pay Later
CAV	Connected and Automated Vehicles
COVID-19	Coronavirus Disease
DER	Distributed Energy Resources
DST	Decision-support tool
EV	Electric vehicle
GDP	Gross Domestic Product
GFC	Global Financial Crisis
GVC	Global Value Chain
i4.0	Industry 4.0 (or 4IR)
ICT	Information and Communication Technology
IIoT	Industrial Internet of Things
ILO	International Labour Organisation
IMF	International Monetary Fund
iMIS	Intelligent Management Information Systems
IoT	Internet of Things

A. Nankervis et al. (eds.), *The Fourth Industrial Revolution*,
https://doi.org/10.1007/978-981-16-1614-3

IT	Information Technology
LNG	Liquefied Natural Gas
MIS	Minimally invasive surgical
MP	Member of Parliament
MUA	Maritime Union of Australia
OECD	Organisation for Economic Cooperation and Development
PPE	Personal Protective Equipment
RBA	Reserve Bank of Australia
SME	Small-Medium Enterprise
TAFE	Technical and Further Education
TEL	Technology-enhanced Learning
UAV	Unmanned Aerial Vehicle
UNCTAD	United Nations Conference on Trade and Development
UUV	Unmanned Underwater Vehicle
VET	Vocational Education and Training
VICT	Victoria International Container Terminal
VR	Virtual Reality
WEF	World Economic Forum
WHO	World Health Organisation

Definitions

Artificial Intelligence A branch of computer science where intelligence is demonstrated by machines, as opposed to natural intelligence displayed by humans and animals.

Augmented Reality The digital augmentation or enhancement of the physical world using computer-generated virtual elements.

Automation Readiness Index A global ranking, created by the *Economist Intelligence Unit*, of the relative ability of countries to develop and apply automated solutions (such as robotics and artificial intelligence).

Blockchain An open, distributed ledger technology that can record transactions and contracts from peer-to-peer in a verifiable and permanent way.

Cloud Computing The technological capability to use on-demand computing services that are not installed on a local computer or server.

Distributed Energy Resources Renewable energy units or systems located at houses or businesses to provide them with power.

Drone Another term for an 'unmanned aerial vehicle', which can fly autonomously.

Edge Computing Open information technology infrastructure that involves data being processed by a device itself, rather than being transmitted to a data centre for processing.

Extractive Industries Industries that involve extracting raw minerals from the earth.

Grabit Free newsreader software that allows users to download data from online newsgroups.

Industrial Internet of Things The extension and use of the internet of things (IoT) concepts in industrial production.

Internet of Things Refers to all smart devices (from computers to coffee machines to motion detectors) which are connected to the internet.

Machine Learning A branch of artificial intelligence (AI) that refers to applications that learn from data and improve automatically through experience.

Nanotechnology A field of applied science involving the control and innovation of matter (such as devices) on the scale of atoms and molecules.

Peaker Plants Power plants that generally operate when there is high demand.

Robotics The research, development, and operation of machines (robots) to perform tasks done traditionally by human beings.

Smart Meter A digital device that measures energy consumption and is capable of recording and transmitting power consumption data.

Soft Skills Personal competencies, such as people skills, social skills, communication skills, which often aid relationships with other people.

Utility 4.0 The utilities sector facing the impact of artificial intelligence (AI) and associated technological changes inherent to the 4IR.

Virtual Reality Computer modelling and simulation whereby a person can interact within an artificial three-dimensional environment using electronic devices.